T0237651

Co-governed Sovereignty Network

Hui Li · Xin Yang

Co-governed Sovereignty Network

Legal Basis and Its Prototype & Applications with MIN Architecture

 Springer

Hui Li
Shenzhen Graduate School
Peking University
Shenzhen, China

Xin Yang
Shenzhen Graduate School
Peking University
Shenzhen, China

To:

The People's Republic of China and every Chinese around the world.

All people, nations, and organizations who love peaceful, secure, open, and cooperative cyberspace.

The coming United Nations of Cyberspace with democracy and rule of law.

Foreword I: From IP to MIN
by Prof. Weimin Zheng

National sovereignty is the basic subject of the theory and practice of contemporary international law, which occupies an important position. In more than 50 years since the emergency of the Internet, the formed cyberspace has become another important basic space following the land, sea, air, and space. Scholars at home and abroad have made a series of achievements in the study of sovereignty in the Internet era, which is of great theoretical significance for promoting the international governance of cyberspace. But on the whole, the research on the sovereignty in the Internet age is still in its infancy.

Confronted with the understanding and practice of network sovereignty, taking national sovereignty as a starting point to promote the formulation of the international code of conduct on the Internet is the best choice that conforms to the interests of most states. In terms of regime, it is necessary to form the legal countermeasures and suggestions to safeguard international cyberspace sovereignty. It is important to shape a cyberspace governance system that is in line with the development realities of all countries. In terms of technology, only by proposing a new network architecture, equal and multilateral cooperative governance among states and sovereignty autonomy in the field of the cyberspace can be realized.

The proposed sovereignty network is an effective means to realize sovereignty autonomy in cyberspace and end centralized management under a single IP identifier. At the same time, current and future needs are better met than IP network due to its identity-centric multi-identifier system, endogenous security architecture, real identity authentication, and privacy protection mechanism for all of the access entity, etc.

In this book, the authors start with traditional sovereignty, cyberspace sovereignty, and its scientific basis, followed by the detailed introduction of the future co-governed sovereignty network with multi-identifier system from the aspects of definition, architecture, operating process, security analysis, and relevant protocols. The book also introduced the key technology of network sovereignty, such as identity-centric network, blockchain, security mechanisms, and other performance guarantee. At present, MIN has passed the principle verification on the large-scale operator network. The prototype of broadcasting and television sovereignty network has also passed the test report of the Planning Academy of the National Radio and Television Administration. The primary application scenarios of MIN are government, military, large enterprises with a high standard for security, as well as private network in the financial, electric, and other vital industry. With further developing, the wide deployment of MIN will constitute the United Nations of Cyberspace with independent sovereignty.

In October 2019, MIN architecture and its prototype proposed by Prof. Hui Li's team were rewarded as the leading technology achievements of the 6th World Internet Conference, Wuzhen, China. MIN won the award for two historical first times: the first award for the original and subversive network architecture protocol system, and the first award given to large-scale prototype systems without mature commercial products and systems. Every year, the award goes to Huawei, ZTE, Tencent, Baidu, Alibaba, 360, Microsoft, Google, Qualcomm, Tesla, Ericsson, and Oracle. This also confirms the expectation of academia and industry on this technology.

From two dimensions of legal theory and technology, the book analyzes and explores the theoretical basis and practical application of sovereignty network. It is the related important resources for network security management, network construction, as well as managers and practitioners. At the same time, for security, network engineering, network space communications professional postgraduate, and senior undergraduate, this book also extremely has the reference value.

March 2021

Weimin Zheng
Professor of Tsinghua University
Academician of Chinese Academy
of Engineering; Former President of
China Computer Federation
Tsinghua Campus, Beijing, China

Foreword II: From MINs to Cog-MIN by Prof. S.-Y. R. Li

The IPv4 network was formally proposed in 1969. With the rapid development of Internet, the exhaustion of the IPv4 address space in the 2010s hindered the furtherance of Internet. To expand the address space, IETF in 1995 proposed RFC 1883, marking the birth of IPv6. However, after more than a decade of transition, IPv6 has not completely replaced IPv4 and, in fact, is still expected to coexist with IPv4 for a long time.

IPv4 binds user identity with location. This disadvantage remains with IPv6. As early as 1989, there had been study on revolutionary post-IP architecture. In August 2010, the US government began to fund the research on the Future Internet Architecture of post-IP. Soon Europe, Japan, Korea, and China all followed up. Exemplifying projects included the content-centric network named data networking (NDN), the identification-centric network mobility first, the service-centric network NEBULA, etc. In all proposals on future network architecture, the existing IPv4 domain name system (DNS) remained the basic anchor to supplements of new identities. The problem of centralized management of the network domain name was set aside.

The identification domain name is the new territorial space after land, sea, and sky. In establishing a universal global network architecture in the post-IP era, Prof. Hui Li advocates three key points. First is national sovereignty on the virtual network space in replacement of the monopoly by a single country or organization. The top-level identity domain name must be jointly governed by international parties. When the top-level identity domain name of a nation is approved by consensus, the nation owns autonomy on low-level identification domain names. Secondly, all individual or organization users, all operators, and their devices must register a uniform ID in the cyberspace with real identity information. Thirdly, the network must be able to trace the source of every data packet so as to keep everybody responsible. The entire virtual space thus transforms from the current exclave into law abiding territory. National cyberspace will be governed by the territorial law and globally shared space by the international law.

Professor Hui Li was a star student at the Department of Information Engineering, The Chinese University of Hong Kong, where he completed the Ph.D. studies in 2000. His doctoral dissertation "On the Complexity of Concentrators and Multi-Stage Interconnection Networks in Switching Systems" was nominated for the Best Doctoral Thesis of the Year. Based on algebraic theory, he completed the research on the lowest complexity of VLSI layout of the broadband switching structure via multi-stage interconnection networks (MINs) and the self-routing model of MINs. Over the last 20 years, he and his team at Peking University have shown original achievement in every layer of the computer network. Many patents have been granted by the governments of both USA and China. Fields of invention include distributed storage coding theory on the physical layer, algebraic structure of packet switching on the datalink layer, united routing, and addressing algorithm on the multi-identifier network layer of the integrated space-and-terrestrial network, adaptive transmission control protocol (TCP) based on network coding theory on the transport layer, system and methods for managing top-level domain names using consortium blockchain on the application layer, anti-attacking quantitative modeling for cyber-mimic-defend systems based on GSPN and martingale theory. These inventions are at the core of Cog-MIN architecture.

I am delighted to see the advancement of his academic career from MINs to Cog-MIN. It is my belief that the Cog-MIN architecture will bring a peaceful and secure cyberspace to the world.

March 2021

Shuo-Yen Robert Li
Professor Emeritus, The Chinese
University of Hong Kong
Distinguished University
Professor, UESTC
N.T., Hong Kong, P.R. China

Preface

The Internet is the most important global infrastructure in the era of digital economy. Human life, work, entertainment, as well as various industries, government management, and services are inseparable from the network. Moreover, technological progress makes the network to constantly expand the breadth and depth of its application, from the earliest information exchange and communication, personal consumption, e-commerce, to value manufacturing, value creation, low-cost credit, and trust development. After the earliest commercial networks, the Internet of Things, the Industrial Internet, the Internet of Vehicles, and the Internet of commercial satellites continue to expand. It can be imagined that it will continue to expand its coverage boundaries with the exploration of the universe and celestial constellation by human beings. As the world moves toward multipolarity, economic globalization, cultural diversity, and IT application, the Internet will play an even greater role in promoting the progress of human civilization.

IP Network and Its Achilles Heel

The Internet originated in the USA, who defines the current IPv4 network standard, leads the world in IP technology and creates a virtual space based on DNS for human society. ICCAN, a private organization in California, is the administrator of DNS. Objectively, the USA has a unilateral monopoly advantage over other countries in cyberspace, and other countries are only users of the US Internet. However, the following three events occurred in the USA:

A. After the bloody clashes that broke out on January 6, 2021, when Congress was invaded by Trump supporters, the nation's biggest online platforms, including Twitter, Facebook, Google, Apple, YouTube, Reddit, Instagram, Snapchat, Discord, Pinterest, blocked all contents posted by President Trump and his team and shut down their social media accounts. The most powerful man in the world, the President of the USA who once authorized American military to launch cyber-attacks on other countries, suddenly lost his online channel to communicate with tens of millions of his voters without judicial process in the last half month of his term, but there was nothing he could do. The US Internet giants easily overrode the US President's freedom of speech! The rule of law system restricted by the separation of legislative, judicial, and administrative powers was gone in the virtual cyberspace. Where is the law and justice?

B. On December 17, the US Department of Homeland Security's Cyber Security and Infrastructure Security Agency (CISA) issued a "highly unusual warning" said that cyberattack against US government agencies and private companies has continued over the past week, reaching the highest "grave" risk level at a critical time for the 2020 presidential election. Data from some Internet-connected Dominion voting machines was mysteriously erased, and even election data was erased from local servers in some counties. It was showed that the ultimate goal of the cyberattack may have been hackers trying to destroy the election fraud data! Was it a hostile state or a hostile domestic campaign? The USA, the birthplace of IP network technology, and its biggest political campaign, the presidential election, was manipulated and molested by its opponents! How is the US government's cybersecurity bureaucracy doing?

C. In 2013, Edward Joseph Snowden, a former CIA employee, fled to Hong Kong to seek political asylum in Russia. He revealed that the National Security Agency (NSA) had been running a top-secret electronic surveillance program, PRISM, since 2007 under George W. Bush. Officially known as US-984XN, the program monitors the Internet communications and activities of all Americans. American citizens have no privacy whatsoever. How can citizens' human rights and privacy be protected and respected? What happened to the natural rights of the US Constitution?

The reason for the occurrence of the above events is that the current IP architecture has congenital defects. The reason for (A) is that the domain name of IP is managed by a single organization, and the accounts of users on each Web site are only managed by the platform itself, so it is easy to erase a user. The reason why class (B) events often occur is that the asymmetric advantage of the adversary is obvious, which comes from the innate deficiency of the IP network architecture—its data packet is untraceable and there is no security guarantee. The reason for (C) is that the privacy of user data on IP network is not guaranteed, which is basically streaking.

IP semantic overload includes dual attributes of identity and location, untraceable data packet, unguaranteed security and unguaranteed service performance, etc., making it unsuitable for the mobile, real-time, and high-security requirements of future Internet. Therefore, powerful as the USA, its government agencies and corporations, senior officials and ordinary citizens are all deeply worried and uneasy about the current state of the Internet, including its technology architecture, operation, management, and governance. Not to mention other countries that use it.

The Sovereignty Network: Appeal from Most Countries in the World

After the Snowden Event in 2013, the EU, the UK, Russia, and China all called for a joint management of human cyberspace, but so far there has been no real progress.

For Russia's own security, in February 2020, President Putin ordered the start broken network test, establish an "internal network," the world's largest Internet infrastructure based on self-built Russia Network (RuNet). The DNS controlled by the Russia government is applied to re-route the domestic traffic, no longer rely on the root of the DNS overseas.

Chinese President Jinping XI pointed out that "no cyberspace security, there is no national security." At the World Internet Conference 2015 Wuzhen, China, he proposed all countries join together to "promote reform of the global Internet governance system, jointly build a peaceful, secure, open and cooperative cyberspace, and establish a multilateral, democratic and co-managed global Internet governance system." This is the common aspiration of all countries in the world.

Cog-MIN: The First Solution to Sovereignty Network in the World

Therefore, in terms of global cyberspace co-governed, the authors of this book proposed the co-governed multi-identifier network architecture (Cog-MIN, or shorter by MIN). We invented a large-scale consortium blockchain based on one vote for one country to manage top-level identified domain names. Extensively, the hierarchical consortium blockchain was used for independent management within each country. User behavior logs at all levels were recorded by the blockchain at all levels. Cog-MIN was proposed to take identity as the indispensable basic core identity. For compatibility with IP, Cog-MIN supported network identification including IP address, content, service, etc., at the same time. It used asymmetric cryptography to support all data traceability, thus high security and reliability became the DNA of Cog-MIN architecture.

Cog-MIN has solved the IP network's dilemma of single identifier and centralized management. Its management plane uses multi-identifier system (MIS), which supports the coexistence of network identifiers including identity, content, geographic information, and IP address. The system is constructed based on the voting consortium blockchain to ensure privacy protection and manageability simultaneously. MIS requires all users to register using their real identities and store the data using modern cryptography techniques. MIN turns the network into a safe, peaceful, democratic, and transparent space, rather than a space without the rule of law.

MIN proposes a traceable data signing and acceptance mechanism on the data plane. The core equipment of MIN is multi-identifier router (MIR) that integrates multiple innovations. The first is an HPT-FIB algorithm by combining hash table and prefix tree that supports inter-translation between different kinds of identifiers in size of tens of billion entries. The second is an addressing model based on coordinate mapping in hyperbolic space, to deal with the exponential growth of FIB table. The third is a tunnel scheme to transport IP packets through MIN, to support the progressive deployment of MIN on IP network.

The MIN architecture proposed in this book supports natural and progressive de-IP, which will be chosen by users and the market without having to de-IP compulsively. It can be predicted that in the future, IP will still be in the mainstream position in the USA, while other countries will gradually abandon IP and use MIN for their own sovereignty in cyberspace. MIN ensures the interconnection between sovereign networks of every country and IP network of USA. In other words, IP becomes America's own internal network, while other countries form a multilateral network system based on MIN.

Co-governed Sovereignty Network: Prototype Based on Cog-MIN

The application scenarios of MIN could be classified into three scales:

(1) the small-scale scenarios such as high-security private networks of enterprises, industries, and government departments;
(2) the medium-scale scenarios of industrial Internet, private network of Internet of vehicles, and smart city;
(3) The large-scale high-security cyberspace for multilateral condominium and sovereign autonomy to replace existing IP network, the United Nations of Cyberspace (UNC) for Sovereign Networks of States based on Cog-MIN.

In March 2019, we have successfully launched the first testing prototype of co-governed sovereignty network in the world based on Cog-MIN on the operators' networks in Great China area. In October 2019, MIN and its prototype system were selected as the leading technology achievements of the Sixth World Internet Conference at Wuzhen, China.

Cog-MIN takes identity as anchor identification and supports multiple identification addressing, routing, and fallback mechanism. Taking identity as an anchor identifier, Cog-MIN and supports multiple identifiers addressing, routing, and fallback mechanism. IPv4, IPv6, IPv9, NewIP, Network 5.0 and known Future Network Identifiers such as content and service can all be integrated on the Cog-MIN architecture.

The multi-identifier management system based on hierarchical large-scale consortium blockchain and multi-identifier translation algorithms support the above requirements of multiple identifiers translating, addressing, and routing. Cog-MIN will put an end to the requirement of continuous upgrading of network architecture by continuous evolution of network layer addressing and routing scheme, which is conducive to the coexistence and natural transition of various identification systems. It will greatly save costs and extend the service cycle of existing equipment to the best of its ability. It is expected that Cog-MIN to the data packet network architecture is what Signaling No. 7 to the telecommunication system. The support of Signaling No. 7 for basic services and various future intelligent services has made it become the terminator of all previous signaling systems since No. 1.

Now the private network based on Cog-MIN, which was deployed on operators' IP network, has already applied on some particular scenario. In terms of its goal to become a truly multilateral co-governing United Nations of cyberspace globally, Cog-MIN is still in its conceptual and infancy, with much pioneering work yet to be done by global peers. The purpose of publishing this book now, according to a Chinese proverb, is to "throw a brick and attract jade." We want to contribute our ideas to building a peaceful, secure, open, and cooperative cyberspace governed by the rule of law for all mankind.

MIN-VPN Versus IP-VPN: Exponential Security Gain Enhancement has been Demonstrated

Since 2020, aiming at high-security requirements, we have developed the first version of this high-security private network MIN-VPN system product based on Cog-MIN to meet the practical needs of users such as mobile office, identity management, rights management, log storage, behavior detection, and identity authentication. It integrates large-scale blockchain, geospatial information, personal biometrics, trusted computing, cryptography, endogenous security, AI, and other technologies. It provides global industry-defined five security features: authentication, access control, data confidentiality, data integrity, and non-repudiation.

It can effectively resist authorization violation, impersonation attack, bypass control, Trojan horse or trap gate, and other attacks. Min-VPN uses a variety of technical authentication means to ensure system security. Illegal users first need to steal the account password and user's private key, then pretend to pass in vivo detection, and finally break through multiple internal security defense mechanisms to steal internal network resources.

MIN-VPN integrates the hierarchical protection architecture of multiple security mechanisms and constructs a dynamic and unified security defense model by means of password verification, certificate verification, in vivo detection, intelligent behavior detection, and endogenous security, which can reduce the success rate of attack to below the order of ten to minor twenty, or 10^{-20} (Fig. 1).

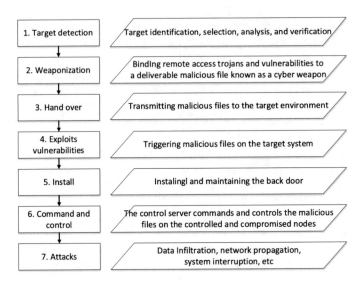

Fig. 1 Classical attack chain model and selection of attack modes

We have deployed the MIN-VPN on the operators' IP network, taking the mainstream IP-VPN as the reference system, and using the classic attack chain and attack methods to carry out various comparative attack tests. After a long time of testing by a number of third-party professional teams, the results show that the MIN-VPN environment can effectively protect and against the traditional IP network attacks in all links of the attack chain under both IP to MIN and MIN to MIN network scenarios, while the IP-VPN cannot. The test results are shown as follows (Fig. 2).

Attack phase	Attack means		IP-IP test result	IP-MIN test result	MIN-MIN test result
Reconnaissance	Host discovery		Can be discovered	Discover hosts that are not CUTV's	Nothing found
	Ping Scan		Can be detected	Undetectable	Undetectable
	Operating system identification		System fingerprint can be obtained	Nothing found	Nothing found
	Port scan		Can detect all port services	can't found any port information.	Nothing found
Exploitation	Trojan implantation	TCP trojan	Connected	Can't connect	Can't connect
		UDP trojan	Connected	Can't connect	Can't connect
		ICMP trojan	Connected	Can't connect	Can't connect
	Web shell		Connected	Can't connect	Can't connect
Actions	ARP poisoning	Sniff	Sniff successfully	Non-intranet	Sniff failed
		Forced disconnection	Disconnected	Non-intranet	Failed

Fig. 2 Results of testing experiments under IP to IP-VPN versus IP to MIN-VPN, MIN to MIN

For further information about our systems and products, please visit the web of MIN.[1] We are willing to provide products or services to customers in various countries for non-military purposes. When the time is right, we may contribute the source code of MIN to the global community.

Chapters Arrangement

The first chapter of this book introduces the concept of traditional sovereignty and sovereignty in cyberspace. The second chapter introduces the understanding, policies, and governance of sovereignty in cyberspace of major countries, especially the security and defense strategies in cyberspace. Especially through the chaos of the US presidential election in 2020, we can find that there is a long way to go for all countries to effectively govern cyberspace. The third chapter summarizes the concept and requirements of the post-IP sovereign Internet architecture and system. The author proposes the basic architecture of Cog-MIN, a multilaterally managed and sovereign independent multi-identifier network architecture, and considers the security of Cog-MIN. The fourth chapter introduces the key technologies of sovereignty Internet based on the Cog-MIN architecture, most of them are from the patent technology of the authors, including voting consensus algorithm, topology structure for large-scale consortium blockchain, hierarchical extensible multi-blockchain to an unity chain, management system of top-level domain name based on consortium blockchain, routing scheme of tens billion of identifiers, the mutual translation of endogenous quantitative model of security, transmission control protocol for multi-semantic supported, routing algorithm for space-terrestrial integrated network, anti-attacking quantitative modeling for cyber-mimic-defend systems based on GSPN and martingale theory. The fifth chapter introduces the application of Cog-MIN to various possible scenarios, including high-security private network MIN-VPN, industrial Internet, Internet of Things, and cyberspace United Nations via co-governing and sovereignty auton-omy, and the future space-terrestrial integrated network.

The readers of this book include officials of the UN World Summit on the Information Society, managers and researchers of the United Nations for a secure and peaceable cyberspace, researchers of the network system, officials and

---

[1]www.cogmin.net or www.cogmin.cn.

technicians responsible for information system planning of national and local governments, chief information officers of enterprises and public institutions, network security managers, and network center managers.

Shenzhen, China

Hui Li
Professor of Peking University
Director of Shenzhen Key Lab of Information
Theory and Future Network; PKU Lab of China
Major Science and Technology Infrastructure
for Future Network

Acknowledgements

This book has crossed the legal theory and network technology. On the one hand, it starts with the historical development of sovereignty and expounds the legal basis of cyberspace sovereignty. On the other hand, based on the high-performance blockchain, a new network architecture is designed to realize co-governance at the technical level. This book consists of five chapters: Prof. Hui Li is responsible for the preliminary planning and the writing of Chaps. 1–4; Ms. Xin Yang is responsible for the writing of Chap. 5.

The authors are very grateful to all our colleagues who have contributed to the publication of this book. In particular, we would like to express our sincere gratitude to those who directly or indirectly engaged in the writing, revising, or supplementary work. In addition to the co-author, we also extend our heartfelt thanks to the following people: Prof. Zining Jin from the School of Transnational Law of Peking University, who put forward valuable opinions on the legal theory part of Chaps. 1 and 2; Lawyer Shufei Wu from Beijing Kangda Law Firm, she revised the English writing of the first two chapters; Ms. He Bai who collected and summarized the related materials of sovereignty in cyberspace and revised the format of the whole book; Ms. Xin Xiao who help to redrew most of the pictures in this book.

The authors would also like to sincerely thank Mr. Xinchun Zhang and Mr. Guohua Wei from the compilation team of Chap. 3 who participated in designing the network architecture and provide the corresponding materials; Mr. Jianming Que, Mr. Bin Yin, and Mr. Feng Wang from the compilation team of Chap. 4 who participate in multi-identifier coexistence scheme based on identity-centric network and provide the corresponding materials; Ms. Han Wang, Mr. Jiansen Huang, and Mr. Zixian Wang from the compilation team of Chap. 4 who participated in proposing blockchain-related scheme and provided corresponding materials; Mr. Jiawei Hu and Ms. Ting Huang from the compilation team of Chap. 4 who participated in proposing the hash table with prefix tree HPT algorithm and provide the corresponding materials; Mr. Yongjie Bai and Ms. Sai Lu from the compilation team of Chap. 4 who participated in constructing the space-terrestrial multi-identifier network and provide the corresponding materials; Mr. Gengxin Li, Mr. Lihong Lin, and Mr. Yao Yao from the compilation team of Chap. 4 who participated in constructing the security situational awareness system and provide the corresponding materials. In addition, we would also like to thank the laboratory team Mr. Huajun Ma, Mr. Xin Xie, Mr. Rui Xu, Mr. KaiXuan Xing, Mr. ChongHui Ning, Mr. Jiuhua Qi, Ms. Xinwei Liu, Ms. Yuanyuan Yang, Mr. Bohui Wang, Mr. Tian Zhao, Ms. Mengchu Shi, Mr. Haiyang Yu, Mr. Tao Liu, Ms. Liu Yang, Mr. Hongyu Guo, Mr. Yaoguang Huo, Mr. Xiangzhen Meng, Mr. Zhenwei Xiao, and Mr. Zhenyuan Yang who provides a large number of materials in writing this book and takes part in system prototype tests.

The authors deeply thank to Mr. Xin Xu, Mr. Zhaohui Wu, Mr. AnBo Dong, Ms. Su Li from Shenzhen Security Test Center for their contribution on testing the functions of MIN-VPN.

Hui Li also extend my sincerely thanks to Academician of the Chinese Academy of Engineering, Prof. Jiangxing Wu from NDSC for his guidance on the development of MIN Architecture; as well as the following people for their support in the prototype verification: Prof. Ke Xu from Tsinghua University; Mr. Shisheng Chen from Shenzhen Branch of China Telecom Corporation Limited; Dr. Wei Liang, Director of Blockchain Laboratory from China Telecom Corporation Limited; Director Jinwu Wei and Senior Engineer Wei Li of Big Data Research Center of China United Network Communications Limited; Fusheng Zhu, President of Guangdong Communications and Networks Institute; Chairman Kaiyan Tian and General Manager Jiang Zhu of Kingsoft Cloud Network Technology Co., Ltd.; Prof. Yiqin Lu from South China University of Technology; Prof. Yijun Liu from Guangdong University of Technology; Prof. Yongxiang Han and Prof. Hanxu Hou from Dongguan Institute of Technology; Prof. Wai-Ho Yeung from CUHK; Prof. Wai Ho Mow from the Hong Kong University of Science and Technology; Prof. Zefeng Zheng from Macau University of Science and Technology; Mr. Tao Sun, Director of Network Information Center of Shenzhen University Town; Mr. Ji Liu, Director of Network Information Center of PKUSZ.

Hui Li has special thanks go to his Ph.D. supervisor, Prof. Shuo-Yen Robert Li, IEEE Fellow, Professor Emeritus of the Chinese University of Hong Kong; and Prof. Weimin Zheng, Academician of the Chinese Academy of Engineering, Professor of Tsinghua University, and Former President of the Chinese Computer Federation for their Forewords to this book.

Hui Li would like to sincerely appreciate following funds include: Foshan Innovation Team No. 2018IT100082, PCL Future Regional Network Facilities for Large-scale Experiments and Applications (LZC0019), China Environment for Network Innovations (GJFGW [2016] No. 2533, [2018] No.775, [2020] No. 386, SZFGW [2019] No. 261), National Keystone R&D Program of China (2020AAA 0104203, No. 2017YFB0803204, 2016YFB0800101, No. 2012CB 315904), NSFC No. 61671001, GuangDong R&D Key Program No. 2019B010137001, YWMZH [2020] No. 1; Shenzhen Research Programs (JCYJ20190808155607340, 20170 306092030521 JSGG20170824095858416); HuaWei No. YBN2017125, TC20 201222002; ZTE 2019ZTE03-01, 2014ZTE03-01-01; Shenzhen Smart City Tech. Group No. SZSCG-HT-2021-012.

Further, we would like to thank all peers inland and oversea, their achievements, which like pearls in the field, have provided us with nourishment and inspiration; so that we could invent a rope to string them together to become a necklace, it is this Cog-MIN architecture!

Finally, we thank all reviewers for their invaluable comments and suggestions that improved the quality of this book and the staff members from Springer for publishing this work. Besides, thank you for reading this book.

Shenzhen, China   Hui Li
March 2021   Xin Yang

Contents

About the Authors

Hui Li is Full Professor of Peking University, School of Electrical and Computer Engineering, and Adjunct Professor of PengCheng Lab, the China National Lab on Network Tech. He was Director of Shenzhen Key Lab of Information Theory and Future Network Architecture, Director of PKU Lab of China Environment for Network Innovations (CENI), the National Major Research Infrastructure. He was elected as Chairman of IEEE Blockchain Technology at Shenzhen Branch in 2019 for his contribution on consortium consensus. He was awarded the 2017 Annual Figure by National Committee of "Scientific Chinese" and reported by its journal due to his contribution on network architecture.

He proposed the first multilateral condominium network architecture in the world for building the United Nations of cyberspace, which is the co-governing multi-identifier network architecture (Cog-MIN or briefly as MIN). He finished MIN's conceptually proving project on operators' network, and this project "MIN: Co-governing Multi-Identifier Network Architecture and Its Prototype on Operator's Network" obtained the award of World Leading Internet Scientific and Technological Achievements by the 6th World Internet Conference (WIC), WuZhen, China, on 2019.

MIN won the award and has created two first times in WIC history: the first award granted to an original and revolutionary network architecture, and the first award given to large-scale prototype systems without mature commercial products and systems. The member of WIC Committee of Expert was composed from all over the world. Every year, the award goes to Huawei, ZTE, Tencent, Baidu, Alibaba, 360, Microsoft, Google, Qualcomm, Tesla, Ericsson, and Oracle.

He was invited as Guest Editor by ZTE COMMUNICATIONS, for publishing a regular issue with topic on "Domain Name and Identifier of Internet: Architecture & Systems," 2020 Vol. 18 No. 1. As First Inventor, he was granted eight US patents and more than 20 China patents. He has published four monographs in Chinese. His research interests include network architecture, cyberspace security, distributed storage, and blockchain. He received his B.Eng. and M.S. degrees from School of Information Eng., Tsinghua University, Beijing, China, in 1986 and 1989, respectively, and Ph.D. degree from the Dept. of Information Engineering, The Chinese University of Hong Kong in 2000.

Xin Yang received the B.Eng. degree from the Department of Computer Science and Engineering, South China University of Technology, in 2016. She is currently working toward the Ph.D. degree in the School of Information Science, Peking University. Her research interests include cybersecurity, future network architecture, and distributed storage system.

Chapter 1
Sovereignty and Network Sovereignty

National sovereignty is the basic subject of the theory and practice of contemporary international law, occupies a crucial position. In order to studying the sovereignty of internet, we need to have an accurate cognition on the traditional concept of sovereignty. In this chapter, we introduce sovereignty from three perspectives: the historical background of traditional sovereignty, the adaptability of sovereignty in cyberspace or network sovereignty, and the sovereignty in the cyber era. Finally, we define sovereignty in cyberspace from the perspective of jurisprudence.

1.1 Historical Background

Sovereignty, the supreme and exclusive political power which a state processes over its jurisdiction. It's the supreme authority for self-determination.

1.1.1 Origin of Traditional Sovereignty

The author of the Dictionary of Taxation, Wang Meihan, pointed out that "National sovereignty is the most important attribute that distinguishes a state from other social groups. It is the inherent supreme power of a nation in the domestic as well as the independence and sovereign right in the international sphere. Any state has the right to choose its social system and state form, organize its government, and independently decide and handle its internal and external affairs according to its discretion and national condition. Any form of aggression or interference by other states is prohibited" [1]. In the United States Declaration of Independence [2], the founders pointed out that the root of national sovereignty lies in all citizens. Before that, the perception of sovereignty has been debated for a long time (Fig. 1.1).

© The Author(s) 2021
H. Li and X. Yang, *Co-governed Sovereignty Network*,
https://doi.org/10.1007/978-981-16-2670-8_1

1

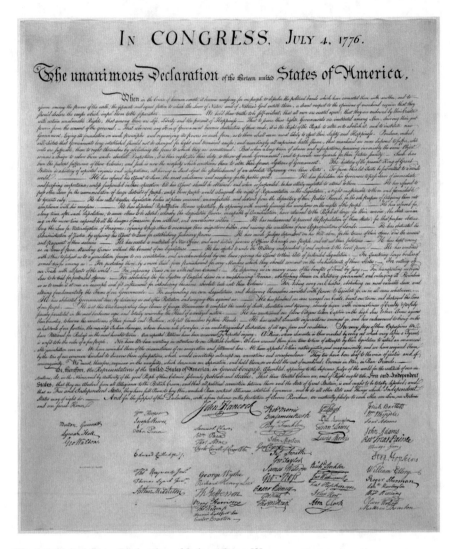

Fig. 1.1 United States Declaration of Independence [3]

Jean Bodin was a French jurist and political philosopher who firstly unequivocally put forwards the concept of sovereignty. His classical definition of sovereignty in The Six Books of a Commonwealth was: "The supreme power to rule over citizens and subjects, which is Non-Divisible, Non-Transferable and Non-Annihilable, not bound by law or time. It is the inherent power of the state, and this inherent power exists forever and represents the legitimacy of the unification of state power" [4]. In other words, states existed for sovereignty rulers. Since its strong monarchical ruling color, this view on sovereignty was called monarchy sovereignty theory (Fig. 1.2).

Fig. 1.2 Portrait of Jean Bodin [5]

Johannes Althusius was a German jurist, he had pointed out that, "The state exercises its sovereignty, but sovereignty belongs to the people, and this power should be vested in its administrators according to the arrangements of the laws of the State", improved the monarchy sovereignty theory (Fig. 1.3).

According to the international relations at that time, Hugo Grotius, a great Dutch jurist and thinker, further generalized the concept of sovereignty: "Sovereignty means that the exercise of power is not restricted by others. When a state handles

Fig. 1.3 Johannes Althusius, engraving by Jean-Jacques Boissard [6]

internal affairs without any others' control, it is manifested as sovereignty" [7] (Fig. 1.4).

The modern significance of sovereign state appeared after the formation of the capitalist nation of centralization of authority. At the end of the three decades of European religious wars, European countries signed the Peace of Westphalia, which established the principles of national sovereignty, national territory and national

Fig. 1.4 Portrait of Hugo Grotius by Michiel Jansz. van Mierevelt, 1631 [8]

independence, and then, the Westphalian System with the state as the basic unit was established [9]. Later, due to the emergence and development of the European Community and other international organizations, more and more western scholars believed that the national sovereignty was non-transferable, and the concept of sovereignty, as the cornerstone of dealing with national political affairs and international relations, was gradually accepted by the international community and evolved into new connotations (Fig. 1.5).

Fig. 1.5 Peace of Westphalia in Münster (Gerard Terborch 1648) [10]

In 1905, renowned German jurist L. F. L. Oppenheim pointed out in his book Oppenheim's International Law that, "Sovereignty is the highest authority of a state, it doesn't mean that it is superior to all states under international law, but implies full independence" [11]. Besides, Article 2 of the UN Charter [12] also had a stipulation of the sovereign equality of member states.

The emergence of the concept of sovereignty promotes the perfection of the international order and international law system (Figs. 1.6 and 1.7).

1.1.2 Traditional Sovereignty

The basic elements of a sovereign state are population, territory, regime and sovereignty. The core of building a nation and state is sovereignty: Sovereignty is the supreme power that a country deals with its internal and external affairs independently. A sovereign state needs to ensure four fundamental rights—jurisdiction, self-defense, independence and equality. Specifically, a state has the power to exercise jurisdiction over all persons and matters within its territory, as well as nationals outside its territory. It has the right to establish a political and socio-economic system combined with its circumstance. To safeguard its political

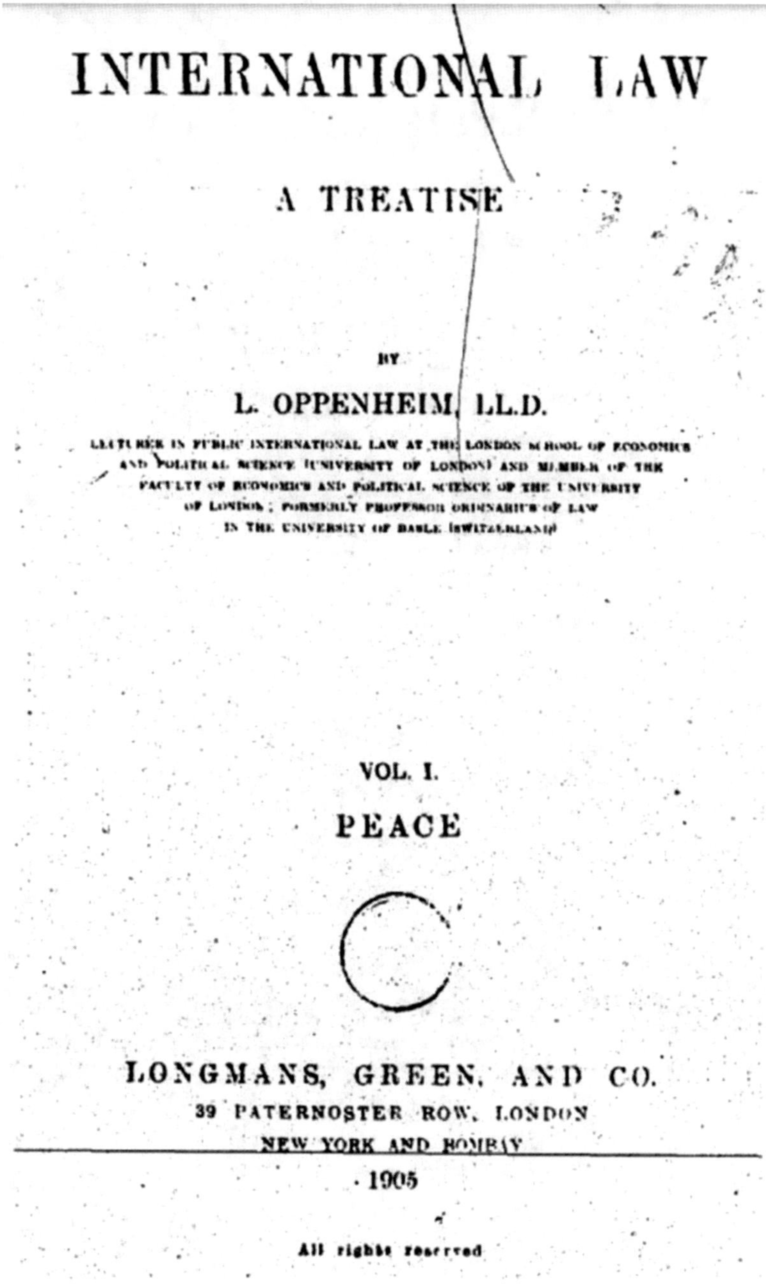

INTERNATIONAL LAW

A TREATISE

BY

L. OPPENHEIM, LL.D.

LECTURER IN PUBLIC INTERNATIONAL LAW AT THE LONDON SCHOOL OF ECONOMICS AND POLITICAL SCIENCE (UNIVERSITY OF LONDON) AND MEMBER OF THE FACULTY OF ECONOMICS AND POLITICAL SCIENCE OF THE UNIVERSITY OF LONDON; FORMERLY PROFESSOR ORDINARIUS OF LAW IN THE UNIVERSITY OF BASLE (SWITZERLAND)

VOL. I.

PEACE

LONGMANS, GREEN, AND CO.

39 PATERNOSTER ROW, LONDON

NEW YORK AND BOMBAY

1905

All rights reserved

Fig. 1.6 International law: a treatise. Vol. 1. Peace by L. Oppenheim, LL.D. [13]

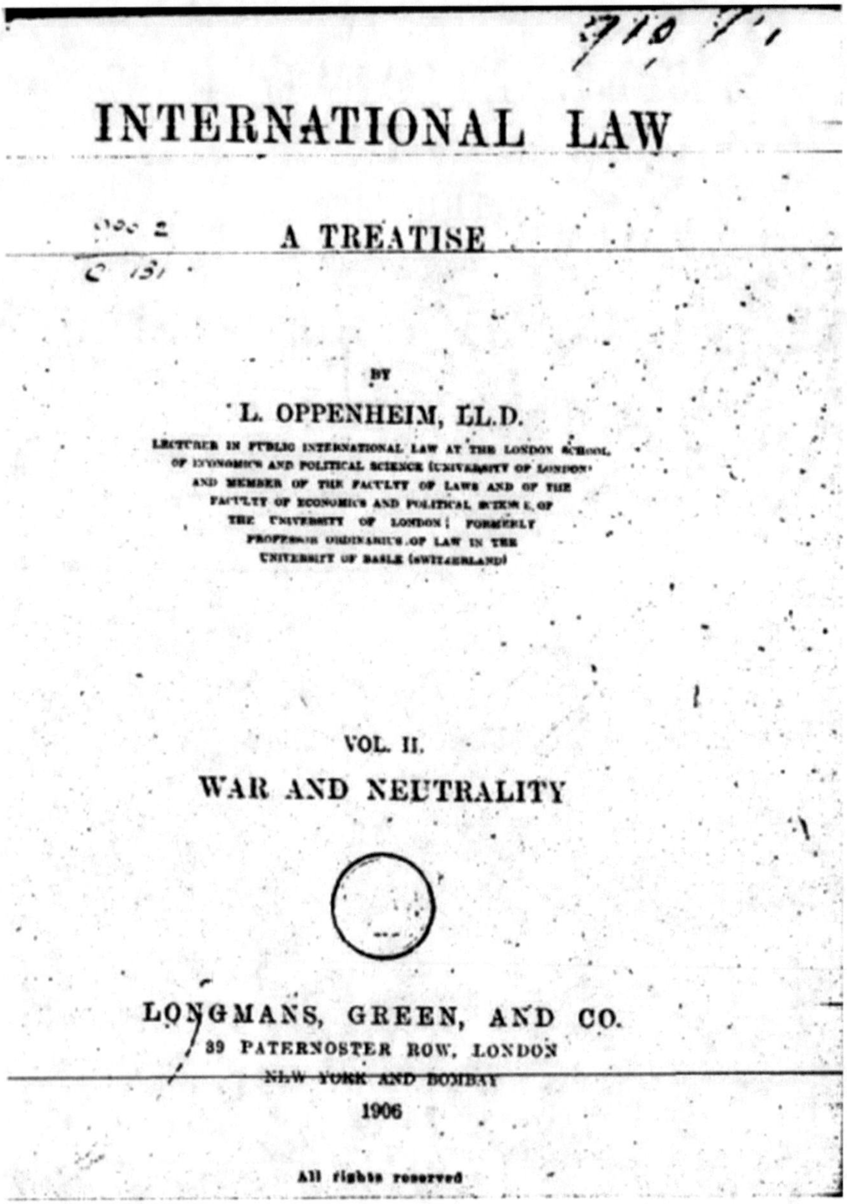

INTERNATIONAL LAW

A TREATISE

BY

L. OPPENHEIM, LL.D.

LECTURER IN PUBLIC INTERNATIONAL LAW AT THE LONDON SCHOOL OF ECONOMICS AND POLITICAL SCIENCE (UNIVERSITY OF LONDON) AND MEMBER OF THE FACULTY OF LAWS AND OF THE FACULTY OF ECONOMICS AND POLITICAL SCIENCE, OF THE UNIVERSITY OF LONDON; FORMERLY PROFESSOR ORDINARIUS OF LAW IN THE UNIVERSITY OF BASLE (SWITZERLAND)

VOL. II.

WAR AND NEUTRALITY

LONGMANS, GREEN, AND CO.
39 PATERNOSTER ROW, LONDON
NEW YORK AND BOMBAY
1906

All rights reserved

Fig. 1.7 International law: a treatise. Vol. 2. War and Neutrality by L. Oppenheim, LL.D. [14]

independence and territorial integrity, a state has the right to defend itself against foreign aggression and threats. It is completely independent and free from external interference to exercising the power of a state. In international law, all sovereign states, whatever size, strength, political, economic, ideological and social system, are equal.

Jean Bodin, the founder of the sovereignty theory, pointed out that, "Sovereignty is the principle of the existence of a state, and it is the non-divisible and non-transferable supreme power of a state within its territory". Sovereignty is of great significance in the exchanges between states. In essence, it is the baseline to distinguish states and thus generates the symbols of sovereign states, such as national names, national flags, national emblems, national borders, national anthems, nationalities, national languages, and nationals.

Overall, sovereignty contains three elements: territory, people and regime, which were explained in articles 78, the first preambular paragraph and the second preambular paragraph respectively of the Charter of the United Nations [12]: "The trusteeship system shall not apply to territories which have become Members of the United Nations, relationship among which shall be based on respect for the principle of sovereign equality." "We the peoples of the united nations determined to save succeeding generations from the scourge of war, which twice in our lifetime has brought untold sorrow to mankind, and to reaffirm faith in fundamental human rights, in the dignity and worth of the human person, in the equal rights of men and women and of nations large and small, and to establish conditions under which justice and respect for the obligations arising from treaties and other sources of international law can be maintained, and to promote social progress and better standards of life in larger freedom, and for these ends to practice tolerance and live together in peace with one another as good neighbors, and to unite our strength to maintain international peace and security, and to ensure, by the acceptance of principles and the institution of methods, that armed force shall not be used, save in the common interest, and to employ international machinery for the promotion of the economic and social advancement of all peoples, have resolved to combine our efforts to accomplish these aims. Accordingly, our respective governments, through representatives assembled in the city of San Francisco, who have exhibited their full powers found to be in good and due form, have agreed to the present Charter of the United Nations and do hereby establish an international organization to be known as the United Nations."

In short, state sovereignty comprises three elements: the land, sea, air, resources, the persons within territory and nationals outside the territory, as well as the equal and independent regime. Only the political unit with a fixed territory, a certain population, a certain form of regime organization, and sovereignty can be called a sovereign state.

1.1.3   Mission of Sovereignty

With the foregoing discussion, sovereignty has both internal and external properties. The highest internal attribute of sovereignty is the political ruling power of a state, which realizes the internal unity of a state through the legislative, administrative, judicial, military, economic, cultural, and other means. The external attribute of sovereignty derives from the highest internal attribute of sovereignty, which consists of the self-determination of a state and integrity of territorial, which is realized by military, legal, diplomatic, economic, and other means. Sovereignty demands governing by law internally and maintaining independence and autonomy externally. The legal form of sovereignty is commonly defined in the constitution or basic law. It has the internal property and the external property. The external property of sovereignty is international mutual recognition. In short, it is the obligatory mission of sovereignty to resist foreign aggression and pacify the interior.

1.2   Adaptability of Sovereignty in Cyberspace

National sovereignty is the basic subject of the theory and practice of contemporary international law, occupies an important position. Cyberspace, a fundamental space in addition to land, sea, and air space, but lacks the international code of conduct. In recent years, more and more attention has been focused on the adaptability of national sovereignty in cyberspace. Especially after the outbreak of vicious cyber incidents such as PRISM, the discussion on the sovereignty in cyberspace continues unabated.

1.2.1   Composition of Cyberspace

The problem of how to divide the boundary of the cyberspace means how to form the cyberspace and establish sovereignty [15]. Before discussing the adaptability of national sovereignty in cyberspace, we introduce the constitution of cyberspace from three aspects: the definition, the legal attributes [16], and the boundaries of cyberspace [17].

Cyberspace is different from the traditional space of sea, land, and air. Different countries hold different positions and views on the legal attributes and the exercise of rights in cyberspace. The International Telecommunication Union (ITU) defined cyberspace as "the physical and non-physical terrain created by and/or composed of some or all of the following: computers, computer systems, networks, and their computer programs, computer data, content data, traffic data, and users" [18]. In 2003, the United States defined cyberspace as "the interdependent network of

THE   NATIONAL   STRATEGY   TO

SECURE CYBERSPACE

FEBRUARY 2003

Fig. 1.8 The National Strategy to Secure Cyberspace (February 2003) [20]

information technology infrastructures" in the National Strategy to Secure Cyberspace [19]. The definition of cyberspace affects the determination of network sovereignty. Network sovereignty determines the rationality of the state jurisdiction over the infrastructure and information content of cyberspace and the right of external defense. The international community needs a unified definition of cyberspace and network sovereignty based on laws (Fig. 1.8).

There are mainly two kinds of legal attributes about cyberspace: infrastructure theory and domain theory at present. In the infrastructure theory, the Internet is regarded as an important infrastructure of a state, and the Internet within national boundaries is under the jurisdiction of the sovereignty. The National Information Infrastructure: Agenda for Action, issued by The US government, clearly defined this concept. And the Chinese government also made a similar statement in relevant documents. In the domain theory, cyberspace is regarded as an area where sovereignty can be exercised, and the government should claim the legitimate right of self-defense against cyber attack, which was stipulated in the International Strategy for Cyberspace promulgated by the U.S. government (Fig. 1.9).

A state's demarcation of the boundary of cyberspace under its sovereignty is also the issue of cyber boundaries. Just as cyberspace is defined as a physical and non-physical domain, the boundaries of cyberspace should also include physical and non-physical boundaries. Cyber boundaries are the collection of the physical geographical boundaries and the non-physical network boundaries. Physical geographical boundaries are the territorial boundaries within the scope of a state's sovereignty, including the territorial boundaries of a state, and the geographical space where the national sovereignty covers, such as consulates and aircraft. Non-physical network boundaries are the intangible boundary established through network technologies, such as firewall, password system, dynamic protection of intrusion detection system, and other technical barriers.

Dividing national jurisdiction over cyberspace is to divide the cyberspace boundary among states in the global cyberspace on the premise of admitting the existence of cyberspace, and to determine national sovereignty in cyberspace.

1.2.2   Network Sovereignty in the New Era

Network sovereignty is the product of the new era, deriving from the existence of cyberspace. Different from the land, sea, and air fields which boundaries are relatively stable, in the Internet world, the national boundaries have expanded to the virtual world, and the network boundaries are invisible and the spatial scope is not clear.

On the one hand, the development of network technology and innovation expands the space of network boundaries. States are competing fiercely for the development, possession, analysis, and application of cyberspace information resources. With the policy game between different states, the strength of information technology capability, and the level of international status altering, the boundaries of network sovereignty are constantly changing and adjusting.

On the other hand, the emergence of international organizations such as the United Nations (UN), the World Trade Organization (WTO), and the International Organization for Standardization (ISO) has brought new opportunities and challenges to the development of network sovereignty. The emergence of these international organizations further expands and strengthens communications and

Fig. 1.9 International Strategy for Cyberspace (May 2011) [21]

coordination among international counterparts. Trade and cultural exchanges provide good opportunities for cultural communication. The increase in communications between the advanced techniques and equipments in the world has created favorable conditions for the network to improve the overall technological level and accelerate technological upgrading. At the same time, in the international competition, cyber powers can effectively expand their sovereign borders by technological strengths, while the relatively weak ones are faced with the constant compression and adjustment of the scope of network sovereignty.

Taking the China Broadcast Network as an example, after China's entering World Trade Organization (WTO), the opportunities and challenges have increased the sense of urgency for the reform and development of the China broadcasting and television system. This helps radio and television industries develop professional video services that meet the personalized needs and the new generation of radio and television types such as high-definition television (HDTV) and interactive television (ITV), which will expand the space for the survival and development of radio and television. China plays an active and constructive role in the WTO [22]. China's accession to the WTO has brought new challenges to the radio and television industries. The competitions between traditional media such as broadcast television, audio-video, books, newspapers, and new media such as the Internet will be increasingly intensified. Advertisement, programs, talent and other resources will be redistributed. With the entry of large foreign media groups, the exotic cultures and values may squeeze the living space of local culture and bring potential and profound influence on the broadcast television industries.

In the process of copyright protection, the China Broadcast Network has continuously strengthened communications and coordination with the world. In 1980, China became a member of the World Intellectual Property Organization (WIPO). In 1992, China acceded to the Berne Convention for the Protection of Literary and Artistic Works and the Universal Copyright Convention. In 1993, China acceded to the Convention for the Protection of Producers of Phonograms Against Unauthorized Duplication of Their Phonograms. China became a member of the world copyright family. China's accession to the WTO has accelerated the process of China's copyright legislation, and further improved the level of copyright protection.

Broadcasting organizations enjoy extensive protection of their programs under the Copyright Law, which further expands their neighboring rights. In terms of copyright protection, both China and other members of WTO, carry out activities within the framework of TRIPS, enjoy the same rights and obligations as each other, enjoy national treatment and most-favored-nation treatment, and provide a dispute settlement mechanism for solving copyright disputes. Besides, accession to the WTO is conducive to promoting the mutual understanding and cooperation between China and WTO member states in copyright legislation and law enforcement, strengthening the communication of copyright information, studying the new issues of copyright protection faced together, and constantly improving the level of copyright protection.

In terms of copyright protection, as cultural products, the programs in broadcast networks are treated by each state with different special policies from general merchandise. In the negotiations for the accession to WTO, China has never made any commitment to the opening of radio and television programs. Even if some overseas TV channels are launched in parts of China, they are only handled as mutually beneficial cooperation cases. This will help enhance cultural exchanges between China and other states and regions on the premise of protecting the copyright of the broadcasting network, to make full use of advantages and avoid disadvantages. China's radio and television industries will further accelerate the pace of reform and opening up, and further, promote the development of network sovereignty in the WTO. In Chap. 3, we propose the sovereignty network architecture based on China Broadcasting Network.

1.3   Exploration of Network Sovereignty

Scholars at home and abroad have made a series of achievements in the study of sovereignty in the Internet era, which is of great theoretical significance for promoting the international governance of cyberspace. But on the whole, the study of sovereignty in the Internet age is still in its infancy.

1.3.1   Theoretical Contend

There are mainly four mainstream views on the theoretical debate of network sovereignty: the theory of negating sovereignty in cyberspace [15], the theory of non-sovereignty in cyberspace, the theory of limited sovereignty in cyberspace, and the theory of complete sovereignty in cyberspace.

1. Theory of Negating Sovereignty in Cyberspace

Internet strategists who are vested interests in the current network architecture, advocate the global commonality or attribute of the Internet. This is to treat cyberspace as an international space similar to the high seas, and not to assert national sovereignty. This concept, though immature and controversial, poses a challenge to state sovereignty in cyberspace. Although this theory advocates network freedom and promotes the "de-government" governance model of cyberspace [23], in essence, it still shows the control of cyberspace sovereignty everywhere.

For example, on Oct. 27, 2015, the U.S. Senate introduced the Cybersecurity Information Sharing Act of 2015. The bill allowed private industries to share information collected on their users with the Department of Homeland Security (DHS). It gave the United States the right to track down and arrest citizens of other states, regardless of their nationality or location [24]. The bill broke the equal relationship between states when tracking criminal suspects. It essentially controls state sovereignty in cyberspace.

In 2018, the U. S. Defense Department released the Cyber Strategy that emphasized the concept of "Defense forward". This has been interpreted by the outside world as the US military would implement network attacking and defense moves in other states. In August of that year, U.S. President Donald Trump signed an order overturning President Barack Obama's Presidential Policy Directive no. 20 (PPD-20), giving the military more freedom to deploy advanced cyberweapons without being blocked by the State Department or the intelligence community. Earlier, the US President also gave the military the freedom to deploy advanced cyber weapons without hindrance.

In short, the vested interests of IP networks have been touting the risk of a "Cyber Pearl Harbor" for years, but they were responsible for the world's first use of cyber-weapons against a foreign facility. As the initiator of cyber warfare, this genre is not only the most powerful state in cyber warfare but also the state that has launched the most cyber warfare.

2. Theory of Non-sovereignty in Cyberspace

Similar as the negating sovereignty theory, the non-sovereignty theory is also one of the important views on the management of cyberspace due to the virtuality of cyberspace. This view holds that cyberspace is a free space for all mankind, and the government and public powers are denied access, thus there will naturally be no issue of national sovereignty. In other words, this view emphasizes individual freedom under rational control, advocates the distinction between individual authority and social authority, and does not restrict individual authority without harming others' interests. It starts from the liberal theory, adheres to the principle of human rights over sovereignty, and advocates network anarchism. The virtuality of cyberspace provides individuals with the convenience of free use of virtual information resources, and to some extent guarantees that citizens' freedom of speech and behavior in cyberspace is not subject to external constraints and control.

Although both the negating sovereignty theory and the non-sovereignty theory advocate network freedom, their starting points are different. From the perspective of network autonomy, the theory of non-sovereignty excludes any intervention of public power from government, "to deny all legislation, all power, all privilege, franchise, official and legal influence" [25].

3. Theory of Limited Sovereignty in Cyberspace

The theory of limited sovereignty in cyberspace originates from the "theory of limited sovereignty" in the "theory of state sovereignty". This theory advocates that states should abide by international conventions in exercising sovereignty, and emphasizes that in the process of exercising power, parts of power can be transferred to international organizations and institutions to expand common interests among states. On the other hand, it advocates that a state should give up its limited sovereign interests and gain greater national interests. Professor Yan Xuetong, a scholar of international relations, pointed out that "Sovereignty is a part of the national interest, which can be called the sovereign interest. Sovereign interests are not always aligned with the interests of all states. For example, to enter the WTO, China would have to give up some of its domestic economic decision-making power and economic jurisdiction, just like other member states, but this does not mean giving up national interests" [26]. Therefore, the theory of limited sovereignty in cyberspace advocates that, "the purpose of safeguarding sovereignty is to achieve greater national interests, rather than sovereignty itself. A small amount of national sovereignty may be appropriately limited or ceded to the greater national interest" [27]. The theory of limited sovereignty in cyberspace affirms that all states have network sovereignty. At the same time, it emphasizes the balance and choice between cyber sovereignty and national interests. This theory advocates that sovereign states should give full play to their enthusiasm and initiative, achieve joint governance under international consensus and treaty provisions, and achieve a dialectical unity between absoluteness and relativity under the framework of the United Nations.

4. Theory of Complete Sovereignty in Cyberspace

The absolute sovereigntists believe that the existence of a sovereign state is based on absolute sovereignty, and safeguarding sovereignty means protecting its right to survive and develop in the international community; all states must adhere to the basic principles of independence, equality, mutual respect, non-aggression, and non-interference. In the development history of international relations, the theory of state absolute sovereignty plays an important role in protecting the formation, consolidation, and development of European states. It has a certain barrier and protective effect on a majority of Asian, African and Latin American states emerging after the "World War II" to defend sovereignty and safeguard national independence and dignity [27]. The theory of state absolute sovereignty has also been completely transplanted into the cyberspace theory. In the international social order, developing countries are often at a disadvantage, whose national sovereignty is in a state of fragility and insecurity, and they are easy to become the object of interference by some big powers' network hegemony. Therefore, weak countries generally claim that cyberspace has complete sovereignty, and the international community needs to strictly govern cyberspace, closely monitor domestic information, resist external information, and safeguard national network sovereignty. However, the rapid development and popularization of Internet technology has put increasing pressure on developing countries to "popularize the Internet with an open attitude or continue to maintain the backward status quo" [28].

In short, cyberspace has the characteristics of virtuality, openness, shareability, and vulnerability, which makes national sovereignty easily weakened in cyberspace. But cyberspace is not a "land beyond law". In any area of sovereignty, observance of the law is a matter of principle. In particular, recent years people have seen the emergence of advanced forms such as cyber terrorism, cyber militarization, and cyber conflicts between states. The international community should actively explore solutions to cyberspace security governance, formulate practical plans, and improve relevant laws and regulations based on equal cooperation. At the same time, cyberspace governance, research of network technologies, and formulation of standards should be actively carried out to ensure that cyberspace has laws to follow.

1.3.2 Exploration and Practice

States have different understandings of network sovereignty, theories, and laws on network. States with strong national strength have more say in the world. Therefore, there are different practical schemes for cyberspace governance at present.

1. Construction of Offensive Internet Hegemony

As mentioned in the previous section, people who are vested interests in the current network architecture, advocate the global commonality or attribute of the Internet. The views on politics, primarily the US, pursue Internet freedom, which is fully demonstrated in its diplomatic strategy. In 2015, the US regarded the diplomatic strategy of Internet freedom as a priority project and included it in the International Strategy for Cyberspace, "When the US or its allies are under cyber attacks, the US will use all possible means of violence (diplomatic, economic or even military) to prevent or retaliate" [29]. Alvin Toffler, a world-renowned futurist, pointed out that, "The Rubik's cube of world politics will be in the hands of people with information power in the future. They will use the rights at their disposal, such as the right to control network and publish information, and take advantage of the strong cultural and linguistic advantages of English to achieve the goal that neither violence nor money can conquer" [30].

In terms of actions, the scheme tries to realize the monitoring of cyberspace on a global scale. In this process, technological advantages will gradually transform into power advantages and help it realize Internet hegemony. To interfere with other regimes and implement cyberspace surveillance on an international scale more conveniently, the common excuse for them is to fight against terrorist forces and promote freedom of expression.

The ultimate goal of them is to achieve network hegemony by monopolizing the international network rulemaking authority. The normal operation of the Internet cannot be separated from the root server and the domain name system. The root server of the existing DNS is in the hands of a few states, who control the distribution of Internet domain names and addresses, and provide legitimacy and compliance for the implementation of the policy of cyber hegemony by manipulating the Internet Corporation for Assigned Names and Numbers (ICANN). The United States is doing its utmost to suppress the interests of emerging Internet countries.

2. Construction of a Defensive Cyberspace Security Strategy

Compared with vested interests in the current Internet system, developing countries have relatively weak overall national strength, low level of network technology, and limited voice in cyberspace. They are committed to promoting the modernization of network governance capacity at the national level.

On the theoretical level, with the advent of the network era, these forces realize the importance of cyberspace. To counter hegemonism and consolidate power, they firmly call for network sovereignty and advocate that the international community jointly establish rules and regulations to safeguard cyberspace sovereignty and achieve the common development of the world. Russia, Brazil, and other countries have called for the regulation of the network, respect for the network sovereignty, and safeguard national sovereignty.

In terms of policy, the scheme mentioned above requires a focus on improving network technology and the level of network governance. At present, the vested interests in the Internet can occupy a favorable position because of its strong comprehensive national strength and advanced technology. On the other hand, developing countries are highly dependent on the Internet. If they want to gain equal status in cyberspace, they must strengthen the technological construction. The improvement of cyber governance is also an important way for developing countries to cope with network hegemonic attacks. The developing countries continue to strengthen the network legislation, legislating a code of conduct in cyberspace. According to statistics, more than 90 countries in the world have formulated special cybersecurity protection laws [31], and in the future, more and more developing countries will legislate a code of conduct in cyberspace and maintain cyber security through legalized means.

3. **International Governance Patterns**

It is difficult for a single sovereign state to maintain cyber security and govern cyberspace on its own. It requires extensive participation and in-depth cooperation among all countries. According to the above description, it can be found that neither of the above two cyberspace security strategies can achieve good governance in cyberspace. In this regard, some international organizations and sovereign states put forward the following international governance patterns of cyberspace [32]:

(1) UN Governance Pattern: as the most authoritative international organization among governments, the United Nations has tried to dominate the international governance of cyberspace, trying to reach an international agreement on network governance. Among them, the UN World Summit on the Information Society has played an important role in the process of international cyber governance, providing a platform for relevant international actors to express their interest demands and playing an active role in promoting the multi-dimensional governance of cyberspace. However, the operation of the United Nations cannot be separated from the financial support of governments, and the coherence of the United Nations policy will be limited to some extent under the condition of being limited by national funds. In 2014, the United States staunchly resisted handing over the control of ICANN to the United Nations. Therefore, the UN governance pattern is difficult to change the monopoly of network resources led by the United States.

(2) "Multi-stakeholders" Governance Pattern: the Tunis Agenda, adopted by the UN in 2005, for the first time proposed a pattern of "multi-stakeholder" governance. At one time, this pattern was regarded as the best approach to Internet governance, and it provided a more universal innovative pattern of global governance [33]. The "multi-stakeholder" pattern recognizes the limited government management in cyberspace, tries to explore the role of

non-governmental organizations, and advocates participatory democratic practice, to determine the forms and rules of the Internet and realize the autonomy of cyberspace. Although this pattern has some effect on accommodating the interests of all parties, it is difficult to practice. The "multi-stakeholder" governance model is uncertain in determining the rights of stakeholders [34], and it is generally questioned whether the participants can achieve diversity and the generation mechanism of representative countries. Therefore, there are still many defects in this pattern in terms of meeting the equity pursued by developing countries.

(3) State-centered Governance Pattern: the state-centered governance pattern advocates the top-down governance of state functions in cyberspace governance, believing that the government is the main actor in cyberspace governance and should fully crack down on network crimes and maintain cyber security. It enables developing countries to enjoy the same rights as developed countries, avoids conflicts of interests among multi-stakeholder and decentralization of organizations, reduces governance costs, and improves governance efficiency.

1.4 Overview of Network Sovereignty

Taking national sovereignty as a starting point to promote the formulation of the international code of conduct on the Internet is the best choice that conforms to the interests of most states. Confronted with the understanding and practice of network sovereignty, it's necessary to form the legal countermeasures and suggestions to safeguard international cyberspace sovereignty. It is important to shape a cyberspace governance system that is in line with the development realities of all countries, and protect the voice of international governance in cyberspace, providing the theoretical basis to fight network hegemony of technology power, defend the network sovereignty, govern cyberspace, and participate in the formulation of relevant international rules.

1.4.1 Legal Connotation of Network Sovereignty

Whether a state can exercise jurisdiction in cyberspace is regarded as the first generation of the issue of cyberspace sovereignty, and how a state exercises jurisdiction is regarded as the second generation of the issue. Western scholars thought that the first-generation problem has been solved, and we are facing the second-generation problem now. As mentioned above, the key disagreement in the international community today is how national sovereignty is exercised in cyberspace.

The existence and development of cyberspace is relatively short, and it has developed rapidly with the development of modern information technology and has a more complex and special structure. People's understanding of cyberspace is still evolving, and the exercise of state sovereignty in cyberspace is also evolving. In combination with the theories of cyberspace, relevant international practices, and the diversified composition of cyberspace, the exercise of state sovereignty in cyberspace should not be generalized but should be analyzed and treated differently in the light of actual conditions.

Firstly, the physical composition of cyberspace is generally considered as network infrastructure. As an artificial space, cyberspace is created by enterprises and individuals from different countries in the real world through various infrastructures such as computers, routers, and servers. These infrastructures are the physical or hardware basis of cyberspace, and they are distributed within the territory of different sovereign states. States have full and exclusive sovereignty over these network infrastructures. Although western countries tend to emphasize sovereign states' obligations to the network infrastructure, such as surveillance and prevention. They have even pushed the United Nations information security government to adopt a consensus document (A/70/174) containing several responsible norms of state conduct in international space. According to legal analysis, no state can use network facilities to engage or direct, control private to engage in acts that breach of national obligations. It has long been agreed upon in international law. Each state should monitor the personal behavior that someone uses the network infrastructure within the state's borders to commit illegal acts against other states, but the obligation to do so should be commensurate with their capabilities and should not be unduly strengthened [35].

Secondly, regarding the virtual information in cyberspace, the Internet has become one of the most important carriers of contemporary information transmission and exchange, which determines that the transmission and storage of massive information is one of the core functions of cyberspace. Due to the global nature of cyberspace and the reproducibility of data, the storage and transmission of data across borders is a common phenomenon, which is also one of the key differences between cyberspace and traditional physical space. Whether a country can exercise jurisdiction over data in cyberspace is a complex and critical issue.

In short, a state's network sovereignty includes both the sovereignty over its physical network infrastructure and the sovereignty over intangible network information and data. In terms of specific regulations, the flag state system of the law of the sea can be used for reference to solve the problems between them.

The international discussion on how to exercise state sovereignty in cyberspace is becoming regularized and concrete. For example, on February 2, 2017, Tallinn Manual 2.0 on the International Law Applicable to Cyber Operations, published by the NATO Cooperative Cyber Defense Centre of Excellence (CCDCOE), expounded the network sovereignty and the jurisdiction and prudential obligations related to it (Fig. 1.10).

TALLINN
MANUAL 2.0
ON THE
INTERNATIONAL
LAW
APPLICABLE TO
CYBER
OPERATIONS

SECOND EDITION

Prepared by the International Groups of Experts
at the Invitation of the NATO Cooperative
Cyber Defence Centre of Excellence

CAMBRIDGE

Fig. 1.10 Front cover of the Tallinn Manual 2.0 [36]

1.4.2 Layers of Network Sovereignty

In the past, the focus of network sovereignty has often been on the evolution and extensibility of sovereignty. However, it has become an indisputable fact that cyberspace, as the fifth frontier, is an important battlefield for all states. Different states have different demands for cyber security, and their terms of network sovereignty are also different. The international community should respect and understand the different views of states. Huang Zhixiong, an expert on International law in China, puts forward a three-layer framework for analyzing network sovereignty, which is used to find the applicable domain before exclusivity and alienation [9].

1. **Bottom Layer**

The bottom layer is the physical layer, which includes a variety of network infrastructures. On this level, international standardization and global connectivity should be pursued. To solve the digital divide, countries need to make collective transfers and developed countries export their results to developing countries.

2. **Middle Layer**

The middle layer is the application layer, which includes many applications of the Internet in real life, and reflects human activities in science and technology, culture, economy, trade, and life. At this layer, the influence of network sovereignty should be more tailored to local conditions, dynamic, peaceful, multilateral co-governance, and achieve a balance between freedom and order.

3. **Top Layer**

The top layer is the core layer includes politics, laws, political security, and ideology, which is related to the foundation of governance. It is the core interest of a state and cannot be challenged. Cyber security should not be used as an excuse to duplicate the division of forces between the enemy and ourselves in the traditional space. All Civilizations, cultures, and states should respect each other and coexist peacefully. As Chinese leader Xi Jinping said in his speech at UNESCO headquarters in 2014, "exchanges among civilizations should not be premised on the superiority or derogation of one civilization".

In a word, in the middle layer and bottom layer of the triangular framework, network sovereignty can be transferred to some extent, while at the top layer, the dominant role of the government is reflected.

1.4.3 Role of Network Sovereignty in Each Stage

China's view of network sovereignty expresses China's position on international relations in the real world. It does not make any explanation beyond the traditional concept of sovereignty. China emphasizes the sovereignty over cyberspace and has a very clear understanding of its stage of development and the historical mission of the government.

At the opening ceremony of the second World Internet Conference (WIC, Wuzhen, China), Chinese President Xi Jinping declared, "Our goal is to make the achievements of Internet development benefit more than 1.3 billion Chinese people and the people of other countries". And he proposed that the development of the Internet in China must be guided by the vision of people-centered development, and mentioned network sovereignty when discussing the relationship between security and development in an important speech on April 19.

Therefore, national development should be regarded as the top priority, and network sovereignty is to serve national development. The state should advocate network sovereignty, ensure that each state can independently formulate policies and plans suitable for their development according to the national conditions at home, strive for equal participation in Internet governance, and make the cyberspace order more just and equitable.

In short, the sovereignty network, including data, should undertake the objectives of promoting national development and national security.

1.5   Necessity of Advocating Network Sovereignty

Under the background of information revolution and globalization, network sovereignty is derived from political sovereignty, economic sovereignty and cultural sovereignty in the formation process of information society and new information concepts represented by the Internet and global electronic communication network. It's a part of modern national sovereignty. Although intercommunication and virtualization are typical characteristics of cyberspace, the reality of its foundation, including the carrier of information, content, and facilities for information transmission, determines that cyberspace is by no means a "land beyond the law" excluding state sovereignty and cannot be allowed to develop indefinitely.

1.5.1   Necessity of Dividing Information Sovereignty

The term "information" was proposed and used as a scientific term dating back to 1928 when L. R. V. Hartley distinguished between "message" and "information" in his essay Transmission of Information. The carrier of information is various, such as signal, intelligence, data, material, knowledge, symbol, and so on. In the legal sense, information as a form of resource is not only a description of the information in the physical world but also a concrete and describable existence, which is a symbol system that satisfies certain conditions. Its concerns are the issues that whether the information content is legal, whether the methods of information production, acquisition, and dissemination are legal, what legal responsibilities should be borne for illegal production, acquisition, and dissemination of information, and how to bear the legal responsibilities.

The core of Internet application is information interchange. Through the application of communication technology, the instantaneous output and transmission of information can be achieved. Everything in the world can be calculated, measured, recorded, and analyzed in the form of data, and then shared around the world. There are complex interest relationships among states in the world. In traditional international law, based on territorial sovereignty, a state has supreme sovereignty over all persons, objects, affairs, and acts within its territory, including the flow of information. Therefore, there is no doubt that human beings have national boundaries when using communication technology to acquire and disseminate resources, especially the content of resources must comply with the legal provisions of sovereign states.

The international community has reached a consensus on the protection of personal privacy and intellectual property rights in the field of online information dissemination, as well as the supervision of matters involving drugs, violence, pornography, and endangering national security. This also proves that although information is a virtual data existence, its content is related to all aspects of a state's economy, politics and culture, and the guarantee of information security affects the state's security and citizens' rights. However, the Internet has greatly weakened the state's control over the dissemination of information and the behavior of individuals within its territory. Network attacks also threaten national network infrastructure and vital information systems, which need protection by the military. If the network sovereignty is abandoned and the state sovereignty that exists above it is not recognized, it is a denial of the existence of information sovereignty and a rejection of sovereignty independence and equal protection of sovereignty in legal values.

1.5.2 Necessity of Network Territory

In the traditional information field, such as newspapers, books, radio, and television, the state can play a role in the control. However, in the Internet world, the contradiction between the regionalism of state sovereignty and the transboundary nature of the network is a difficult problem for the state to control the spread of Internet information.

Cyberspace exists virtualized in life based on the data carrier. There is no doubt that its content and the source or means of data transmission are of practical significance. More and more people present their identity, behavior, property, and interests in cyberspace. An increasing number of financial payments and international trade is carried out through online platforms. The real space and cyberspace show a trend of gradual fusion. At the same time, people's geographical location and space environment are dependent on the territory and jurisdiction of the state. In a word, the cyberspace cannot become an out-of-reality existence.

The network brings enormous convenience to people's production and life. However, there have also been illegal acts such as hacker attacks, network viruses, and so on. Some people use the Internet to engage in acts that breach of international law, such as human trafficking, drug trafficking, and arms trading. Besides, some people take advantage of the convenience and difficulty in monitoring the Internet to commit crimes. These dilemmas affect the state's economic, political, and cultural security. If the security of cyberspace cannot be guaranteed, it will be difficult to solve complex network disputes, and the security of states and citizens will be threatened for a long time, which is not conducive to the development of information technology.

Cyberspace has become the state's fifth frontier, besides the four frontiers of land, sea, sky, and space. The security of cyberspace affects and determines the security of other territories to a certain degree. Strengthening the concept of network sovereignty enables the government, in the position of safeguarding national sovereignty, and have the right to establish national information security in the network boundary and to review the information exported and imported.

1.5.3 Necessity of Making Rules Under the Law

Information technology was invented by human beings. Code can control the identity, time, place of using the network. Input different code will output different results, which determining the difference of network activities. Therefore, controllability is one of the foundations of Internet architecture. The Internet needs certain operating rules to guarantee its basic functions, such as authentication, compatibility, interconnection, and so on. From the operating rules of the Internet, we can also see the controllability of the cyberspace. Cyberspace involves technological, political, economic, cultural, and other factors, so rules need to be formulated.

The national legal system has great significance to the adjustment of network behavior, but there are also many limitations. Especially, when virtual space carries real legal relations, the characteristics of the Internet bring a series of difficulties for the implementation and application of laws, and the feasibility and legitimacy of traditional region-based laws are challenged. Therefore, the concept of network sovereignty makes it easy to legislate in cyberspace and provides theoretical support for the application of existing laws in cyberspace.

The world of code cannot be separated from legal regulation. Legal governance should be combined with technical governance. Legal governance takes precedence over technical governance, and technical governance should not break through the framework of legal governance. There have been a lot of precedents to prove the significance of formulating network rules under the law. For example, the Virginia Court of the United States ruled that cnnews.com, a domain name registered by Shanghai Meiya Company, violated the trademark right of CNN. When the court decided to suspend the domain name, it indicated that the government had already intervened in the governance of cyberspace. At the same time, because of the controllability of the network, it is possible to control the behaviors related to the national interests, to achieve the purpose of protecting the security of the national cyberspace. Besides, some cases, such as Germany's filtering requirement on the dissemination of illegal information on the Internet and Singapore's cracking down on extremist statements through the Internet model, prove the controllability of cyberspace and demonstrate the necessity of formulating rules under the law. From the perspective of safeguarding national security and maintaining world peace and security, it is necessary to regulate cyberspace appropriately at the national level and recognize the existence of network sovereignty.

References

1. Wang MH (1991) The dictionary of tax revenue. Liaoning People's Publishing House, Shen Yang
2. Wikipedia (2021) United States Declaration of Independence. https://en.wikipedia.org/wiki/United_States_Declaration_of_Independence. Accessed 28 Jan 2021
3. Wikipedia (2020) United States Declaration of Independence. https://en.wikipedia.org/wiki/File:United_States_Declaration_of_Independence.jpg. Accessed 29 Dec 2020
4. Bodin J (1992) On sovereignty: four chapters from the six books of the commonwealth. Cambridge University Press
5. Wikipedia (2018) Jean Bodin. https://en.wikipedia.org/wiki/Jean_Bodin. Accessed 29 Dec 2020
6. Wikipedia (2020) Johannes Althusius. https://en.wikipedia.org/wiki/Johannes_Althusius. Accessed 29 Dec 2020
7. Grotius H (1625) The law of war and peace. Chinese edition: Grotius H (2005) The rights of war and peace (trans: He QH). Shanghai People's Publishing House, Shanghai
8. Wikipedia (2020) Hugo Grotius. https://en.wikipedia.org/wiki/Hugo_Grotius. Accessed 29 Dec 2020
9. Huang ZX (2017) On cyber sovereignty jurisprudence, policy and practice. Social Sciences Academic Press, Bei Jing
10. Wikipedia (2020) Peace of Westphalia. https://zh.wikipedia.org/wiki/%E5%A8%81%E6%96%AF%E7%89%B9%E4%BC%90%E5%88%A9%E4%BA%9A%E5%92%8C%E7%BA%A6. Accessed 29 Dec 2020
11. Oppenheim L, Watts A (1992) Oppenheim's international law. Longman, London
12. United Nations (1945) Charter of the United Nations. https://www.un.org/en/charter-united-nations/index.html. Accessed 9 Nov 2020
13. Oppenheim (1905) International law: a treatise. Peace by Oppenheim L, vol 1. Longmans, London
14. Oppenheim (1906) International law: a treatise. War and neutrality by Oppenheim L, vol 2. Longmans, London
15. Hu L (2018) On the construction of national cyberspace sovereignty strategic system. Legal Econ 3:45–46 + 58
16. Deng J (2013) On the basic legal issues of cyberspace. Soc Sci Hunan 2:101–104
17. Xu KY (2015) Governance of cyberspace border: the new sphere of maintaining national political security. Stud Marxism 7:128–136
18. Westby JR (2010) ITU toolkit for cybercrime legislation. International Telecommunications Union
19. Bush GW (2003) The national strategy to secure cyberspace. The White House, Washington

20. U.S. government (2003) The national strategy to secure cyberspace. https://us-cert.cisa.gov/sites/default/files/publications/cyberspace_strategy.pdf. Accessed 29 Dec 2020
21. U.S. government (2011) International strategy for cyberspace. https://obamawhitehouse.archives.gov/sites/default/files/rss_viewer/international_strategy_for_cyberspace.pdf. Accessed 29 Dec 2020
22. Zhu H (2003) China's accession to the World Trade Organization and the protection of radio and television copyright. TV Res 4:4–6 + 1
23. Lu CY (2014) Challenges and adjustments to the Obama administration's cyberspace strategy. Contemp Int Relat 5:54–60
24. Congress, U. S. (2015) Cybersecurity information sharing act of 2015. Bills, S, 754
25. Bakunin MA (1970) God and the state. Courier Corporation, East China Normal University Press, Shanghai
26. Yan XT (1996) Analysis of China's national interests. Tianjin People's Publishing House, Tianjin
27. Yang HS (2000) Three different theoretical positions on state sovereignty: sovereignty interference theory, sovereignty absolute theory and sovereignty restrictive theory. World Econ Polit 3:18–22
28. Schmidt E, Cohen J (2013) The dark side of the digital revolution. Wall Street Journal
29. Zhang ZH, Cai RY, Zhang LK (2017) Analysis and enlightenment of the network information security strategy of the major developed countries. J Mod Inf 37(1):172–177
30. Toffler A (1990) Powershift. Plaza & Janes. Chinese edition: (2006) (trans: Wu Yingchun). China Citic Press, Beijing
31. World Internet Conference Panel (2014) Xi Jinping: respect the sovereignty of the network and seek common governance and win-win results. Shanghai Morning Post, 9–20 Nov 2014
32. Liu X, Zhu YN (2017) Network sovereignty theory: theoretical contention and international practice. J Southwest Minzu Univ (Human Soc Sci) 38(7):129–133
33. Bygrave LA, Bing J (2009) Internet governance: infrastructure and institutions. Great Lakes Entomol 3:137–140
34. Mueller ML (2010) Networks and states: the global politics of Internet governance. MIT Press. Chinese edition: (2015) (trans: Zhou Cheng). Shanghai Jiaotong University Press, Shanghai
35. Huang ZX (2017) On cyber sovereignty: jurisprudence, policy and practice. Social Sciences Academic Press (China), Beijing, p 71
36. Schmitt MN (ed) (2017) Tallinn manual 2.0 on the international law applicable to cyber operations. Cambridge University Press

Chapter 2
Interpretation of Network Sovereignty

In recent years, with the integration of the Internet and various economic and social fields, the security situation in cyberspace has been changing rapidly. There are more and more network games at the national level and the network attack and defense have become more intense. Network sovereignty has become one of sovereignty that all states are striving for.

2.1 International Community and Network Sovereignty

Since the establishment of the principle of national sovereignty by the Westphalian Peace Council in 1648, upholding sovereignty and opposing hegemony have been the important contents of international governance practice. More than 30 years after its birth, the DNS system has proved more robust than expected as the infrastructure of the Internet. However, root domains, important top-level domains, and root certificates were previously controlled by the U.S. government or by the U.S. government-authorized nonprofit ICANN due to some historical factors. Besides, attacks on the domain name system have become one of the most significant threats to global Internet security. The autonomous capability of the Internet in various regions, namely the network sovereignty, is always under threat, and the international community has long been concerned about this.

In 2003, the World Summit on the Information Society (WSIS) was held in Geneva. The Conference adopted the Geneva Declaration of Principles, which outlined the network sovereignty of states, "policy authority for Internet-related public policy issues is the sovereign right of States. They have rights and responsibilities for international Internet-related public policy issues" [1].

On February 2, 2017, the NATO Cooperative Cyber Defense Centre of Excellence (CCDCOE) announced on its website that the Tallinn Manual 2.0 was officially published. Compared with the initial version, Tallinn Manual 2.0 divided cyberspace into three layers: the physical layer, the logical layer, and the social

© The Author(s) 2021
H. Li and X. Yang, *Co-governed Sovereignty Network*,
https://doi.org/10.1007/978-981-16-2670-8_2

layer, and specified that all the objects, facilities, and personnel involved in these three layers could be controlled by states under the principle of sovereignty [2]. At the same time, the Manual also affirmed that states had external sovereignty in the field of cyberspace and states were free to engage in network activities and accede to international network treaties.

Since the core of the US strategy shifted from comprehensive defense to attack and deterrence in 2015, the competition among states for dominance and discourse power in cyberspace is more intense. On December 14, 2017, the Federal Communications Commission announced the abolition of the principle of net neutrality. In the same year, the UK used cyber attack and jamming for the first time in a joint military operation. On February 12, 2019, the State Duma of Russia passed a bill, which was designed to ensure the operation of the Internet in the country if access to servers abroad is cut off. The Japanese government released a new Medium-Term Defense Force Readiness Plan, which planned to set up a command to coordinate professional forces in space and cyberspace from 2019 to 2023 to enhance the size and capability of the network defense forces.

The International Code of Conduct for Information Security (the "Code") was an international effort to develop norms of behavior in the digital space, submitted to the UN General Assembly in 2011 by China and Russia. In 2015, China together with the United Nations permanent representatives from the member states of the Shanghai Cooperation Organization wrote to the Secretary-General of the United Nations and submitted the revised Code, the content of which was reflected in the resolution of the United Nations General Assembly that year. The resolution reaffirmed that, "Policy authority for Internet-related public issues is the sovereign right of States, which have rights and responsibilities for international Internet-related public policy issues", and claimed that "comply with the UN Charter and universally recognized norms governing international relations, including respect for the sovereignty, territorial integrity and political independence of all states", and "All states have rights and responsibilities to protect, under relevant laws and regulations, their information space and critical information infrastructure from threats, disturbance, attack and sabotage" [3].

On the opening ceremony of the second world Internet Conference, China's leader Xi Jinping pointed out that, "International community should strengthen dialogue and cooperation based on mutual respect and trust, promote the reform of the global governance system of the Internet, and jointly build a peaceful, secure, open and cooperative cyberspace, and establish a multilateral, democratic and transparent global Internet governance system".

2.2 International Comments on Network Sovereignty

Alvin Toffler, a famous sociologist, predicted in his book the Third Wave in the 1980s that, "Whoever masters the information and controls the Internet, will have the world". Today, with the development of the network information field, this prediction has been verified. After entering into the twenty-first century, states carried out a variety of network actions, such as the phishing case of Syrian Electronic Army, the test of Russia's unplugged internet and so on, games between states are being played in cyberspace.

2.2.1   Age of Cyber Warfare

National security and stability are closely related to network sovereignty. Since the end of the twentieth century, the construction of network forces in various states has been continuously strengthened, and the technology and means of network attack have emerged one after another (Fig. 2.1).

Estonia

Estonia was the first country in history to experience a massive cyber attack on its government and critical infrastructure. In three weeks from April to May 2007, Estonia was hit by a massive network attack, which focused on the websites of the Estonian president and parliament, various government departments, political parties, three of the six major news organizations, the two largest banks, and communications companies. When the attack broke out, it caused great shock in the local area, and almost all websites were paralyzed, causing great losses. The scale and intensity of the cyber attack in Estonia had brought it to the attention of the

Fig. 2.1   Cyber warfare now—tales from the digital battlefield (Lima Charlie news) [4]

international military community, and it was regarded as the first cyber warfare at the national level.

Iraq

In terms of the operation of the Internet, as the network in Asia and Europe passes through the United States, the United States can control the root server to count and monitor the relevant information resolved by all the servers, such as the number of visits and the frequency of website clicks. During the Iraq War in 2003, the United States used the resolution rights of the root server to cancel all application parsing work of Iraqi domain name "iq", and all Iraqi domain names with the suffix "iq" could not be searched from the Internet, which dealt a major blow to the network sovereignty of Iraqi.

Libya

In April 2004, the United States launched a network attack that brought down the top-level domain name of Libyan, making sites with the suffix "ly" (Libyan abbreviation) unsearchable on the engine, and Libya disappeared from the Internet for three days.

Syria

In 2013, the Syrian Electronic Army accessed the Twitter account of the Associated Press (AP) by including malicious links in phishing emails. The email was sent to the employee of AP in the name of a colleague. Hackers then posted a fake news report on the AP account that said there had been two explosions at the White House and that President Barack Obama had been injured. The reaction was so dramatic that the stock market fell 150 points in five minutes.

Iran

In August 2010, Iran's Bushehr nuclear power plant was attacked by a computer network virus of unknown origin. At least 30,000 Iranian computers were attacked, so that, Iran's Bushehr nuclear power plant, which had just been capped, had to take out the nuclear fuel and delay its start. Iran's nuclear development plans had also been put on hold. The computer virus later came to be known as Stuxnet.

Israel

As early as 1998, Israel recruited young men who successfully invaded the U.S. Department of Defense and began to step up the research into cyberwarfare. In the Palestine-Israel conflict and Lebanon-Israel conflict, Israel used the way of network attacks to tamper with web pages and attack TV stations to influence the direction of public opinion. The Israeli military hacked into military computers to steal secrets to determine the focal points and precise coordinates of fire strikes. They blocked the communication and command system of the enemy to grasp the best combat time. All of this was a snapshot of the Israeli military in the cyberwarfare.

Venezuela

In early March 2019, Venezuela experienced a massive power outage that affected 18 out of 23 states, directly paralyzing transportation, health, communications, and infrastructure. Venezuelan President Nicolas Maduro accused that the United States orchestrated this network attack on the Venezuelan power system to create chaos and force the government out of office through a nationwide blackout. Some analysts believed that in the absence of direct and indirect military intervention, launching network attacks on Venezuela may be the best option for the United States.

The United States

The United States has dominated the Internet for decades, and its network discourse power has been impacted by governments and groups of all states. The United States is the region with the highest incidence of transnational network crimes. It is also the most popular state for top hackers in the world, while it is actively hacking into networks around the world. The United States Department of Energy was hacked 1131 times between 2010 and 2014, 159 times successfully. Julian Assange, the founder of WikiLeaks, once hacked into the U.S. military and obtained 90,000 classified U.S. military emails. Some criminal groups, such as Anonymous and the New World, frequently challenged the network sovereignty of the United States. In October 2016, public institutions and social networking sites in California, New York, Boston, Seattle, and other areas in the United States were hacked by Anonymous for several hours, causing nearly half of the network in the United States to crash. It was one of the largest attacks in history.

2.2.2 Governance of Network Sovereignty

According to the principle of cyberspace sovereignty, the state plays a leading role as the most important subject in the governance of cyberspace. At present, national governance of network sovereignty is mainly carried out at both internal and external levels. Internally, through legislation and the establishment of special regulatory agencies, cyberspace can be formally brought under the jurisdiction of the national legal system to achieve effective governance of cyberspace and establish national authority in cyberspace. Externally, national network security can be guaranteed through network security defense measures, establishing the dominant position of sovereign states in network security [5].

1. Domestic Legislative and Regulatory Policies

Since 1995, South Korea has amended the Telecommunications and Commerce Law, passed the Basic Law on National Informatization and the Regulations on Network Security Management, and other new laws and regulations. South Korea started to implement the Internet real-name system in 2002. Through a series of legislative activities, the national jurisdiction has been extended to the Internet field [5].

Since the establishment of the European Union, a series of relevant policies and regulations have been introduced. Besides, to proceed with some legislative activities, many states have set up specialized agencies to manage the cyberspace. As early as March 2004, the European Union established the European Network and Information Security Agency (ENISA). In January 2013, the European Union established a special police department, the European Cybercrime Centre (EC3), to combat online child pornography and organized network fraud activities [5].

The government of the United States has set up six special network security agencies to monitor cyberspace. The outbreak of the PRISM (surveillance program) showed that the U.S. government's control of cyberspace has never been interrupted.

Other states, such as Thailand and Japan, have also set up institutions to regulate cyberspace. Many states have adopted legislation and institutional construction to regulate the behavior in cyberspace. National sovereignty and government regulation have never been far from cyberspace governance.

2. External Multilateral Co-government

The Internet Corporation for Assigned Names and Numbers (ICANN) is a nonprofit organization set up to manage domain name systems, IP address allocation, protocol configuration, and master server systems. It is managed under contract by the Internet Assigned Numbers Authority (IANA) and other entities together with the U.S. government now. For a long time, it was unilateral control by the United States, inconsistent with neither the industry's expectations of Internet freedom nor other states' expectations of network sovereignty. As a result, calls for the reform of ICANN have continued unabated. Since 2014, many states, including China, Russia, Brazil, and India, have proposed multiple multilateral cooperation programs on global governance of cyberspace under the principle of network sovereignty [5].

In April 2014, at the Conference in Sao Paulo, Brazil and other states proposed a more moderate improvement plan within the framework of ICANN, requiring promoting the position of the Governmental Advisory Committee (GAC) of ICANN, enhancing the voice of states in ICANN, and confirming the independent jurisdiction over the limited number of services in ICANN.

The East West Institute of the United States submitted a work report at the Berlin summit, which required that the governments of sovereign states should be given substantive management authority in the ICANN system.

At the Pusan conference in 2014, India proposed to transfer the main functions of global governance in cyberspace from ICANN to the International Telecommunication Union (ITU), which was explicitly refuted by the United

States, claiming that it would never transfer the management authority of ICANN to the management agencies composed of one or more states.

These schemes introduced the principle of multilateralism, compared with schemes of the United States. These proposals sought to enhance the role of sovereign states in the global governance of cyberspace. The first two proposals called for enhancing regulatory authority for sovereign states under the original ICANN framework, while India's proposal directly called for sovereign states and international organizations among them to become the main body of global governance in cyberspace, replacing the functions and status of the former ICANN.

Therefore, in the network space governance, adhering to the principle of national sovereignty, establishing international multilateral cooperation mechanism, with governments around the world hand in hand, and through the way of negotiation mediation, jointly participating in the global governance in cyberspace, is the most effective and legal way. Only the principle of state sovereignty in cyberspace governance is truly clear, can states ensure the security right in cyberspace, and participate equally in the global governance in cyberspace. Through the establishment of multilateral cooperation mechanisms, international conflicts on cyber issues can be effectively avoided and all sovereign states in the world can coexist peacefully and achieve win-win cooperation in cyberspace [5].

2.2.3 Strategic Layout of Some States

1. Germany

Germany has been forming a hacking force since 2006, and it was described as an effort to close the gap with other states. In a 2012 document submitted to the Bundestag, the German military said it had the initial capability to attack enemy networks. On April 1, 2017, the German Armed Forces formally established the Cyber and Information Command. The command, together with the army, navy, air force, and medical services, constitutes the Bundeswehr system, which will play a leading role in the NATO alliance.

In 2019, to ensure the digital sovereignty of European users of cloud services, the German Federal Ministry for Economic Affairs and Energy launched the GAIA-X project, which aimed to develop an efficient and competitive, secure, and trustworthy data infrastructure for Europe, and reduce the reliance on cloud services from Amazon, Microsoft, Google, and other American companies (Fig. 2.2).

The project was supported by representatives of business, science, and administration from Germany and France, together with other European partners. The founding members on the German side included Beckhoff Automation, BMW, Bosch, DE-CIX, Deutsche Telekom, German Edge Cloud, PlusServer, SAP, and Siemens. The project objectives were that combining existing central and decentralized infrastructures to form a system, which can offer a uniform data and service room. Bundesverband Information swirtschaft, Telekommunikation und neue

Fig. 2.2 GAIA-X project [6]

Medien (BITKOM), declared that the GAIA-X project would make an important contribution to strengthening digital and data sovereignty in Europe. "The next stage will be for Germany to invite other EU member states to join the project", German Economy Minister Tomas Altmaier said.

2. **Russia**

Russia is one of the states that are actively preparing for the sovereignty network. It has tested its unplugged internet and strengthened the supervision of network information through national legislation and other means.

The Russian government has a long history of tight control over the network environment. As early as 2006, the government restricted the use of websites and apps such as the professional social network LinkedIn, the chat app Zello, the instant messaging tool Telegram, and required foreign companies to give the system access right to the government for monitoring user data. The Russian government required all Internet facilities to pass through an official control center, and allowed itself to cut off external connections at any time, closed unapproved websites, and monitored all Internet traffic. The Russian government is also preparing to adopt a series of technical measures and formulate more related policies in the future.

In November 2019, Russia formally promulgated and implemented the Sovereign Internet Law, which stated that it was necessary to be prepared to use the Russian sovereignty network RuNet to safeguard national network security in case of external network attacks. Under the bill, government agencies and security agencies, as well as all communications operators, messaging, and email providers, would have to take part in the test, but it would not affect regular Internet users. The law stipulated that the Internet infrastructure of Russia should gradually be free

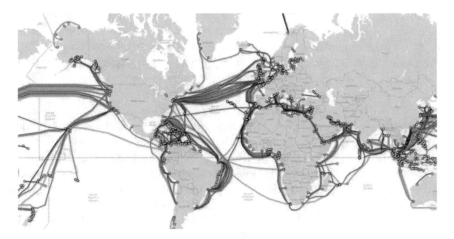

Fig. 2.3 A map showing undersea internet cables around the world [7]

from dependence on foreign nodes, especially in the case of external attacks, Russia can cut off the connection with the outside world and operate the regional Internet independently. Russia is currently building its domain name system (DNS), which is expected to be completed by 2021 (Fig. 2.3).

On December 24, 2019, Russia successfully tested its unplugged internet. The results showed that the Internet services in Russia could still work when isolated from the rest of the Internet. This test took a few days and was conducted on a specially designated network. This is the first time for Russia to conduct network tests against the risk of being disconnected from the Internet. The tests also examined the stability of communications, the security of cellular communications, including issues of protecting personal data, preventing calls and SMS from being hijacked, intercepting traffic, and the security of using the Internet of Things [8].

Meanwhile, Russia's setting up its homegrown version of Wikipedia and is requiring all smartphones to come with Russian software pre-installed.

3. **The United States**

As early as the late 1990s, the U.S. government began to pay attention to the challenges brought by the development of the Internet, attaching importance to the construction of the information security mechanism in cyberspace, setting up several network security institutions, and issuing several laws and regulations, striving to maintain the information security in cyberspace.

In November 2008, President Obama announced the creation of a cyberspace Policy review panel to review the state of U.S. network security. In December 2009, the White House Office of Cybersecurity was established. In May 2010, the U.S. military established the Cyber Command to coordinate and safeguard the operations in cyberspace. In May 2011, the U.S. government published International Strategy for Cyberspace, which combined Internet policy with International policy goals for the first time. In July 2011, the U.S. Department of Defense issued the Strategy for Operating in Cyberspace, which provided specific operational guidelines for the deployment and implementation of U.S. military network operations. In 2013, President Obama issued Executive Order 13,636, which explicitly proposed the mechanism for sharing security information in cyberspace. Then, the National Institute of Standards and Technology (NIST) led a partnership with the private sector to develop the Framework for Improving Critical Infrastructure Cybersecurity (FCIC), and the U.S. government had an agreement with the private sector on cybersecurity issues. In February 2016, the U.S. government issued the Cybersecurity National Action Plan (CNAP) and established the Commission on Enhancing National Cybersecurity to ensure greater information security capabilities for the United States in the digital age [9]. On March 23, 2018, President Trump formally signed the Clarify Lawful Overseas Use of Data Act (CLOUD Act), which provided a legal basis for the U.S. to obtain foreign data and the eligible foreign governments to obtain data in the U.S [10].

The U.S. government attaches great importance to network sovereignty by maintaining network and information system security through policy promulgation, institution establishment, law enforcement, and other means.

4. France

In 2013, in the White Paper on Defense and National Security, France identified network attack as one of the most serious external threats to national sovereignty and called for the establishment of network defense forces. France planned to set up a chain of network defense operations and invested 1 billion euros by 2019 for network security and defense research. At the same time, France planned to reserve a civilian network security and defense force, training civilian network defense experts to serve the government and the military when necessary [11] (Fig. 2.4).

5. The United Kingdom

The United Kingdom has set up the UK Office of Cyber Security, which is directly responsible to the Prime Minister, to draw up the development plan of cyberwarfare forces and the action platform for cyber security at the strategic level. The UK's Cyber Security Operations Centre (CSOC) is affiliated with the Government Communications Headquarters (GCHQ) and is responsible for providing intelligence support for military cyber warfare operations. The UK's National Cyber Force is affiliated with the Ministry of National Defence, it's mainly responsible for training and operation planning related to military cyber warfare, and coordinating military technical experts to carry out security protection for military network targets [11].

Fig. 2.4 2013 French white paper on defence and national security [12]

FRENCH WHITE PAPER

DEFENCE AND NATIONAL SECURITY

2013

foreword by
François Hollande
President of the French Republic

Liberté • Égalité • Fraternité
RÉPUBLIQUE FRANÇAISE

2.3   Safeguarding Network Sovereignty

Network sovereignty is an important part of national sovereignty as well as the extension of national sovereignty in cyberspace. Just as the principle of national sovereignty constitutes the foundation of the modern international order, the principle of network sovereignty is also the cornerstone of the international order in cyberspace. In the tide of globalization, technology is changing at a rapid pace, and the Internet is one of the best. If a state can take the lead in cyberspace issues, it can take the lead in the building of order and the game of rules in cyberspace. Therefore, we should respond to the demand of most states for network sovereignty and firmly safeguard network sovereignty.

2.3.1 Strengthen the Awareness of National Network Sovereignty

Cyberspace is the fifth frontier, besides the four frontiers of land, sea, sky, and space, and the research on cyberspace is still in its infancy. States have different understandings about how to apply sovereignty rules in cyberspace, but growing voices are calling for greater attention to network sovereignty (Fig. 2.5).

The European Union advocates jurisdiction over the security of citizens' data. German Chancellor, Angela Merkel, has long, and lately more openly, been defending the need for Europe to shield its digital sovereignty. The UK has launched the National Cyber Security Programme (NCSP) to protect the UK from network attack and develop sovereignty in cyberspace. Russia has introduced the Sovereign Internet Law, which established the autonomous and controllable network sovereignty of the Russian Network from five aspects, including domain name autonomy, regular exercises, platform control, and active disconnection of the Internet. China is the initiator and advocate of national sovereignty in cyberspace. In June 2010, China issued a white paper, named "the State of the Internet in China", which clearly stated that the Internet in China was under the jurisdiction of Chinese sovereignty, and Chinese Internet sovereignty should be respected and upheld [14]. On July 1, 2015, the National Security Law of the People's Republic

Fig. 2.5 Cyberspace [13]

of China came into effect, and China defined cyberspace sovereignty in the form of law for the first time [15].

On December 16, 2015, at the Second World Internet Conference, Xi Jinping, the Chinese President, attended the opening ceremony and delivered a speech, and elaborated on the four principles and made a five-point proposal concerning Internet development and governance. The four principles included respecting sovereignty in cyberspace, upholding peace and security, promoting openness and cooperation, and building a sound order. The five-point proposal includes accelerating the building of global Internet infrastructure for greater connectivity, building an online platform for cultural exchanges and mutual learning, promoting innovative development of the digital economy for common prosperity, maintaining cybersecurity to promote orderly development, building a system of global governance in cyberspace to promote equity and justice (Fig. 2.6).

On December 27, 2016, the China national network information office issued the National Network Security Strategy, which called for the network security strategy as a national strategy, specified that the network sovereignty was the new frontier of national sovereignty. "The Internet was the new field of human activity as important as land, sea, sky, and space, and national sovereignty had been extended to cyberspace, and cyberspace sovereignty had become an important part of national sovereignty. It has become the consensus of the international community to respect the sovereignty of cyberspace, safeguard network security, seek joint governance and achieve win-win results" [17]. Like national sovereignty, network sovereignty is inviolable. Therefore, the strategy also required that, "Chinese citizens should

Fig. 2.6 Location of the world internet conference at Wuzhen, China [16]

resolutely safeguard the sovereignty of cyberspace. All network activities within the scope of China's sovereignty are subject to the constitution, laws, and regulations. We should take all measures, including economic, administrative, scientific, technological, legal, diplomatic, and military measures, to protect the security of China's information facilities and resources, and unswervingly safeguard China's cyberspace sovereignty. We are firmly opposed to any act that subverts China's state power or undermines China's national sovereignty through the Internet" and "we should respect the right of all states to choose their development path, cyberspace management model and cyberspace public policy and to participate peacefully in international cyberspace governance. The cyberspace affairs of each state are up to its people. States have the right, in light of their national conditions and drawing on international experience, to enact laws and regulations on cyberspace and take necessary measures under the law to manage their information systems and network activities within their territory". On March 1, 2017, China launched the International Strategy of Cooperation on Cyberspace, addressed China's position on issues related to international cyberspace governance, and claimed that, "a clear definition of cyberspace sovereignty not only reflects the responsibilities and rights of governments to govern cyberspace under the law, but also helps promote the building of a platform for benign interactions among governments, enterprises, and society, and creates a healthy ecological environment for the development of information technology and international exchanges and cooperation" [18].

2.3.2   Opposing the Theory of Negating Sovereignty in Cyberspace

Different states have different attitudes towards network sovereignty, based on their development level of network technology and status in the international community.

Developed countries, the US, for example, believes that cyberspace, outer space, international waters, and space, constitute the infrastructure of the global system and belong to the global commons [19], so states should not exercise national sovereignty there. The view of the United States' denial of network sovereignty is inseparable from its global cyberspace strategy, which aims to establish hegemony in the global cyberspace and strive for national interests to the maximum extent. But at the same time, the United States has enacted several strategies and laws about cyberspace. In short, the network developed states, represented by the United States, adopt the double standards on the issue of network sovereignty. In the international network space, the network is considered the global commons, when they need to collect other information for their national interests. At this time, they claim that the United Nations is not competent for the task of cyberspace governance, and a new international mechanism for conducting global governance of cyberspace should be established, the purpose of which is to introduce American global strategy through the network. However, when it is necessary to strengthen the domestic network supervision, they claim that cyberspace is a sovereign domain, and their state has absolute and exclusive sovereignty jurisdiction over cyberspace.

In the international community, emerging network states, such as Russia, have certain strengths in some network technologies and infrastructure and have become the developed states in network science and technology by vigorously developing network business. These emerging network states believe that the network should have explicit sovereign attribute.

Besides, there are some network developing states with relatively backward development of network technology. These states attach more importance to the role of network sovereignty so that they can protect relevant interests as far as possible in relatively backward areas. Network developing states have taken an active part in the governance of cyberspace issues and made up for their shortcomings in network technology through legislation. Meanwhile, they have actively carried out cooperation with emerging network powers to jointly safeguard national sovereignty in cyberspace.

The conflict between these network ideas is typically reflected in the struggle for control of the domain name system. Cheng Weidong, a Chinese scholar, said that the theory of negating sovereignty in cyberspace, which some developed states insist on, ignores the essential characteristics of the network, and ignores the principal contradiction and the main aspects of contradiction, has violated the basic Marxist materialist dialectics, also does not have the practical basis of network field, and cannot stand the test of practice. In essence, the theory of negating sovereignty in cyberspace reflects the special interests of a few states and attempts to use the assertion of network freedom to spread western values [20]. As Professors Goldsmith and Wu Xiuming of Harvard Law School have pointed out, a few sovereignty holdouts, while talking about the top-down governance, Internet community and other things, have never actually ceded control of the root domain name, and the root domain name is still under their control and ownership. No matter how powerful a single country is, it does not have the right to control the root domain name. Therefore, talking about privatization or internationalization can divert the attention of critics. But the United States has never meant to give up its power over such an important resource [21]. Other scholars believe that the leapfrog technology cannot be the natural reason for the borderless and super-territorial cyberspace, and the global commons theory of cyberspace undermines the basis for international cooperation on cyberspace governance [22]. The principle of sovereignty is a basic principle that should be upheld in international cyberspace governance. Cyberspace within the territory of a state is governed by this state and is not subject to any other factors. The academic circles criticize the theory of negating sovereignty in cyberspace, which illustrates the foundation of network sovereignty from the perspective of theory and jurisprudence.

2.3.3 Peace and Stability in Cyberspace

Safeguarding cyber sovereignty in the age of globalization requires more comprehensive international cooperation. In international exchanges in the field of cyberspace, the use and development of cyberspace should be conducted peacefully. This is conducive to the development of the overall international network environment and is a manifestation of the peaceful development of the Charter of the United Nations and the principle of prohibition of the use of force. Nowadays, there are endless network attacks in international cyberspace, despite the Tallinn Manual 2.0 has provided a detailed analysis of the right of self-defense against network attacks, it is more important to advocate the peaceful use of cyberspace. We should oppose all forms of cyber warfare and non-peaceful activities by taking advantage of information technology. We will continue to advocate the importance of sovereignty in cyberspace, uphold the principle that network sovereignty brooks no foreign interference, and firmly oppose the intention of a few states to interfere in the internal affairs of other states by taking advantage of the international nature of the Internet. We advocate that all states abandon the Cold War mentality in cyberspace governance and the double standards of cyber commons and sovereignty, seek peace through consultation and cooperation based on full respect for other states' network sovereignty, and further enhance their security through the peaceful use of cyberspace.

On the other hand, the innovation of core technologies is the most important for determining whether a state can become a network powerful nation, perform the defense power in cyberspace, and safeguard the independent right and jurisdiction in cyberspace. Internet is a sunrise industry to promote economic development, as well as an important field to safeguard national interests. Only when a state has technological advantages in the field of international cyberspace can its voice be enhanced.

Therefore, only by proposing a new network architecture from the technical level can the current domain name system truly remove its control over the network, realize equal and multilateral cooperative governance among states, and realize sovereignty autonomy in the field of the Internet.

2.3.4 Expanding the Network Sovereignty Concept

Only by respecting the network sovereignty can states, regardless of their size or strength, conduct dialogue and exchanges on an equal footing, fully safeguard their interests in cyberspace and effectively promote the solution of various network problems. The current global Internet governance system has yet to be improved. China puts forward the claim of network sovereignty, which has been widely praised by the international community.

Safeguarding sovereignty equality in cyberspace can accommodate different interests of different states, eliminate potential conflicts among states, and create opportunities for mutual benefit and win-win outcomes among states. While the Internet has integrated the world into a global village, it has also created a pattern of mutually dependent interests among states in the world. Every state's sovereignty rights and interests in the field of information should not be infringed upon by others, and every state has the right to safeguard its information security. We should foster the sense of building a community with a shared future in cyberspace and abandon the old concept of zero-sum games and winner-takes-all in cyberspace. Each state cannot seek its absolute security at the expense of the security of other states. All states must follow the principle of equality in network sovereignty, respect the major interests of other states, and stick to the principle of working together, mutual trust, and mutual benefit. Thus, a realistic basis for international cooperation will be established, and more states and people can ride the express train of the information age and share the fruits of Internet development. States need to foster consensus in cyberspace, expand the interests of cooperation in cyberspace, strengthen exchanges among the international community on network security technologies, institutional building, and management experience. We should work hand in hand to build a multilateral, democratic, and transparent global Internet governance system.

On December 3, 2017, at the fourth world Internet conference, representatives from China, Egypt, Laos, Saudi Arabia, Serbia, Thailand, Turkey, and the United Arab Emirates jointly launched the "Belt and Road" Digital Economy International Cooperation Initiative. With the help of the "Belt and Road" initiative, China can combine geographical advantages with network technology [23], promote the concept of network sovereignty, and promote the building of a community with a shared future in cyberspace (Fig. 2.7).

Many states along the "Belt and Road" route have maintained good bilateral relations with China for a long time, and they also face some threats in terms of economic and social development and national security. For example, some states have a low level of network infrastructure construction, which needs to be improved urgently. China has comparative technological advantages and can carry out in-depth cooperation in such fields as network infrastructure construction, to strengthen support and assistance for the popularization of Internet technology and infrastructure construction in backward areas. On the premise of respecting each other's network sovereignty, we should vigorously develop and build our cyberspace, narrow the digital divide [25], and then build the "Information Silk Road" with the vast developing states and some developed states along the "Belt and Road" (Fig. 2.8).

Fig. 2.7 "The belt and road" Digital economy international cooperation initiative launching ceremony (2017), by Shuqiong Pan [24]

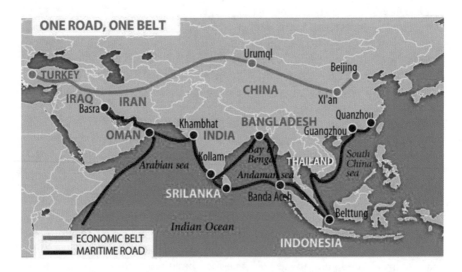

Fig. 2.8 Belt and road initiative [26]

2.4   Current Situation of the Sovereignty of Broadcasting TV Network

Broadcast TV network is the key link of three networks convergence of cable television network, telecom network, and computer network. Moreover, it's the representative of an efficient and cheap comprehensive network. Broadcast network has the advantages of wide frequency band, large capacity, many functions, low cost, strong anti-interference ability, and supports various services to connect thousands of families. Its development has laid a foundation for the development of information superhighway.

Broadcast TV network has covered a vast area. In 2003, the number of Chinese Community Antenna Television (CATV) subscribers exceeded 100 million. After eight years of rapid development, the number exceeded 200 million in 2011. By the end of 2016, the actual number of CATV users was 252 million, among which the number of digital TV users also reached 210 million, with a digitalization rate of 83.3%. Television has become one of the information tools with the highest household occupancy rate, and the CATV network has become the most popular multimedia in the home. However, the CATV network still uses coaxial cable to deliver TV programs to users at an analog level. The development direction of the CATV network includes the two-way broadband TV on demand (VOD), access to the Internet through CATV network for TV on demand, CATV call, etc. The ultimate development target is to make the CATV network become a broadband bidirectional multimedia communication network.

With the rapid development of new media formats such as IPTV, Internet TV and mobile TV, broadcast TV networks are facing unprecedented challenges. For example, in terms of video business architecture, flexible and convenient services of Internet video can meet the rapid changes of user needs and consumer psychology under the information development, which makes the traditional TV camp split. As the main promoter of digital TV reform in the radio and television industry, the cable network is in the situation of network segmentation and decentralization, and the national operation subject is still unformed.

In fact, the broadcast network has some inherent advantages, such as safe and reliable network transmission, stable and clear transmission quality, the exclusive copyright of some programs, and strong credibility. However, due to the lack of supervision on content, the openness of the telecommunication network and the Internet is too casual.

In a word, the signal transmission of public radio and television channels is one of the basic services of the broadcast TV network. As an important national information infrastructure, the broadcast TV network is an important national strategic resource and an important barrier against network risks. Therefore, the broadcast TV network should provide technical means for the national guidance of public opinion in cyberspace, and stabilize the sovereign equality in cyberspace. We must build, strengthen, and enhance its role in the national network security

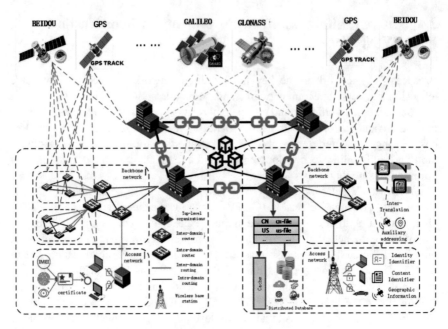

Fig. 2.9 The architecture of sovereignty network [47]

system, strengthen the broadcast TV network based on the sovereignty network research and construction.

This book proposes and sets up the sovereignty network, a new future network architecture, from the technical level. It makes the cyber space dynamic, peaceful, multilateral co-governance, and achieve a balance between freedom and order. The sovereignty network based on MIN is the first technically viable sovereignty Internet architecture in the world. The architecture of sovereignty network is shown as Fig. 2.9. We describe its architecture, core technologies, application and diffusion, and choose the broadcast TV network as a typical application scenario to introduce.

2.5 The 4th Power: United States Presidential Election in 2020 and Network Sovereignty

2.5.1 United States Presidential Election and the Storming of the United States Capitol

The 2020 United States presidential election was the 59th quadrennial presidential election, held on November 3, 2020. All 435 seats in the House of Representatives and 33 seats in the Senate were also be elected to form the 117th United States

Fig. 2.10 2020 US elections [28]

Congress. The general election in November was also an indirect election, in which voters cast ballots for a slate of members of the Electoral College, these electors then directly elected the president and vice president. On December 14, 2020, electors voted to confirm Joe Biden as the 46th president of the United States and Kamala Harris as vice president [27] (Fig. 2.10).

Trump secured the Republican nomination without serious opposition, while Biden secured the Democratic nomination over his closest rival, Senator Bernie Sanders, in a competitive primary that featured the largest field of candidates for any political party in the modern era of American politics. Biden's running mate, Senator Harris from California, was the first African-American, first Asian-American, and third female vice presidential nominee on a major party ticket. In addition, there were some nominees representing other political parties and independent nominees. Central issues of the election included the public health and economic impacts of the ongoing COVID-19 pandemic; civil unrest in reaction to the killing of George Floyd and others; the U.S. Supreme Court following the death of Ruth Bader Ginsburg and confirmation of Amy Coney Barrett; and the future of the Affordable Care Act [27].

The election saw a record number of ballots cast early and by mail due to the ongoing pandemic. As a result of the large number of mail-in ballots, some swing states saw delays in vote counting and reporting; this led to major news outlets delaying their projection. After Election Day, Trump and numerous Republicans attempted to subvert the election and overturn the results, alleging widespread voter fraud. On November 7, 2020, all major US news outlets announced that Biden and Kamala Harris had won the election, receiving the minimum 270 electoral votes needed after winning Pennsylvania's 20 Electoral College votes. On November 9, 2020, even after the major US news outlets had declared that Biden had won the election, the General Services Administration had not certified the winner and

Fig. 2.11 The storming of the United States Capitol [29]

refused to approve documents to begin the transition process. On November 23, 2020, the General Services Administration officially approved the documents for the transition process to proceed with the handover, and stated that its role was not to certify the elect, but that the real elect would be determined by the electoral process prescribed by the Constitution of the United States [27] (Fig. 2.11).

Trump said he would leave the White House if the Electoral College voted for Joe Biden. On December 14, the Electoral College voted to choose the president and vice president. The voting results confirmed Joe Biden as the 46th president of the United States and Kamala Harris as the 49th vice president of the United States. Congress was scheduled to meet in joint session on Jan. 6, 2021, to formally count the electoral college votes submitted by states, which was known as certifying the voting result of each state. Under the Constitution of the United States, the count and certification of the electoral votes by both houses of Congress was the final step in formally confirming the president's election. But the Capitol was attacked by extremists that day, rioters breached police perimeters and stormed the United States Capitol Complex.

It was the first time the U.S. Capitol had been attacked since the British invaded in 1814. A large number of demonstrators gathered outside the Capitol and carried pro-Trump flags to protest the election. The demonstration then escalated into a riot, with protesters clashing with security guards and tear gas was in the air. Some demonstrators even broke the windows of the Capitol and entered the inside of the building. Five people were killed during the riot. The counting of the electoral votes by Congress was interrupted by pro-Trump rioters storming the Capitol [30]. This riot led to the suspension of the joint session to certify the election results. After the

Fig. 2.12 Supporters of President Donald Trump climb the west wall of the U.S. Capitol on Wednesday, Jan. 6, 2021, in Washington (Jose Luis Magana/Associated Press)

joint session of the United States Congress confirmed Joe Biden and Kamala Harris in the early hours of January 7 local time, Trump immediately issued a statement promising an "orderly" transfer of power on January 20, 2021 (Fig. 2.12).

2.5.2 Social Media Platforms Banned Trump's Accounts

After the storming of the United States Capitol on January 6, 2021, which was carried out by a mob of supporters of President Donald Trump, many social media platforms and technology companies suspended or banned Trump's and his team's accounts from their platforms, and many business organizations cut ties with him [30]. On January 9, 2021, Fox News listed the social media platforms which has "banned" or "restricted" Trump, these platforms took different measures to block Trump's and related accounts.

According to the statistics of American media Axios, the platforms that had taken measures to ban or restrict Trump and his related accounts include Twitter, Facebook, Google, Apple, YouTube, Reddit, Instagram, Snapchat, Discord, Pinterest and other platforms [31]. Some platforms and websites had taken "Trump" as a sensitive word and removed posts as soon as they detected it. The account of Trump's teenage youngest son, Barron, was suspended after he sent a tweet "Hello Twitter" (Fig. 2.13).

@realDonaldTrump

Account suspended

Twitter suspends accounts which violate the Twitter Rules

Fig. 2.13 Twitter has suspended President Trump from its platform [32]

"After close review of recent Tweets from the @realDonaldTrump account and the context around them we have permanently suspended the account due to the risk of further incitement of violence," Twitter said. "In the context of horrific events this week, we made it clear on Wednesday that additional violations of the Twitter Rules would potentially result in this very course of action." [33] (Fig. 2.14).

After Twitter had banned his @realDonaldTrump account, Trump tweeted from the US president's official @Potus account suggesting he would "look at the possibilities of building out our own platform in the future" and railing against Twitter. But the tweets were removed from the platform as soon as they were posted [35] (Fig. 2.15).

"If it is clear that another account is being used for the purposes of evading a ban, it is also subject to suspension," Twitter said in a statement. "For government accounts, such as @POTUS and @WhiteHouse, we will not suspend those accounts but will take action to limit their use. However, these accounts will be transitioned over to the new administration in due course and will not be suspended by Twitter unless absolutely necessary to alleviate real-world harm." Twitter's policy would also prohibit Trump from directing a third party to operate a Twitter account on his behalf [33].

Trump supporters have been migrating to niche social media platforms such as Parler for days. Parler briefly topped the app download charts. In response, Internet giants targeted Parler. Google removed Parler from the App Store and Apple issued

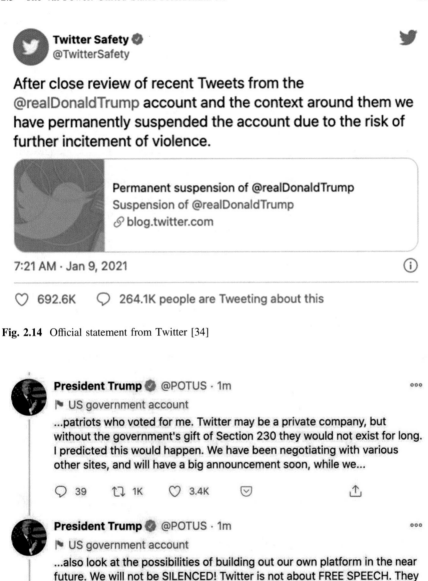

Twitter Safety ✔
@TwitterSafety

After close review of recent Tweets from the @realDonaldTrump account and the context around them we have permanently suspended the account due to the risk of further incitement of violence.

> Permanent suspension of @realDonaldTrump
> Suspension of @realDonaldTrump
> 🔗 blog.twitter.com

7:21 AM · Jan 9, 2021   ⓘ

♡ 692.6K   💬 264.1K people are Tweeting about this

Fig. 2.14 Official statement from Twitter [34]

President Trump ✔ @POTUS · 1m   000
⚑ US government account

…patriots who voted for me. Twitter may be a private company, but without the government's gift of Section 230 they would not exist for long. I predicted this would happen. We have been negotiating with various other sites, and will have a big announcement soon, while we…

💬 39   ⟲ 1K   ♡ 3.4K   ⌄   ⬆

President Trump ✔ @POTUS · 1m   000
⚑ US government account

…also look at the possibilities of building out our own platform in the near future. We will not be SILENCED! Twitter is not about FREE SPEECH. They are all about promoting a Radical Left platform where some of the most vicious people in the world are allowed to speak freely…

Fig. 2.15 Trump's tweets after his account had been suspended by Twitter [35]

an ultimatum to Parler. Amazon stopped offering Parler web services such as hosting. According to a report by Agence France Presse (AFP) on January 11, 2021, the Parler platform could not be accessed after midnight on that day, showing that it was disconnected [36].

Twitter boss Jack Dorsey has said banning US President Donald Trump was the right thing to do. He reiterated that removing the president from Twitter was made after "a clear warning" to Mr. Trump. "We made a decision with the best information we had based on threats to physical safety both on and off Twitter," Mr. Dorsey said. But he accepted that the move would have consequences for an open and free internet [37] (Fig. 2.16).

Political figures in Europe disapproved of the social media platforms' decision to block Mr. Trump's account, such as German Chancellor Angela Merkel. Steffen Seibert, Merkel's chief spokesman, said the operators of social media platforms "bear great responsibility for political communication not being poisoned by hatred, by lies and by incitement to violence", at a regular news conference in Berlin, on January 11, 2021. He said it's right not to "stand back" when such content is posted, for example by flagging it. But Seibert also said that the freedom of opinion is a fundamental right of "elementary significance." "This fundamental right can be intervened in, but according to the law and within the framework defined by legislators—not according to a decision by the management of social media platforms," he told reporters in Berlin. "Seen from this angle, the chancellor considers it problematic that the accounts of the U.S. president have now been permanently blocked" [38].

Bruno Le Maire, France's finance minister, said he was "shocked" by Twitter's decision to ban Trump, adding that "digital regulation should not be done by the digital oligarchy… (and) is a matter for the sovereign people, governments and the judiciary" [39].

 jack ✔
@jack

I do not celebrate or feel pride in our having to ban @realDonaldTrump from Twitter, or how we got here. After a clear warning we'd take this action, we made a decision with the best information we had based on threats to physical safety both on and off Twitter. Was this correct?

8:16 AM · Jan 14, 2021

♡ 115K   💬 66.7K people are Tweeting about this

Fig. 2.16 Twitter's chief said he did not celebrate or feel pride in the ban—which came after the Capitol riot [37]

Cédric O, France's digital minister, expressed similar concerns. He wondered about these social networks which "may decide to censor someone followed by 88 million people completely unilaterally". "They intervene in the public debate without any democratic supervision, without action of justice, by referring only to their general conditions of use", he estimated. "Imagine that Twitter or Facebook becomes politicized and considers that it is on this or that political side, he explains. They could change their terms of service by saying, for example, 'you are not allowed to make pro-Democrat or pro-Republicans, or pro-party or party in France. In such cases, they would censor an entire expression without any supervision since they are beyond the control of justice and the plurality of democratic expression" [40].

Thierry Breton, the European Union's commissioner for the internal market, said in a Politico opinion piece: "Just as 9/11 marked a paradigm shift for global security, 20 years later we are witnessing a before-and-after in the role of digital platforms in our democracy". Breton said the incidents in Washington revealed "the fragility of our democracies—and the threat that under-regulated tech companies can pose to their survival". He expressed serious doubts about whether social media companies alone should have the power to block accounts of a US president. "The fact that a CEO can pull the plug on (Trump's) loudspeaker without any checks and balances is perplexing," Breton wrote. "It is not only confirmation of the power of these platforms, but it also displays deep weaknesses in the way our society is organized in the digital space," he added. Breton also defended the EU's recent proposals to more closely regulate big tech, including the Digital Services Act that could see platforms face fines for failures to curb illegal content [41].

"Who decides free speech?" 20 Minuten AG said that free speech was not just a legal issue. The worry is that in the digital world, the Internet giants have the final say. Der Spiegel said the Internet giants had allowed their platforms to be abused for too long over the years, allowing false and incitement to violence to spread on their platforms in an effort to monopolize and expand, and that some politicians in power enjoyed special protections. But the fact that these billionaires from Silicon Valley can decide for themselves who will be banned and who will be allowed to speak online is frightening [36].

2.5.3   Regulating the Power of Social Media Platform

The fourth power, also known as the 4th power, refers to the fourth political power in addition to "executive power, legislative power, judicial power", refers to the media, the public and thereby. The 4th power theory emphasizes the freedom of speech stipulated by the press. The 4th power theory points out that "the purpose of the freedom of the press guaranteed by the constitution is to maintain the autonomy of the media, so that the media can provide information, public opinion and entertainment programs that are not controlled or influenced by the government, promote people to care about the work of the government and discuss public affairs, so as to play the function of supervising the government."

In network age, individual free speech should be under the control of national sovereignty, not determined by digital platforms. Although states have always been and will continue to play a central role in international affairs, the non-state actors such as multinational corporations are also becoming increasingly important, and some enterprises even have more powerful associative power than sovereign states. For example, the market value of Google's parent company Alphabet is equivalent to the combined GDP of Belgium and the Netherlands. Twitter, Facebook, Apple and others have access to information about hundreds of millions of netizens around the world.

Internet giants have gained a stronger position in front of the country and the public. It depends on the vast amount of data they have, the user engagement brought by their services, and the political and social power of the platforms themselves. The blocking of Trump's account by some social media in the United States is precisely the exercise of their super power [42].

Global information, communication technologies and industries are growing more rapidly than global governance and the regulatory forces of sovereign states. How to define the authority boundary and legal responsibility of the digital oligarchy has become a problem and it's difficult to reach agreement among states. The influence of related enterprises on national politics, economy, society and other aspects as well as the challenges brought by them are increasing day by day. Uncontrolled digital power has caused a certain negative impact on the traditional political life, social opinion and economic activities [42].

The legal environment in the United States is relatively friendly to digital platforms. Following the tradition of the First Amendment to the United States Constitution, American politics and society are very cautious about public power interfering with the dissemination of public opinion. Section 230 of Communications Decency Act (CDA) provides immunity from liability for providers and users of an "interactive computer service" who publish information provided by third-party users. The statute in Section 230(c)(2) further provides "Good Samaritan" protection from civil liability for operators of interactive computer services in the removal or moderation of third-party material they deem obscene or offensive, even of constitutionally protected speech, as long as it is done in good faith [43]. This means that the judicial authorities cannot hold Internet companies accountable for what users say on the Internet platforms, on the other hand, users cannot hold Internet companies accountable for their posts being deleted or blocked on the Internet platforms. This regulation is designed to prevent the Federal Communications Commission (FCC) from interfering with the Internet, and also allows websites to censor content according to their own needs [44].

For more than 20 years, Section 230 has been criticized by politicians and civil rights activists as condoning cyberbullying, but many in the tech industry believe it creates the foundations of modern Internet services. While the U.S. Department of Justice (DOJ) has proposed legislation in 2019 to change the division of responsibility for content censorship, it has faced fierce opposition from some companies such as Facebook. On October 14, 2019, Facebook and Twitter again restricted the sharing of two scandalous reports about Hunter Biden, son of former vice president Joe Biden, citing violations of the platform's rules. This move brought the debate over whether to alter Section 230 of the Communications Decency Act to the surface again [44].

Twitter's decision to suspend of U.S. President Donald Trump's account was pushing European leaders to stress the need to regulate social media companies [45]. Thierry Breton, EU Commissioner for Internal Market, raised concerns about the "deep weaknesses in the way our society is organized in the digital space". Manfred Weber, chairman of the EPP group at the European Parliament, pointed out that "we cannot leave it to American Big Tech companies to decide what we do and do not discuss, what can and cannot be said in a democratic discourse. We need a stricter regulatory approach" [46].

Europe has taken a very different stance to regulating Big Tech than the U.S., where companies are often left to regulate themselves and typically enjoy a significant degree of legal immunity though protections like Section 230. This most recent criticism against large social media platforms could be interpreted as a warning shot [39]. The European Commission has taken a double initiative in this direction on behalf of EU member states [46]. The Digital Services Act and the Digital Markets Act are two crucial steps ahead for Europe, and they are mainly aimed at Internet giants known as "gatekeepers" rather than ordinary enterprises [44]. The Digital Services Act will regulate the business models and behaviors of Internet giants in line with European standards, stressing that Internet giants have a legal obligation to censor content, which could lead to huge fines of hundreds of millions of euros if breached. These two laws will also create a precedent for major states to establish rules for the regulation of digital enterprises, and have a strong leading significance for the formulation of legal norms in relevant fields around the world.

For some time, US Internet companies, represented by Silicon Valley giants, have been the target of EU regulatory "focus". In February 2020, the newly appointed President of the European Commission, Ursula Gertrud von der Leyen, explained the concept of "digital sovereignty", "EU must have the ability to make its own choices based on its own values and rules in the digital field". Many European media believed that the General Data Protection Regulation (GDPR) and the Digital Services Act, will be a key legal tool for the current leadership of the EU to ensure digital sovereignty [44].

At the same time, EU is also striving for the construction of its own Internet infrastructure [44]. In their speeches last year, Ursula Gertrud von der Leyen, Merkel and the French President Macron all mentioned Europe's huge dependence on U.S. Internet companies such as Google, Facebook and Twitter. They announced that EU would launch the "GAIA-X" cloud computing platform as a platform to store data, based on the joint development of France and Germany.

In conclusion, Trump's accounts suspension shows that digital sovereignty should be strictly governed by national network sovereignty, and the consolidation of national network sovereignty needs to be implemented in the construction of sovereign network, so as to ensure the effective protection of network sovereignty and national security.

References

1. World Summit on the Information Society (2003) Geneva declaration of principles. https://www.itu.int/net/wsis/docs/geneva/official/dop.html. Accessed 18 Nov 2020
2. Schmitt MN (2017) Tallinn manual 2.0 on the international law applicable to cyber operations. Cambridge University Press
3. Su JY (2013) A brief comment on the draft international code of conduct for information security. China Inf Secur 8:88–92
4. Lima Charlie News (2019) Cyber warfare now—tales from the digital battlefield. https://limacharlienews.com/cyber/cyber-warfare-now-tales-from-the-digital-battlefield/. Accessed 29 Dec 2020
5. Qiang YH (2020) Multilateral and multi-participant governance in global cyberspace based on national sovereignty. J Weinan Normal Univ 35(1):69–75
6. German Federal Ministry for Economic Affairs and Energy (2019) GAIA-X: a federated data infrastructure for Europe. https://www.data-infrastructure.eu/GAIAX/Navigation/EN/Home/home.html. Accessed 29 Dec 2020
7. TeleGeography (2020) Submarine cable map. https://www.submarinecablemap.com/. Accessed 29 Dec 2020
8. Woollacott E (2019) Russia cuts off its internet, with mixed results. https://www.forbes.com/sites/emmawoollacott/2019/12/24/russia-cuts-off-its-internet-with-mixed-results/?sh=234ac00b619d. Accessed 18 Nov 2020
9. Zhuang XC (2016) Research on American information security mechanism from the perspective of network sovereignty. China Foreign Affairs University Press
10. He ZL, An HJ (2019) US extraterritorial law enforcement reform and China's response of the network sovereignty view. J Inf Secur Commun Priv 12:37–47
11. Sun Y, Wang CH (2019) The Internet domain and Frontier from the perspective of general frontier science and discussing the basis of establishing national network sovereignty. Borderland Stud China 1:23–44
12. French Ministry of Defence (2013) French white paper on defence and national security. http://www.defense.gouv.fr/english/content/download/206186/2393586/file/White%20paper%20on%20defense%20%202013.pdf. Accessed 29 Dec 2020
13. Chile Desarrollo Sustentable (2020) Obvious challenges in terms of access and privacy in the 25th anniversary of the founding of the "world wide web".http://www.chiledesarrollosustentable.cl/noticias/noticia-internacional/la-world-wide-web-cumple-25-anos-con-claros-desafios-en-acceso-y-privacidad/. Accessed 29 Dec 2020
14. The State Council Information Office of the People's Republic of China (2010) The situation with the internet in China. People's Publishing House, Bei Jing
15. The National People's Congress (NPC) of the People's Republic of China (2010) The cybersecurity law of the People's Republic of China. http://www.npc.gov.cn/wxzl/gongbao/2017-02/20/content_2007531.htm. Accessed 18 Nov 2020
16. World Internet Conference (2020) 2020 World internet conference. http://www.wuzhenwic.org/. Accessed 29 Dec 2020
17. Cyberspace Administration of China (2016) National network security strategy. http://www.cac.gov.cn/2016-12/27/c_1120195926.htm. Accessed 18 Nov 2020

18. Ministry of Foreign Affairs of the People's Republic of China (2017) The international strategy of cooperation on cyberspace. https://www.fmprc.gov.cn/web/ziliao_674904/tytj_674911/zcwj_674915/t1442389.shtml. Accessed 18 Nov 2020
19. Jasper S (2010) Securing freedom in the global commons. Stanford University Press
20. Cheng WD (2018) A critical analysis of negative views on cyber sovereignty. Chin J Eur Stud 36(5):61–75 + 7
21. Wu JX (2017) Introduction to cyberspace mimic defense. Science Press, Bei Jing
22. Hu L, Qi AM, He JH (2018) The national cyberspace sovereignty strategy (A draft of scholar's proposal). Hebei Law Sci 36(6):80–88
23. Wang P (2017) Firmly safeguarding cyberspace sovereignty. Social Sciences Weekly, 001-19 Jan 2017
24. Office of the Central Cyberspace Affairs Commission (2018) "The belt and road" Digital economy international cooperation initiative launching ceremony. http://www.cac.gov.cn/2018-05/11/c_1122775756.htm. Accessed 29 Dec 2020
25. Yang J (2013) The role of the rising economies in bridging the international digital divide: a case study on the IT cooperation between China and the African countries. Shanghai Inst Int Stud 4:24–29 + 87–88
26. Linked in (2020) Belt and road initiative. https://www.linkedin.com/company/onebeltoneroad/. Accessed 29 Dec 2020
27. Wikipedia (2021) 2020 United States presidential election. https://en.wikipedia.org/wiki/2020_United_States_presidential_election. Accessed 18 Jan 2021
28. Skandinaviska Enskilda Banken AB (publ) (2021) 2020 US elections: 15 questions and answers. https://sebgroup.com/press/news/2020-us-elections-15-questions-and-answers. Accessed 18 Jan 2021
29. Netease Technology Report (2021) US Capitol riots revealed by foreign media: planned online for weeks. https://tech.163.com/21/0107/16/FVOIJG7T00097U7R.html. Accessed 18 Jan 2021
30. Wikipedia (2021) 2021 storming of the United States Capitol https://en.wikipedia.org/wiki/2021_storming_of_the_United_States_Capitol. Accessed 21 Jan 2021
31. Axios (2021) All the platforms that have banned or restricted Trump so far. https://www.axios.com/platforms-social-media-ban-restrict-trump-d9e44f3c-8366-4ba9-a8a1-7f3114f920f1.html. Accessed 21 Jan 2021
32. cnBeta.com (2021) Research: Fake traffic dropped sharply after Twitter blocked Donald Trump's account. https://www.cnbeta.com/articles/tech/1079019.htm. Accessed 18 Jan 2021
33. CNN Business (2021) Twitter bans President Trump permanently. https://edition.cnn.com/2021/01/08/tech/trump-twitter-ban/index.html. Accessed 19 Jan 2021
34. The Washington Post (2021) Twitter bans Trump's account, citing risk of further violence. https://www.washingtonpost.com/technology/2021/01/08/twitter-trump-dorsey/. Accessed 19 Jan 2021
35. BBC (2021) Twitter 'permanently suspends' Trump's account. https://www.bbc.com/news/world-us-canada-55597840. Accessed 18 Jan 2021
36. China Youth Online (2021) Blocking of Trump leads to "freedom of speech" debate, and Internet giants such as Twitter and Facebook are criticized for "excessive power". http://news.cyol.com/app/2021-01/12/content_18915745.htm. Accessed 18 Jan 2021
37. BBC (2021) Twitter boss: Trump ban is 'right' but 'dangerous'. https://www.bbc.com/news/technology-55657417. Accessed 19 Jan 2021
38. The Associated Press (2021) Germany's Merkel: Trump's Twitter eviction 'problematic'. https://federalnewsnetwork.com/world-news/2021/01/germanys-merkel-trumps-twitter-eviction-problematic/. Accessed 21 Jan 2021
39. Forbes (2021) 'Problematic' and 'perplexing': european leaders side with Trump over Twitter ban. https://www.forbes.com/sites/roberthart/2021/01/11/problematic-and-perplexing-european-leaders-side-with-trump-over-twitter-ban/?sh=6e18cba913b5. Accessed 21 Jan 2021

40. Archyde (2021) Cédric O wants to "create a legislative framework" for social networks. https://www.archyde.com/cedric-o-wants-to-create-a-legislative-framework-for-social-networks/. Accessed 21 Jan 2021

41. AFP (2021) Capitol attack will go down in history as social media's '9/11': EU commissioner. https://www.timesnownews.com/international/article/capitol-attack-will-go-down-in-history-as-social-medias-911-eu-commissioner/705802. Accessed 21 Jan 2021

42. Dong YF (2021) Dong YF: Blocking Trump, what is Europe really concerned about. https://opinion.huanqiu.com/article/41WEOM0iPM2. Accessed 18 Jan 2021

43. Wikipedia (2021) Section 230. https://en.wikipedia.org/wiki/Section_230. Accessed 22 Jan 2021

44. Sina Technology (2021) Power and regulation of tech giants: what does Europe see from blocking Trump. https://finance.sina.com.cn/tech/2021-01-13/doc-ikftpnnx6351112.shtml. Accessed 18 Jan 2021

45. Politico (2021) Merkel among EU leaders questioning Twitter's Trump ban. https://www.politico.eu/article/angela-merkel-european-leaders-question-twitter-donald-trump-ban/. Accessed 22 Jan 2021

46. Martens Centre (2021) Safeguarding the algorithm of democracy. https://www.martenscentre.eu/blog/safeguarding-the-algorithm-of-democracy/. Accessed 23 Jan 2021

47. Li H, Wu JX, Xing KX et al (2019) Prototype and testing report of a multi-identifier system for reconfigurable network architecture under co-governing. Scientia Sinica Informationisnis (49):1186–1204

Chapter 3
Architecture of Sovereignty Network

Although the early design concept of the Internet was decentralized, but the current control of the basic technology architecture showed a strong centralized form. Therefore, it is imperative to put forward a new network architecture to meet the demand of future network development and realize decentralized management of domain names by technical means. Sovereignty network effectively realizes multilateral co-management and co-governance of cyberspace, and terminates centralized management under the single IP identifier. At the same time, it protects the network of all countries from the risk of DNS disappearance and blinding caused by the smear of ICANN root zone or hacker attack. With the construction of the sovereignty network, the co-governance and self-management of all parties in cyberspace can be truly realized.

3.1 Sovereignty Network

3.1.1 Definition of Sovereignty Network

The sovereignty network with the new architecture, is an identity centric national network that can be used to autonomously and controllable register, generate, manage and resolute the domain name of an identity of both natural person or corporate organization.

According to international regulations, cyberspace business is governed by Radio and Television laws which are stricter than telecommunications laws of various countries. The news release of telecom network is relatively arbitrary, which results in the large number of false information in the network, indicates that telecom is not enough in content supervision. The national broadcasting network represents the voice of the national government, and the supervision of its ideological field has always been the top priority for various departments or industries.

H. Li and X. Yang, *Co-governed Sovereignty Network*,
https://doi.org/10.1007/978-981-16-2670-8_3

Therefore, this book chooses the broadcast television network as a typical application scenario to deploy a completely autonomously managed sovereignty network with a new identity centric architecture that is safe, reliable, manageable, autonomous and intelligent.

3.1.2 Functional Requirements for Sovereignty Network

To build the sovereignty network, it is necessary to ensure that users within the network can access the Internet and obtain Internet content. At the same time, to conform to the tide of the future network development, the sovereignty network should provide new functions to support the new needs of users. While ensuring to provide rich content resources, sovereignty network also needs to provide higher security level than the existing network architecture.

The functional requirements of the sovereignty network are listed as follows:

(1) Multilaterally managed top-level identifiers to support connectivity.
(2) Identifiers belong to a state can be managed independently by the state. Each virtual cyberspace in a state is independent of each other.
(3) The classification user management should be supported. According to users of different ages and jobs, the classification user purview control mechanism ensures a clean and safe network environment.
(4) Users can access their authorized Internet content. For example, the production and broadcasting staff can access all contents on the Internet except codes and software, and ordinary adult users can access all non-sensitive contents on the Internet, but ordinary minor users can only access specific resources.
(5) The sovereignty network can support 5G requirements and provide both wired and wireless data transmission.
(6) The security of resources and content data within the sovereignty network should be guaranteed, that is, the sovereignty network should effectively prevent existing network attacks (such as worms and malicious traffic), as well as ensure the stable operation of the system.
(7) The production and broadcasting network of radio and television programs can run online in real time.
(8) The sovereignty network can provide a better user experience for watching videos, such as faster video acquisition rate and more stable video playback.
(9) The electronic games, e-commerce, voice calling, video calling and other services should be supported.
(10) The content within the sovereignty network can still meet the basic user needs after being physically isolated from the Internet, that is, users can still access some previously accessed contents published on the external Internet.
(11) Users in the sovereignty network can publish content actively.

(12) The sovereignty network should support various functions, such as video live broadcast, on-demand broadcast, playback, doubling speed and time-shifting, just like the existing system.

(13) Other basic businesses.

3.2 Existing Technologies

3.2.1 IPv9

Now some researchers use IPv9, namely the decimal network, to design the sovereign network. The decimal network is a modified version of the IETF proposal by Mr. Jianping Xie, director of the Shanghai General Chemical Research Institute.

The decimal network system is mainly composed of the IPv9 address protocol, IPv9 header protocol, IPv9 transition protocol, digital domain name specification and other protocols and standards. The digital domain name refers to the use of 0–9 Arabic numerals instead of traditional English letters as the name of domain name. The digital domain name, which is a part of the decimal network system, can also be used directly as the IPv9 address [1].

IPv9 protocol requires to use 0–9 Arabic numerals as the virtual IP address, and use the decimal system as the text representation method, which is easy to find the Internet users. To improve the efficiency and convenience for the use of end users, some addresses can be directly used as domain names. Since IPv9 classifies and codes the services of the original computer network, cable broadcast network and telecommunication network, IPv9 is also known as the "new generation of secure and reliable information integration protocol".

The decimal network refers to a new network using the decimal algorithm and text representation method. It connects various computers using decimal algorithm into a network, and can be intercommunicated with the existing network.

The decimal network system uses decimal, multi-protocol in the domain name system to map English, Chinese and other domain names to globally unique IP addresses. Besides, IPv9 established a distributed root domain name system, introducing the concept of country and region, so that each country has its root domain name system, in order to establish and maintain its status and image as a sovereign country on the Internet.

IPv9 increases the address length of IP from 32 and 128 bits to 2048 bits to support more address levels, more addressable nodes, and provide a simple automatic address configuration. At the same time, the 32-bit address length of IPv4 is reduced to 16 bits, which solved the cellular communication problem in mobile communications. IPv9 addresses specify 256-bit identifiers for interfaces and interface groups, and can be divided into three types. The three types of addresses are as follows:

(1) Unicast: A single interface has an identifier. The package sent to a unicast address is passed to the interface identified by the address.
(2) Arbitrary VoD: Generally, a group of interfaces belonging to different nodes have an identifier. The package sent to an arbitrary VoD (Video-On-Demand) address is passed to the interface identified by the address and measured according to the distance of routing protocol.
(3) Multicast: A group of interfaces belonging to different nodes generally have an identifier, but the package, which is sent to a multicast address, will pass all interfaces of that address. There is no broadcast address in IPv9, and its function is replaced by the multicast address.

There are five types of IPv9 addresses:

(1) IPv9 address: This address takes the form Y[Y[Y [Y[Y [Y[Y [Y], where each Y represents a decimal integer between 0 and 2^{32}.
(2) IPv9 addresses compatible with IPv4: This address takes the form of Y[Y[Y [Y [Y [Y[Y [D.D.D.D, where each Y represents a decimal integer between 0 and 2^{32}, and each D represents a decimal integer between 0 and 2^8 from the original IPv4.
(3) IPv6 compliant IPv9 addresses: This address takes the form Y[Y[Y[Y [X:X:X: X:X:X:X:X. Where each Y represents a decimal integer between 0 and 2^{32}, and each X represents a hexadecimal number between 0000 and FFFF from the original IPv6.
(4) Special compatible address.
(5) Full decimal address: For the convenience of logistics code and full decimal address application.

IPv9 has the following characteristics:

(1) IPv9 adopts fixed-length and non-positioning methods like the telephone, which reduces the network overhead.
(2) IPv9 adopts a specific encryption mechanism to ensure the network security. The IPv9 network is more secure because IPv9 has more addresses, more address modes (variable length, and unique IP address encryption technology), and more IPv9 extension header definitions. The address header, message and protocol number information are not disclosed, but have their system. Even if the protocol is disclosed, only the civilian part will be disclosed, and the military part will be decided by the army. Compared with IPv9, various security measures in the IPv4/IPv6 network system cannot be decided by themselves, and it is still difficult to guarantee security despite IPv4/IPv6 uses IPsec (Internet Protocol Security), SSL (Secure Sockets Layer), and other measures. Theoretically, it is more difficult to crack the special protocol than the cryptographic algorithm. Besides, according to the current IPv4/IPv6 standards, 32-bit/128-bit addresses cannot be encrypted due to the loss of destination.
(3) IPv9 adopts the TCP/IP protocol of absolute code class and long stream code, which solves the contradiction between audio and video transmission in packet

switching circuit. IP addresses can be used as domain names, which suit the mobile phones and family wide-band network.

(4) IPv9 has an emergency category, which can ensure unblocked of transmission lines in the case of war and national emergencies. In addition to ciphertext transmission of network communication, the IPv9 protocol also sets the emergency bit due to its protocol standard. In the case of partial destruction of military network in wars, relevant civilian routers can be urgently requisitioned, then routing tables are modified through router broadcasting, so as to achieve the purpose of war requisition.

(5) As IPv9 adopts a point-to-point circuit, the protection of user privacy is strengthened.

(6) IPv9 is especially suitable for wireless network transmission.

In addition to the above features, IPv9 is also independent of the original IPv4 and IPv6 network, so the network security and information security can be independently controlled and managed by the new architecture. As a result of independent networking, relevant departments can develop public information services independently and flexibly according to national policies. This is conducive to the development of Chinese information retrieval in the future based on advanced application business system expansion.

In order to comply with user habits, IPv9 is compatible with both IPv4 and IPv6. On the one hand, IPv9 has realized the function of using IPv4 as a tunnel to carry data transmission between two IPv9 subnets. On the other hand, they have also realized the function of using IPv9 as a tunnel to carry data transmission between two IPv4 subnets. In this way, the interconnection between IPv9 and IPv4 is achieved.

The main advantages of IPv9 are as follows. Firstly, IPv9 has an independent intellectual property system and huge cyberspace resources. Secondly, the decimal network system can translate the original binary address directly into decimal text, which is compatible with users' daily habits. Thirdly, IPv9 comes up with a design scheme, that the domain name and IP address are integrated, as well as the identity code of people and objects is unified. That makes the telephone, mobile phone, domain name and IP address, IPTV, IP phone and so on merge into one number. In this way, the translation process between network domain name and IP address is avoided, which makes the network communication fast and direct, and improves the communication capability of existing network switching equipment. Fourthly, by using specific encryption mechanisms, IPv9 guarantees network security. Fifthly, from the standpoint of safeguarding sovereignty, IPv9 firstly proposes the concept of "sovereignty equality" of cyberspace. The proposed decimal, multi-protocol digital domain name system is compatible with English, Chinese and other domain names that are mapped to globally unique IP addresses.

Although IPv9 has many advantages, there are many criticisms about it in the industry, which are listed as follows:

(1) The base bits of source addresses and destination addresses used in IPv9 messages are 256 bits, and the maximum is 2048 bits. The 256-bit address space is 2^{256}, and the total number of atoms of ordinary matter in the observable universe is about 10^{80}. Its address space is comparable to the total number of atoms of ordinary matter in the observable universe. Using 256 bits as an address space is big enough, and 2048 bits is unimaginable. The actual network does not need such a large amount of address space.

(2) The address space of IPv9 is too long leading to the problem of inefficient use of address space. There will be a lot of idle addresses without being effectively used.

(3) Since IPv9 uses the source address and destination address with a 256-bit base bit, which leads to the large message header, and causes many problems in network transmission efficiency and congestion control. An IPv9 header is always required for transmission even for very small data, resulting in low network transmission efficiency. Moreover, the current size of the Ethernet frame based on IPv4 and IPv6 is 1500 bytes. If the IPv9 header takes up too much space, the amount of data transmitted by each frame will be reduced.

(4) The memory and computing capacity of devices in the Internet of Things and Industrial Internet is limited, and the storage space is usually less than 10 KB. IPv9 with a long header for data transmission is difficult to meet the application requirements of the Internet of Things and other scenarios.

(5) IPv9 requires that each link on the Internet has an MTU of at least 576 bytes. On any link, if it cannot transmit 576 bytes of data in a data packet, link-related data segments and reassembly must be supported at a level below IPv9.This undoubtedly increases the data processing pressure of the link layer.

(6) IPv9 directly uses the address as the domain name for content requests, and it has a huge domain name address. How to quickly search, match and forward content requests on the router will be a problem.

(7) The naming and addressing method used in IPv9 is a big challenge in searching and addressing quickly with huge amounts of identifiers. At the same time, the geographical location addressing scheme proposed by IPv9 requires the conversion of IP address and geographical location address. As the geographical location address and IPv9 address are both long, it is also a challenge in quick search.

(8) IPv9 adopts a new "decimal" address format, which is different from IPv4 and IPv6, resulting in a barrier to its connection to the Internet.

(9) IPv9 does not guarantee actual security of the network. The purpose of the TCP/IP protocol family is to help computers in different networks (such as Ethernet, token ring, FDDI, ATM, etc.) to communicate with each other in a virtual "common network", different protocols are realized differently. Therefore, IPv9 is essentially a different version of the protocol derived from the same technology and different conventions as IPv6. IPv9 does not avoid the inherent defects of IPv4 and IPv6.

(10) There is no broadcast address in the IPv9 protocol, so the multicast address is used instead of the broadcast address. Using IPv9 to construct a sovereignty network will result in the limitation of real-time, extensibility and flexibility of data transmission.

3.2.2 New IP

In order to support emerging network applications, Huawei Technology Co., LTD. [2] proposed a new protocol framework called "New IP" in 2019. New IP aims to fundamentally support the variable-length, multi-semantic address in network layer and allows user to define and customize networking behavior [3].

New IP studies the following four functional requirements and four performance requirements proposed by four target scenarios of future network 5.0, including ICT infrastructure, industrial Internet, mobile carrier, and holographic communication.

The four functional requirements mainly include endogenous security, network programming and predictable performance, perception and controllable based on large connections, and ubiquitous mobility support.

Traditional security mechanisms mainly protect the system against known vulnerabilities and threats. Different from them, the goal of endogenous security mechanisms is to establish a complete set of endogenous security architecture for the future network. The system should not only guarantee the trustworthiness of communication entities and network infrastructures, but also guarantee the authenticity, suitability, privacy, integrity and confidentiality of end-to-end communication, as well as provide certain availability in case of network failure and attack.

Different applications have different requirements for network transmission quality. According to the characteristics and requirements of different applications, the future network should provide planned, predictable, customizable and differentiated access and transmission rules based on deterministic network behavior. In this way, the service quality of certainty and differentiation is guaranteed.

Perception and controllable beyond large connections refer to the overall consideration of network connections, storages and computing resources under the premise of the explosive growth of the number of communication links caused by the increase of scale and complexity of communication entities.

In the IoT era, classes of business are complex and diverse leading to mobility requirements. Mobility support is also required for some large connection services, so the future network will require efficient, high-speed, large-connection-based mobile communication schemes.

The requirements of the four performances are mainly measured in terms of bandwidth, delay and jitter, packet loss rate.

Based on inheriting existing IP capabilities, the researchers of New IP have proposed many prospective technologies for future needs. New IP aims to provide deterministic network technology and protocol with low delay, security and privacy, connection of everything [4] for the industrial Internet, which is mainly based on future intelligent machine communication. New IP promotes the continuous evolution of network protocols, and supports the technical requirements of 6G and other future businesses. At present, the main research points of New IP [2, 5] are listed as follows:

(1) The address length of New IP is flexible and variable, which provides diversified routing and addressing schemes. In this way, problems caused by the fixed-length address and the single topology routing mode in the traditional IP network are alleviated. This flexible routing solution satisfies the low consumption of IoT devices through short-address addressing, adapts to the highly dynamic nature of satellite networks through geographic routing, and achieves optimized services in edge computing scenarios through a service-based routing scheme. Flexible and diversified addressing schemes enable New IP to be applied to a variety of heterogeneous cyber scenarios, to realize the interconnection of all things on the Internet.

(2) Based on reusing the traditional IP network, New IP tries to add a deterministic forwarding mode beyond the current "best effort" service mode. End-to-end deterministic service capabilities are provided at the network layer to ensure deterministic low latency and jitter for specific traffic flows. Through this mode, many future applications with stringent requirements for network service quality assurance will be satisfied, such as intelligent manufacturing, telemedicine, autonomous driving and so on.

(3) The original Seven Design Principles of IP network did not include security factors. The current IP network is vulnerable to address forgery, privacy exposure, DDoS attacks and other security threats. Based on the STRIDE security model (represents six security threats including Spoofing, Tampering, Repudiation, Information Disclosure, Denial of Service and Elevation of Privilege), New IP analyzes and studies the network architecture to build the endogenous security mechanism, which can ensure user privacy. Through the construction of a solid distributed trust foundation, the demand for privacy protection represented by GDPR (General Data Protection Regulation) and the demand for security and trust of industry interconnection can be met.

(4) To alleviate problems of current transport protocols such as insufficient bandwidth utilization, inability to perceive application requirements and network status and so on, New IP proposes a new transport layer architecture combined with concurrent multi-channel transmission, network coding and cross-layer collaboration mechanism. For future applications such as holographic and full-consciousness communication and AI video processing, New IP can realize ultra-high flux, super-large data burst and differentiated service transmission of business flows.

(5) New IP explores a user definable network architecture. By carrying instructions and metadata information in messages, users can express more fine-grained and diversified business requirements to the network, such as qualitative

transmission and synchronization between multiple business streams. Different from the traditional IP network that can only meet user needs of topology addressing, the New IP can customize data packets according to user definable instructions to support more complex business scenarios in the future.

Although New IP meets the needs of variable-length, multi-semantic address in the network layer and provides a user-customized network as a new architecture, there are many criticisms in the industry due to privacy security, free access and other issues.

3.3 Architecture of Sovereignty Network

3.3.1 Framework

Given the above background and functional requirements, the self-designed architecture MIN (Multi-Identifier Network) [6, 7] is adopted as the main architecture of the sovereignty network. In this book, we use a broadcast television system as the application case to introduce the operational process of the sovereignty network.

There are two primary deficiencies of the existing IP architecture: (1) There is the risk of centralization because IP addresses and Domain Names are allocated and managed by a single agency. (2) The semantic overload of IP addresses reduces its scalability and mobility, which further hinders the security of the system. Global community requires a new form of co-governing network.

To solve the two primary deficiencies of the traditional network, we propose a sovereignty network based on Multi-Identifier Network (MIN) architecture. MIN decentralizes the management of post-IP identifiers by using consortium blockchain with real identity registration [8]. Moreover, MIN is a revolutionary network architecture supporting the coexistence of multiple Network Identifiers, including identity, content, service, geographic information, and IP address, etc. At the same time, MIN supports the compatibility which implies that MIN can be deployed directly over existing IP networks and will gradually replace the IP network by naturally substituting IP traffic with traffic of other identifiers. The primary identifier in MIN is identity. Each resource should be bound to an identity when being uploaded or published.

Sovereignty network uses Multi-Identifier System (MIS) as its management plane. MIS manages users and identities within its domain and balances individual privacy protection and operators' management with cryptography. MIS has a top to bottom hierarchy: the top domain were implemented by countries through consortium blockchain to achieve MIN co-governing. Each subordinate domain is managed by the corresponding country or organization to ensure systemic security and flexibility in a low-coupling way, as well as the particularity and customization among different domains. Multi-Identifier Router (MIR) is the core equipment of MIN, providing identifiers inter-translation and routing services.

In the MIN network, the function of a complete node is to participate in the in-domain user management and identifier registration on the blockchain, as well as provide services such as identifier transformation and identifier addressing; those nodes are called multi-identifier routers. Besides, there are regulatory nodes, individual users, and enterprise users in the network. The supervisor node is set up in each domain as an interface for data access between the upper and lower domains. Supervisor node takes the charge of multi-identifier, such as identity, content, service, geographic information, and IP address.

We describe the MIN network with a four-layer architecture shown in Fig. 3.1, and our work focuses on the application layer MIS and multi-identifier layer MIR.

The function of MIS is responsible for the generation and management of multiple identifiers. The identifier is sent to the supervisor node. After verification and consensus reached by the Consensus Algorithm, its attribution information and operation information will be recorded on the blockchain. Blockchain technology makes the content of the whole network unified and traceable, and prevents content from being illegally modified. The application layer is mainly managed by MIS, which divides the whole network into hierarchical domain networks from top to bottom. Its role in MIN is similar to DNS in the IP network, but DNS functions are

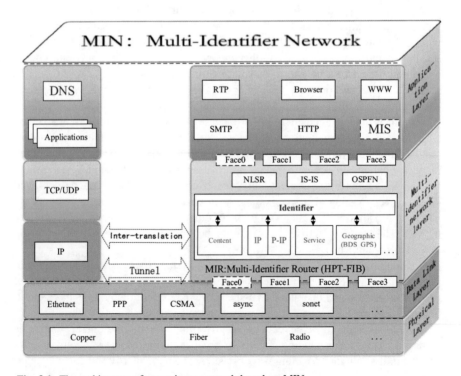

Fig. 3.1 The architecture of sovereignty network based on MIN

only a subset of MIS. Each node of MIS holds a complete identifier database for its domain.

The multi-identifier layer provides resolution service for identifiers, and is also responsible for packet forwarding and filtering. It supports tunnel transmission (IP-MIN-IP, MIN-IP-MIN) and mutual accessing (IP-MIN, MIN-IP) between various identifier scenarios. Each MIR maintains a library of recently used identifiers. Besides there are some technologies proposed by authors to improve the performance, such as HPT-FIB algorithm improving the efficiency of multi-identifier translation and addressing, Hyperbolic Routing model supporting addressing in large scale network, and Transmission Control scheme guaranteeing high quality service.

One of the differences between the sovereignty network and the IP network is the MIN's security mechanisms. Users register with their personal identity information, such as ID cards, mobile phone numbers, fingerprints. User registration information will be stored in blockchain nodes for subsequent user management. New users have to register with their real identities to access the sovereignty network. Then they can actively publish content in the sovereignty network. But the blockchain system will record a behavior log for each user. Besides, there are a set of security mechanisms in the sovereignty network, such as content retrieving mechanism by blockchain, identity authentication mechanism based on cryptography, the multi-identifier router with content audit procedures, cyberspace mimic defense (CMD), and distributed storage system with endogenous security to guarantee the security of data backup. The security of MIN is analyzed in the third part of the next chapter.

Based on the above architecture, we propose a multilateral co-governing sovereignty network. As a future network architecture, MIN was granted as a World Leading Internet Scientific and Technological Achievements of the 6th World Internet Conference at Wuzhen, China, in 2019. The proposed architecture has been implemented in the operators' network to test the multi-identifier management functions and VoD function of network transmission. Through the above prototype and experiments, its compatibility with the IP network and progressive deployment has been verified.

3.3.2 Multi-identifier System

MIS divides the whole network into hierarchical domains from top to bottom. The nodes in the top-level domain belong to the organizations of the major countries which jointly maintain a consortium blockchain. The respective regional organizations govern the other domains. Among them, the registration and management mode of identifiers and the specific implementation details can vary. This low coupling guarantees the security of the network and enables customization of each domain [8]. MIS subsystem realizes the storage and co-governance of user information and identification through blockchain technology. Main modules of MIS are listed as follows:

(1) User registration module. After receiving a user registration request from the client, the request is voted by multiple consortium nodes. If consensus verified, each blockchain node will store the user registration information in a local database and store the registered user information in a user information table.
(2) User query module. After receiving the query request from the client, this module will query the user information from the user information table and return it to the client.
(3) Identifier generation module. After receiving a content publishing request from the client, the request is voted by multiple consortium nodes. If the consensus is successful, each node of the blockchain stores the network identity and real address in the local database and transmits them into the mutual translation information table.
(4) Identifier querying module. After receiving the client's identifier querying request, this module queries the corresponding real address of the network identifier from the HPT-FIB table and returns it to the client.

The registration process is as follows:

(1) Step 1: The user who owns the resource submits a request for identifier registration to the node of a regulatory organization.
(2) Step 2: After receiving the user's request, MIR transmits the registration data to its corresponding domain according to a specific routing protocol.
(3) Step 3: The blockchain node of the corresponding domain reviews the compliance of the resource after receiving its identifier registration request. If so, the resource's identifier is then voted by all the blockchain nodes in the domain to reach a consensus.
(4) Step 4: The blockchain node then returns the registration result to the original requesting node. Since the complete identifier information is stored in the off-chain database rather than the on-chain block, all databases are synchronized frequently throughout the network to ensure consistency.

MIR's process to resolve the identifier is as follows:

(1) Step 1: MIR judges that the identifier is (1) IP address, then query in HPT-FIB. If it exists, it will be resolved. Otherwise, access the traditional IP network through proxies; (2) identity, content and other identifiers, then query in the cache and HPT-FIB. If it exists, it will be resolved. Otherwise, go to Step 2.
(2) Step 2: If MIR cannot find the identifier, recursively query the upper domain until acquiring it.
(3) Step 3: If the identifier is not found up at the top-level domain, then query the lower domain according to the information carried by the identifier until the lowest domain. If it exists, MIR will return the resolved result. Otherwise, return an error message.

In MIN, users' behaviors of publishing and accessing are protected and managed by MIS, and the blockchain undeniably records illegal actions. Only approved content is allowed to be published. At the same time, different identifiers can be defined by different sovereignty subnetworks. The application for an electronic visa for translation between identifiers and content communication between different sovereignty networks of different countries is completed by the blockchain. MIS credibly records transaction history which can be tracked and queried. Thus, MIS ensures that user information and behavior cannot be tampered with and non-repudiation [9].

Therefore, MIN will make the cyberspace in an orderly and secure state, which will direct traffic to the post-IP multi-identifier network tied to the user's identity. The framework of MIS is shown in Fig. 3.2.

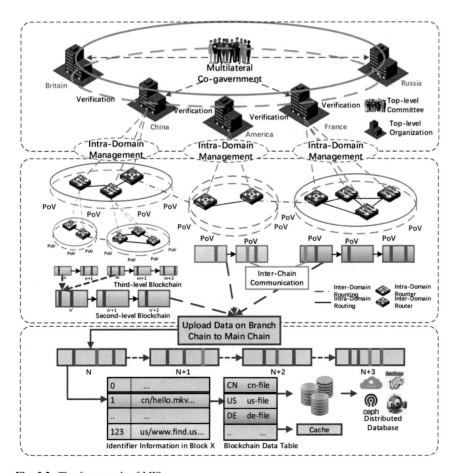

Fig. 3.2 The framework of MIS

3.3.3 Multi-identifier Router

The data plane is mainly composed of switches and MIRs. As the core equipment of the data plane, MIRs are mainly used for identifier inter-translation, routing and addressing, content filtering, data protection, and other functions. To fit different scenarios, MIR supports multiple network identifiers and multiple transmission modes simultaneously. Multiple identifiers include identity, content, service, geographic information, IP address, and other variants. Various transmission modes include the "push" mode represented by IP network architecture and the "pulling" mode represented by Content Centric Network (CCN) architecture.

Due to the large scale of the existing IP network, it cannot be replaced by the new network architecture in one day. Many of the network protocols above the network layer in IP networks are not directly compatible with the content centric network architecture. First, TCP is an end-to-end protocol that communicates through IP addresses and port numbers, which contradicts CCN's content-based philosophy. Second, in CCN, communication is a user-initiated process of "pulling" the required data. However, in TCP, it is a "push" process in which the sender sends data, and the receiver replies to the acknowledgment message. The two are fundamentally different in semantics. Third, TCP ensures reliable end-to-end transmission, which CCN does not address.

To realize the progressive deployment, TCP and CCN need to communicate mutually in MIN. The MIR scheme is divided into two parts, including the IP network compatibility scheme and the development of new network architecture. A comprehensive transmission scenario should be considered, including IP-MIN-IP, MIN-IP-MIN, IP-MIN and MIN-IP.

(1) The tunnel between IP-MIN-IP. This module imitates the idea of using IPv4 as a tunnel to transmit IPv6 packets to realize a tunnel of the MIN network. The tunnel enables the MIN network to transmit IP packets, which provides a compromise for the progressive deployment of sovereignty networks whose transmission process is similar to MIN networks. The architecture of this module is shown in Fig. 3.3. The tunnel agent module is deployed on several agent nodes, each of which is both an IP node and a MIN node. One side of the agent node is the IP network, and the other side is the MIN network. The IP network domains in each test are isolated from each other. The communication between them is completely dependent on the packets forwarded by each agent node to each other. For the nodes in the IP network, the tunnel is transparent. The communication mode of IP nodes between different domains is the same as the traditional IP communication mode. This tunnel module is only responsible for transporting packets from one domain to another.

(2) The tunnel between MIN-IP-MIN. Because the IP network adopts bidirectional "pushing" architecture, this module can directly use the function of transmitting MIN packets with TCP packets as an example. The principle is shown in Fig. 3.4.

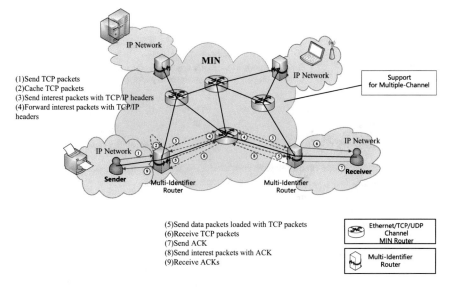

(1)Send TCP packets
(2)Cache TCP packets
(3)Send interest packets with TCP/IP headers
(4)Forward interest packets with TCP/IP headers

(5)Send data packets loaded with TCP packets
(6)Receive TCP packets
(7)Send ACK
(8)Send interest packets with ACK
(9)Receive ACKs

Fig. 3.3 Connection of IP-MIN-IP transmission

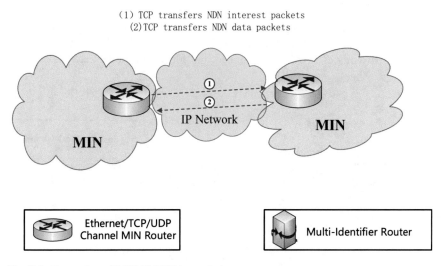

(1) TCP transfers NDN interest packets
(2) TCP transfers NDN data packets

Fig. 3.4 Connection of MIN-IP-MIN transmission

(3) The tunnel between IP-MIN. IP-MIN communication means the transmission process that the host sending the request is in the IP network and the data it requests is in the MIN. Its architecture is shown in Fig. 3.5. The module is installed on the MIR at the junction of MIN and the IP network to obtain data from MIN for all IP nodes that can communicate with. This module

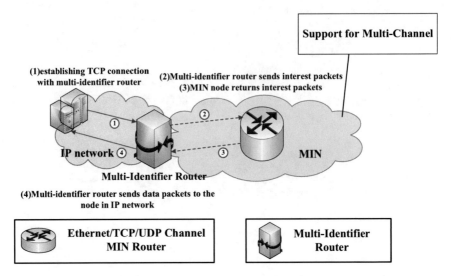

Fig. 3.5 Connection of IP-MIN transmission

communicates with the IP node through TCP protocol and pulls data from the MIN node through the exchange of interest packets and data packets.

(4) The tunnel between MIN-IP. Its architecture is shown in Fig. 3.6. This module is installed on the MIR router at the junction of MIN and IP network, which helps MIN nodes in the same domain pull files from the IP network.

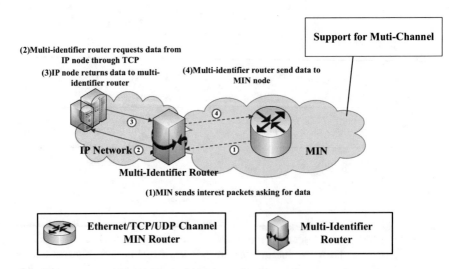

Fig. 3.6 Connection of MIN-IP transmission

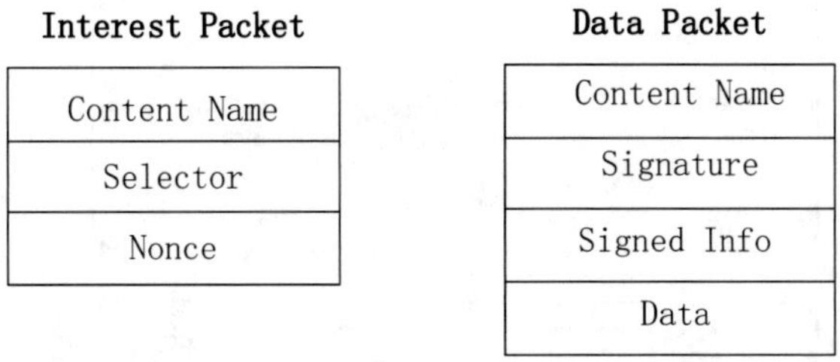

Fig. 3.7 Packet types [11]

Interest Packet

Content Name
Selector
Nonce

Data Packet

Content Name
Signature
Signed Info
Data

The data transmission of the bottom layer of MIN is similar to Information Centric Networking (ICN) [10]. Communication in ICN is driven by data consumers. There are two types of grouping in ICN including interest packets and data packets [11, 12] shown as Fig. 3.7.

All data transmission in the MIN network is carried out through these two groups.

3.3.4 Security Situation Awareness System

With the increase of network scale and complexity, the attack technology is constantly innovated, and a large number of new attack methods emerged. In recent years, a variety of security incidents emerged in endlessly. Usually, enterprises need to react until the attack happens, which is difficult to prevent beforehand. Because security regulators cannot control the security situation of the enterprise in real time, they cannot take effective measures in the early stage of threat formation to avoid loss [13].

Security devices, such as firewalls, WAF (Web Application Firewall), IDS (intrusion detection system) and UTM (Unified Threat Management), are deployed independently in enterprises, governments, and financial institutions. So, they handle security incidents independently based on their device capabilities. At present, many security attacks or penetrations are combined or simulate normal access behavior, such as CC (Challenge Collapsar), APT (Advanced Persistent Threat) attacks, etc. This kind of attack threat cannot be protected or identified by a single system, so it needs to be unified protected by association and analysis of multi-system. Therefore, the security state of the entire network and its trend should be attention by network security personnel.

In addition to the endogenous security architecture [14] of the sovereignty network, a MIN security situational awareness system combined with blockchain has been designed and completed to further ensure the security and control of the network. The network status is monitored in real time by the proposed system, which is deployed on the boundary router of MIN. The proposed system senses the security threats that exist at all levels of the server in real time. Specifically, advanced machine learning, deep learning and high-performance computing models are

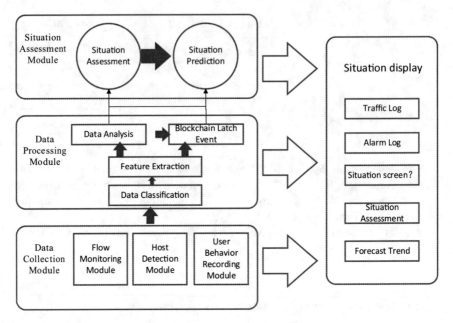

Fig. 3.8 The architecture of security situation awareness system

combined to improve analysis efficiency and accuracy. On the other hand, block-chain technology is combined to latch and accurately locate events. The system can help network analysts assess the risk profile and predict future trends (Fig. 3.8).

The system is divided into three layers including a data collection module, data processing module, and situation assessment module. The data collection module monitors and collects real-time traffic of the network, as well as detects and collects abnormal data of the IP and MIR through the NetFlow tool and TCP dump. The data processing module analyzes, classifies, extracts, and stores the collected data with the Kafka and Scapy. Besides, deep learning algorithms and machine learning algorithms based on single vector machine classification are combined to improve the efficiency of the process. For the host detection, we adopt a comprehensive feature database for testing whose characteristics of library can detect 84 kinds of common abnormal behavior to effective capture of attackers. Then the data will be analyzed with AI technology immediately. According to the result, abnormal traffic and events are recorded and reported to the administrator. The situation assessment module is responsible for assessing and predicting the security situation of the system in real time. The critical security information will be fed back to the administrators to adjust the defending strategy.

Besides, all abnormal events are locked in the PPoV_blockchain to ensure that the record of security threat events is not tampered with, and the attacker's behavior trajectory cannot be erased, which ensures the integrity of the system security log and further improves the security of the system itself.

The security situation awareness system integrates various security technologies such as packet processing technology based on big data, AI modeling, blockchain, and Cyberspace Mimic Defense. These technologies help decision-makers understand the system security situation in real time. The security situation awareness system traces network behavior and supervises the whole traffic in the global domain to guarantee the security of MIN.

3.4 Processes in Sovereignty Network

The sovereignty network supports a variety of functions, each of them is described in this section with selecting Broadcast TV network as a typical application scenario.

3.4.1 Registration Process

Users need to authenticate and register with real information such as ID number, mobile phone number, and face when they register a MIN account. The system uploads and stores user information in the blockchain. The user registration interface is shown in Fig. 3.9.

3.4.2 Publishing Content by Ordinary Users

In the sovereignty network, the core production and broadcast network can publish video, audio and other content, authorized users can also publish content. The content filmed or produced by the authorized user is transmitted to the blockchain node for voting. If the vote is approved, the content can be published on sovereignty networks. The process of authorized users to publish content is shown in Fig. 3.10.

(1) Authorized users log into the network with fingerprint, iris and face.
(2) After authorized users have logged into the network successfully, they can send the content to be published to the blockchain node. The blockchain node can be deployed on an ID-ICN router, or it can be deployed as a separate server.
(3) Vote on blockchain. After a vote has been passed, authorized users can publish the content. Information about users and their published content will be stored in the blockchain.
(4) The user successfully publishes the content. Users can publish content in a distributed storage system with endogenous security or in a localhost.

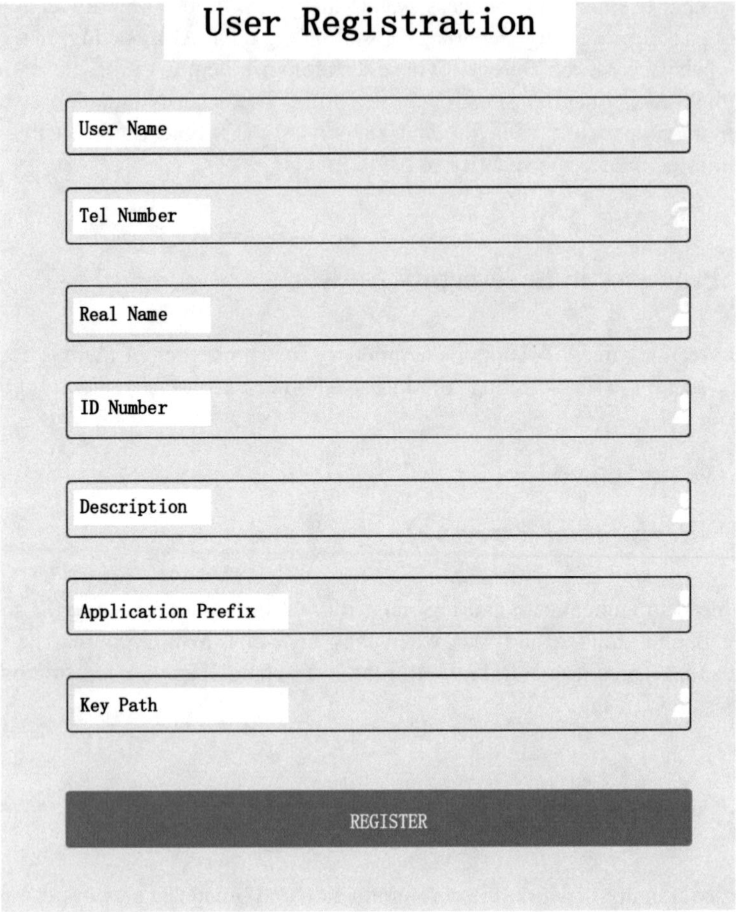

User Registration

User Name

Tel Number

Real Name

ID Number

Description

Application Prefix

Key Path

REGISTER

Fig. 3.9 Registration interface

3.4.3   Publishing Content by Broadcast Network Staffs

Another major source of content published on the sovereignty network is the production and broadcast network, which is shown in Fig. 3.11.

(1) Staffs of the Production and Broadcasting Network obtain content resources from the Internet through Edge Multi-Identifier Router (EMIR) of the sovereignty network.
(2) Staffs of the Production and Broadcasting Network will produce the content and then publish the content to the network.
(3) The content reached the Edge ID-ICN router EMIR node is sent to home or business users.

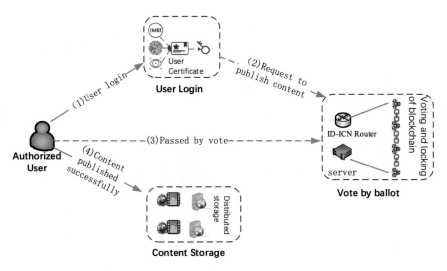

Fig. 3.10 Ordinary users publish content

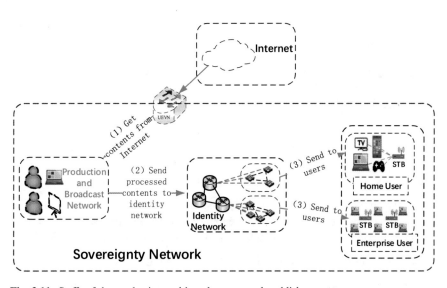

Fig. 3.11 Staffs of the production and broadcast network publish content

3.4.4   Obtaining Content by Ordinary Users

Enterprise users and home users are collectively referred to as ordinary users. The process of ordinary user gets data can be divided into two classifications. The first is that the data provider is on the IP network. When the ordinary users of the

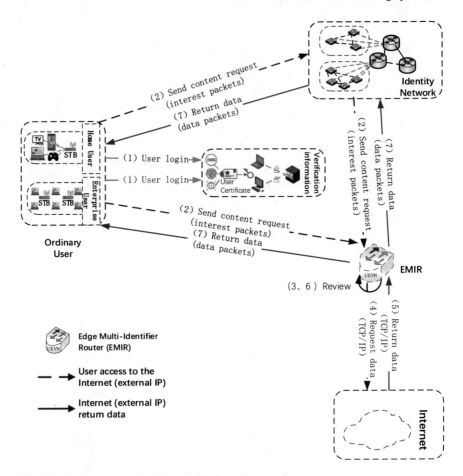

Fig. 3.12 Ordinary users obtaining content from IP network

sovereignty network acquire data for the first time, they need to obtain data from the IP network through EMIR. The data transmission process is shown in Fig. 3.12.

(1) Ordinary users in the sovereignty network log into the network with fingerprint, iris, face, etc.
(2) After ordinary users have logged into the network successfully, they can send content requests to MIR, and MIR sends the request to EMIR. Or ordinary users can directly send the request to the EMIR connected to it. The user and corresponding requested content will be recorded by blockchain nodes.
(3) EMIR reviews the permissions of users in content requests. Its audit method mainly by the following two kinds. One is to record user information in the signature, and EMIR verifies whether the content requested by the user conforms to the scope of authority. Another option is to add a permission domain to the interest packet. EMIR verifies that the content requested by the user

Table 3.1 The permission domain levels

Authority control domain level	Allowed access scope	Suitable crowd
0	All Internet content	Managers, state authorized personnel, ordinary adult users
1	All Internet content except download code and software	Radio and television production and broadcasting staffs
2	Text, video, audio, pictures, web pages and other daily basic content	Specific department or company personnel, specific personnel
3	Content within the specified range	Ordinary minor users and users with internet criminal record

conforms to the permission scope based on the permission domain, which can control the scope of its access content according to different levels. The permission information is shown in Table 3.1. If the requested content exceeds the user's permission, the request is discarded. While it is within the permission, then proceed to the next step.

(4) EMIR extracts content information of content request, and then requests the content from the IP network in the traditional way.

(5) Content providers provide the requested data to EMIR in the traditional way.

(6) EMIR preliminary audit data with filtering technology, such as keyword filtering, AI classification and identification.

(7) EMIR encapsulates the requested data in packets of the identity centric network, and then returns them to ordinary users according to the path of the content request.

The second situation of the ordinary user acquiring data is that the content provider is within the sovereignty network (the content publisher is the sovereignty network user). Or the requested content has been cached in the nodes of the sovereignty network, that is, users themselves or other users have requested the same content before. Hence the data can be directly obtained within the sovereignty network. The data transmission process is shown in Fig. 3.13.

(1) Ordinary users in the sovereignty network log in using fingerprint, iris, face, etc.

(2) Then ordinary users send requests to network nodes or EMIR within the sovereignty network.

(3) If the sovereignty network node or EMIR has cached the requested content, the content is directly returned to the user. Otherwise, the data will be requested from the original data and returned to the requesting user.

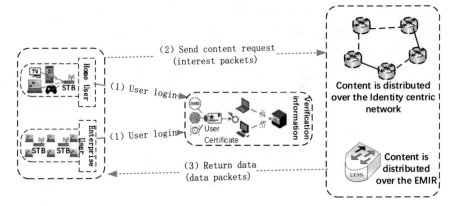

Fig. 3.13 Ordinary users obtain content from the sovereignty network

3.4.5 Obtaining Content by Broadcast Network Staffs

Staffs of the Production and Broadcasting Network obtain resources from the IP network for producing and publishing. Therefore, they access resources mainly through the IP network. The process of data processing is shown in Fig. 3.14.

(1) Staffs of the Production and Broadcasting Network log in with the fingerprint, iris, face, etc.

(2) Then the staff sends a content request to MIR, and MIR sends the request to EMIR. Or the staff can directly send the request to the EMIR connected to it. The staff and corresponding requested content will be recorded by blockchain nodes.

(3) EMIR verifies the permissions of the staff in the content request. If the requested content exceeds the staff's permission, the request will be discarded. If it within the permission, we proceed to the next step.

(4) EMIR extracts content information of content request, and then requests the content from the IP network in the traditional way.

(5) Content providers provide the requested data to EMIR in the traditional way.

(6) EMIR preliminary audit data with filtering technology, such as keyword filtering, AI classification and identification.

(7) EMIR encapsulates the requested data in data packets of the identity centric network, and then returns them to the staff according to the path of the content request.

(8) Staffs of the Production and Broadcasting Network produce and publish contents according to the returned data.

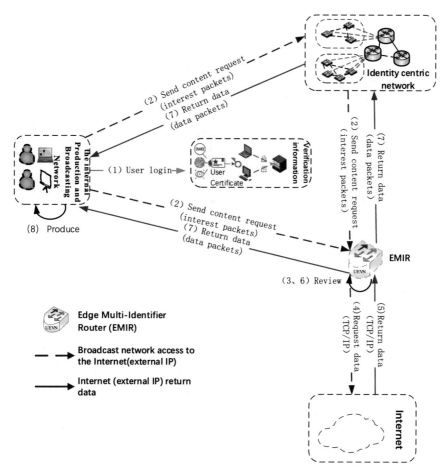

Fig. 3.14 Staffs of the production and broadcasting network obtain content

3.4.6 Assessing to Sovereignty Data by Extranet Users

Users in the sovereignty network can access to data in the IP network, and users or attackers in the IP network can also access the sovereignty network. However, to guarantee the security of the sovereignty network, EMIR strictly examines active requests from the external IP network. The process is shown in Fig. 3.15.

(1) IP users send requests to EMIR.
(2) EMIR review request packets.

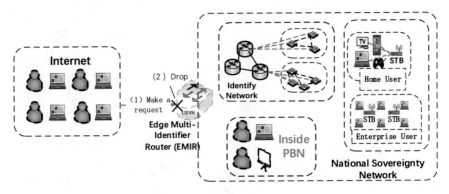

Fig. 3.15 EMIR examines active requests from the external network

3.4.7 Signature Algorithm in MIN

When the data is transmitted in the MIN based on Identity Centric Network (ICN), each data packet will be signed and decrypted, which is shown in Fig. 3.16.

(1) When issuing ICN packets, the content publisher uses some hash function to calculate the hash value of the packets.
(2) The specific signature algorithm is used to sign the hash value with the user's corresponding private key (i.e., the private key is used to encrypt the hash value asymmetrically). The signature can be appended to the end of the packet or placed between the content name and the data block.
(3) The content publisher sends the signature and packet together to the content requester.
(4) Then the requester separates the data signature from the packet. The packet is used to calculate its hash using the same hash algorithm as the content publisher.
(5) The public key, hash value and signature of the content publisher are used to verify the data integrity and reliability of the signature. If the validation passes, the packet is received; otherwise, the packet is discarded.

3.5 Assessing the Security of Sovereignty Network

3.5.1 Anti-attacking Analysis

One of the main usages of the sovereignty network is to construct secure and private networks. How to ensure the security of the kernel private network is an important issue to be considered in the construction of a sovereignty network. The sovereignty network based on blockchain technology will guarantee the security

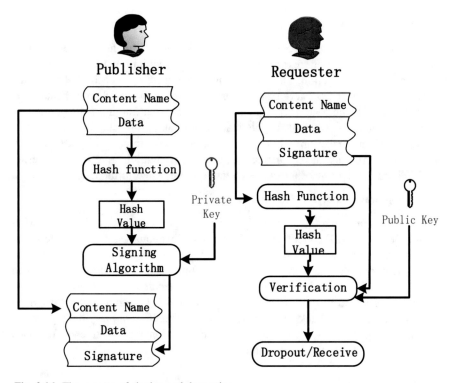

Fig. 3.16 The process of signing and decrypting

and reliability from three aspects: identity centric networking, audit filtering mechanism, and endogenous security mechanism.

1. Identity Centric Networking

Firstly, the sovereignty network is an identity centric network and it does not rely on IP system. All attacks against IP constructed by using IP security defects are invalid in the sovereign network. Secondly, the public key is used to sign each packet. Thirdly, because the identity centric network is driven by data consumers, only content that has been requested can be sent to consumers, and content producers cannot actively send data. If the external network wants to send the request or the attacker wants to send the data actively, they need to crack the signature of the consumer. The cracking process is mainly to crack the related cryptography algorithm. The attack difficulty of existing encryption algorithms has reached exponential level. For example, the most common RSA algorithm would take decades to run on today's highest performance supercomputers. Besides, user information, user behavior information is stored in the blockchain in identity centric network. If there is a problem with the published content or the requested content, it can be accurately located to the individual to ensure that the behavior and resources can be managed and controlled.

2. **Audit Filtering Mechanism**

Starting from EMIR, the sovereignty network will set up filtering functions such as firewall, packet detection, text recognition, audio recognition detection, image and video recognition detection, and natural language processing at each MIR where the packet will pass. These filtering functions will filter the harmful data. If attackers want to attack the core network, they need to attack each filtering MIR on the link in turn. An attacker walks along the attack chain taking one step down the chain each time when breaks through a filter. If the attackers are caught by a filter, they move one step back along the attack chain. Through the multi-layer filtering mechanisms, the spread of attacks is effectively prevented in the network.

3. **Endogenous Security Mechanism**

The core equipments of the sovereignty network are constructed with the Cyber Mimic Defense (CMD) architecture which has endogenous security characteristics. In the field of cyber defense, similar to the biological mimic defense, CMD changes its architecture under the premise of its service function and the target object, which improves the difficulty of attack. The common architecture reconfigures the internal structure, redundant resources, operating system, core algorithm, and environment to avoid the unknown back door or Trojan virus. Therefore, a plausible scenario is presented to the attacker, which disrupts the construction and effectiveness of attack chains to multiplicate the cost of attack.

3.5.2 Security Mechanisms

The security of the sovereignty network can be analyzed from the above three aspects, among which the main security mechanism is listed as follows.

(1) The resources in the sovereignty network can only be actively obtained by the users within the sovereignty network. IP network users cannot actively force the data into the sovereignty network. Hence the attacker cannot scan and attack the system continuously as in the IP network, and cannot even send malicious information to the sovereignty network. This will be guaranteed by the following two mechanisms:

   - The sovereignty network adopts a "pull" mode, namely the receivers pull data actively.
   - If users want to pull data in the sovereignty network, they need to sign in with their real identity information. Therefore, harmful data flowing into the sovereignty network can be traced to a specific user avoiding the intentional introduction of harmful data from the IP network by users in the sovereignty network.

(2) For users in the sovereignty network, blockchain will record requested contents, published contents, and corresponding users. The information stored in the blockchain cannot be tampered with, so the abnormal content can be quickly and accurately located to individuals with high reliability.

(3) The identity centric network is used within the sovereignty network, and the transmission mode is completely different from the IP network. Therefore, the operating environment will be disabled in the sovereign network for some malicious viruses and traffic that bypass the filtering mechanism to enter the sovereignty network, as well as attack methods that make use of the IP network for destruction. For example, the network worm that can replicate in the IP network, cannot propagate in an identity centric network. Malicious manipulation of a host through a TCP port will also fail. Traditional IP attacks may lead to EMIR failure at most, but the security and reliability of users, resources and equipments within the sovereign network can be guaranteed and protected against attacks.

(4) The address space of the sovereignty network is huge leading to the large computational complexity of running the malicious address scanning program, which makes the scanning not feasible.

(5) Various filtering mechanisms are used on EMIR to prevent harmful data from entering the sovereignty network, such as AI content audit procedure.

(6) After the content is transmitted into the sovereignty network, firewall, packet detection, text recognition detection, audio recognition detection, image and video recognition detection, natural language processing, manual review and other mechanisms are used to filter the transmitted content layer by layer, to further ensure the security and reliability of the core network.

(7) The CMD architecture is used for constructing the storage and core equipments to further ensure system security and real-time operation in the core network.

(8) Other routine security mechanisms.

3.6 Protocol Architecture of Sovereignty Network

Since the sovereignty network adopts an identity centric network as its architecture of the core network, it is completely different from the traditional IP network. Protocols in the IP network may not be applicable in the sovereignty network. But the link layer and physical layer of the IP network are similar to the sovereignty network, so both of these two layers can be applied in the sovereignty network without any changes. Protocols in the application layer of the IP network need to be modified to adapt the sovereignty network.

To make the applications of the sovereignty network take full advantage of the characteristics of the multi-identifier network, the network architecture should be redesigned. As shown in Fig. 3.17, the network architecture consists of four layers: application layer, multi-identifier network layer, data link layer and physical layer.

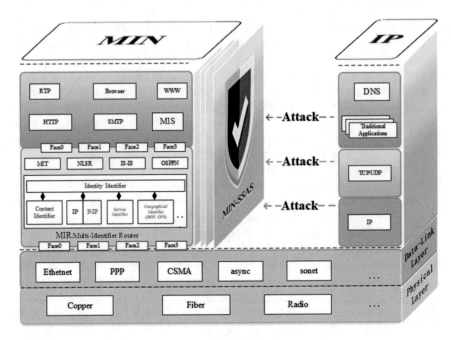

Fig. 3.17 The protocol architecture of sovereignty network

Table 3.2 Protocols in sovereignty network

Protocol	Layer	Function
OSPF	Transport layer	Routing protocol
IS-IS	Network layer	Routing protocol
BGP	Application layer	Routing protocol
NLSR	Network layer	Routing protocol, generating FIB tables
ARP	Link layer	Corresponding analysis of ICN name and MAC
Reverse ARP	Link layer	correspondence analysis of Mac and ICN name
DNS	Application layer	ICN content and ICN real address resolution
PPP	Link layer	Point-to-point protocol
NCP	Link layer	Network control protocol
LCP	Link layer	Link control protocol
CSMA/CA	Link layer	Conflict avoidance protocol
……	……	……

This architecture is compatible with traditional applications, but does not correspond exactly to the TCP/IP model. The protocols used in the sovereignty network are shown in Table 3.2.

We describe the protocol architecture shown in Fig. 3.17.

The sovereignty network adopts an identity centric network as the core network and takes the identity identifier as the core authentication identifier. Compared with the current IP network protocol stack, the sovereignty network establishes the multi-identifier network layer which combines and simplifies the transport layer and the network layer in the IP network. The protocols in the application layer of the sovereignty network are roughly similar to those in the application layer of IP network, while authentication is added in the network layer, and identity is taken as the prior condition of routing. By adding the content identifier field, the translation of content and identity identifier has been realized. Identity information represents the personal information of the publisher, such as ID number, mobile phone number, MAC address of the publisher's device and so on. Among them, the packet forwarding among multi-identifier network layer, application layer and data link layer is through the Face. Face is an abstraction of the network communication channel, which represents not only the interface connection information of physical devices, but also the port information between communication process protocols. The data link layer and physical layer are roughly similar to the current IP network, including CSMA, PPP, Copper, etc.

The identifiers in MIN (Multi-Identifier Network) support a variety of communication modes with different semantics such as push and pull semantics. To guarantee the transmission performance in different communication modes, we propose MIT (Multi-Identifier Network Transmission Control Protocol), which allows the MIR nodes to participate in transmission control to balance the network load.

MIT exploits the explicit congestion detection and notification scheme. The MIR nodes periodically detect its congestion status by using the AQM (Active Queue Management) algorithm. In order to notify the current network status to downstream nodes, the MIR node marks data packets through setting the congestion tag. Once receiving the explicit congestion message, the end host will adjust its packets sending rate correspondingly to make full use of network resources and avoid network congestion. For packets with pull semantics, the receiver adjusts its sending rate according to the congestion mark in received data packets. For packets with push semantics, the receiver marks the reply packet through the congestion mark in the received data packet, so the sender can fully perceive whether their packets cause network congestion through the reply packet.

MIN realized the multilateral co-governing and sovereignty autonomy in cyberspace for the first time. In 2019, MIN and its prototype system were awarded as the leading technological achievements of the sixth World Internet Conference at Wuzhen, China [15] (Figs. 3.18 and 3.19).

Fig. 3.18 The 6th World Internet Conference

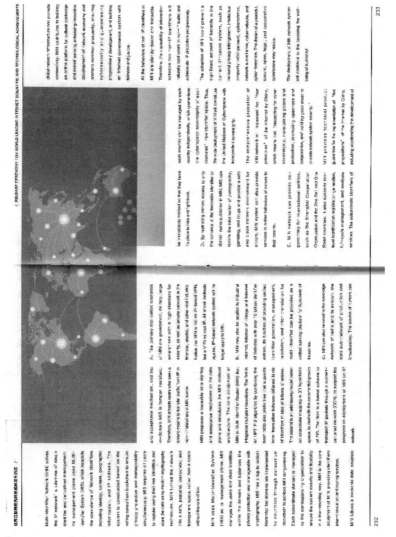

Fig. 3.19 The 6th World Internet Conference-MIN

References

1. Decimal Network Information Technology Co. Ltd (2006) Decimal network working group. http://www.em777.net/. Accessed 14 Jan 2020
2. Zheng X, Jiang S, Wang C (2019) New IP: new connectivity and capabilities of upgrading future data network. Telecommun Sci 35(9):2–11. https://doi.org/10.11959/j.issn.1000-0801. 2019208
3. Li R, Clemm A, Chunduri U et al (2018) A new framework and protocol for future networking applications. In: Association for computing machinery, pp 21–26. New York, USA
4. Huawei (2019) New IP. https://www.huawei.com/cn/industry-insights/innovation/new-ip. Accessed 14 Jan 2020
5. Zheng X, Tan J, Jiang S, Wang C (2019) Analysis on the requirements of future data network. Telecomm Sci 35(8):16–25. https://doi.org/10.11959/j.issn.1000-0801.2019204
6. Li H, Wu JX et al (2019) MIN: Co-governing multi-identifier network architecture and its prototype on operator's network. In: The 6th World Internet Conference
7. Li H, Wu JX, Yang X et al (2020) MIN: Co-governing multi-identifier network architecture and its prototype on operator's network. IEEE Access 8:36569–36581
8. Li H, Wu JX, Wang XG et al (2019) System and methods for managing top-level domain names using consortium blockchain. US Patent. US: 10178069B2. 2019.01.08
9. Li H, Wu JX, Xing KX et al (2019) Prototype and testing report of a multi-identifier system for reconfigurable network architecture under co-governing. SCIENTIA SINICA Informationisnis 49:1186–1204
10. Ahlgren B, Dannewitz C, Imbrenda C et al (2012) A survey of information-centric networking. IEEE Commun Mag 50(7):26–36
11. Jacobson V, Smetters DK, Thornton JD et al (2012) Networking named content. Commun ACM 55(1):117–124
12. Lan JL, Cheng DN, Hu YX (2014) Research on reconfigurable information communication basal network architecture. J Commun 35(1):128–139
13. Wu JX, Lan JL et al (2013) Novel network architecture. J Commun Post Telecom Press 1:120–122
14. Jiang WY, Liu BY, Wang C (2019) Network architecture with intrinsic security. Telecommun Sci 35(009):20–28
15. World Internet Conference (2019) The 6th World Internet Conference. https://2019. wicwuzhen.cn/. Accessed 29 Dec 2020

Chapter 4
Key Technologies of Sovereignty Network

In order to realize all functions of the sovereignty network while guarantee the security at the same time, what key technologies should be used in the architecture? This chapter will elaborate on the key technologies of the sovereignty network.

Sovereignty network is mainly composed by a traceable data signing and acceptance mechanism and combined with the MIN protocol architecture. A variety of innovations were proposed and integrated into the Multi-identifier Router (MIR) as the core device of MIN, and the construction is carried out around supporting multi-identifier coexistence, co-governance, endogenous security, as well as supporting network evolution.

On the data plane of sovereignty network, in order to support the operation of identity centric network, we proposed the data transmission scheme and designed the user access process based on identity centric network, which are described in Sect. 4.1. In order to meet the needs of various communication scenarios, we proposed and realize the inter-translation scheme supporting multiple identifiers coexisting equally in MIN. Then to guarantee endogenous evolution ability of MIN, we designed an identifier extension mechanism that allows the gradual extension of MIN identifiers. Details are presented in Sect. 4.10. In general, the above new identifiers are much longer than IP address, so the inter-translation and addressing process of multi-identifier will face great pressure in computing and storage. To this end, we proposed a hash table with prefix tree algorithm HPT, accelerating the backtracking process of FIB query algorithm and effectively improving the efficiency of multi-identifier translation and addressing. HPT-FIB has a significant storage overhead when the network scale further expands. Therefore, we proposed a hyperbolic identifier and routing scheme instead of forwarding table to reduce storage overhead in MIR. Those are described in Sect. 4.3. Further, in order to meet the demand of the development of future network towards space-terrestrial integrated, we proposed a greedy routing strategy based on hyperbolic routing technology and light-weight distributed self-adaptive satellite routing algorithm based on delay to construct the Space-Terrestrial Multi-Identifier Network (ST-MIN).

© The Author(s) 2021
H. Li and X. Yang, *Co-governed Sovereignty Network*,
https://doi.org/10.1007/978-981-16-2670-8_4

ST-MIN takes advantages of the feature that satellite communication is not affected by time, location or environment, which is described in Sect. 4.9.

Moreover, considering the communication reliability and transmission efficiency of the sovereign network under different scenarios, we proposed MIT–Transmission Control Protocol, a transmission control scheme for MIN. MIT supports the transmission control in both push semantic and pull semantic, which is described in Sect. 4.8.

On the management plane of MIN, in order to realize co-governance of user information and identification, we proposed PPoV (Parallel Proof of Vote) as a non-forking consensus algorithm for consortium blockchain. The core idea is the separation of voting rights and bookkeeping rights, which is presented in Sect. 4.2.

In addition to the construction of the architecture, the sovereignty network is required to protect user privacy and system security while managing users. To this goal, we designed a variety of security mechanisms. To guarantee the privacy of users and traceable of behaviors, combined with asymmetry encryption technology, we proposed an identity authentication scheme of the sovereignty network based on human biological characteristics. To provide a hierarchical security and reliability guarantee for network, we adopted three kind of protection mechanisms: network censorship, cryptography, and Cyberspace Mimic Defense (CMD) for designing six levels of defense barriers. Besides the above structural security, we design a Security Situation Awareness System to monitor the network state in real time, and establish a mathematical analyzing model based on random process to assess the network security and optimize the security policy. The above security mechanisms are described in Sects. 4.4, 4.5, 4.6, and 4.7.

4.1 Identity Centric Network

Identity centric network is one of the key technologies of the sovereignty network. Data transmission in the sovereignty network is based on the identity centric network.

4.1.1 MIN Based on Identity Centric Network

The core conception of MIN is that multiple identifiers and transmission semantics can coexist in the network layer at the same time. In order to illustrate the concrete meaning of multiple identifiers, the identifiers are classified by two dimensions, including the identifier form and the identifier semantic. In terms of the dimension of the identifier form, identifiers can be classified into the following three types:

(1) Flat identifiers. Flat identifiers are usually composed of a series of irregular values or characters. So, such identifiers are difficult to aggregate in the routing

table. Some network architectures (such as XIA) use the hash value of a public key or data slice as the identifier for routing, which is a typical example of Flat identifiers.

(2) Hierarchical identifiers. Hierarchical naming dictates that each content usually has an identifier that is similar to the Web URL, such as "/lab/pku/icon.jpg". This kind of identifier is used in the Network layer of Named Data Networking (NDN) for routing. Identifiers in IPv4 or IPv6 can also be seen as hierarchical identifiers.

(3) Spatial coordinate identifiers. Each node in the network is mapped into a geometric space with a coordinate. In the hyperbolic routing model, the hyperbolic coordinate is used to guide routing, such as (R_1, θ_1).

On the other hand, in terms of the dimension of the identifier semantic, there are at least two types of transmission semantics listed as follows:

(1) Point-to-point push semantic. It is a kind of semantics expressed by the traditional IP address identifier, which is characterized by that the data sender can actively push data to the data receiver without the request from the data receiver. Routers simply forward packets when dealing with such semantic network packets.

(2) Point-to-multi-point pull semantic. It is a kind of semantics expressed by ICN identifier, which is characterized by that data sender can only transmit data to receiver on the premise that the receiver requests data. When a router deals with packets in push semantic, it will record the return path of packet and cache the data.

Network devices can process different types of identifiers. Devices that support the same identifiers can be divided into one area named identifier space. In order to support the extension of the new identifiers in the future, the current network must have one or more basic identifiers. The most typical basic identifier is the identity identifier, which directly uses the hash value of public key of the network device as the identifier for routing. It belongs to the flat identifier, and we define its transmission semantic is the point-to-point transmission semantic. Each device in the network must support identity identifiers, and each device will be bound to an identity identifier. A formal definition of the identifier space is given below.

1. The Definition of Symbols

(1) $I = \{i_0, i_1, i_2, \ldots, i_k\}$, represents the set of all identifier that exist in MIN space. i_0 refers to the identity identifier of network devices, which is the most indispensable one. $\{i_1, i_2, \ldots, i_k\}$ contains other extensible identifiers, such as the content identifier, service identifier, geographic identifier, IP, and so on.

(2) V represent all device sets in MIN.

(3) N is the subset of I, which is consist of several identifiers, for example, $N = \{i_0, i_1\}$.

(4) $S^N = (V_N, N)$. S^N represents the identifier space, which is a 2-tuple. V_N represents a subset of network device V in identifier space, and N represents a subset of all identifiers that are supported by identifier space S^N.

2. **The Definition of Identifier Space**

The set $S^N = (V_N, N)$ can represent an identifier space in MIN if and only if S^N meets the following conditions:

(1) Restrictive: $V_N \subseteq V, N \subseteq I$;
(2) Atomicity: $i_0 \in N$;
(3) Consistency: $\forall v \in V_N, \forall i_j \in N$. v supports i_j;
(4) Closure: if $\exists v \in V$, and for $\forall i_j \in N$, v supports i_j, then $v \in V_N$.

4.1.2   Data Transmission Scheme

The characteristic of data transmission scheme in MIN is that it supports various transmission semantics coexisting on the network layer at the same time, including pull semantic and push semantic. MIR processing the incoming packet with different methods according to their identifier type, and this mechanism enable MIN's network layer to be compatible with various transmission semantics.

Identity identifier is the basic identifier of MIN, and it has two features. Firstly, the transmission semantic of the identity identifier is push semantic. Secondly, identity identifier can be the hash value of public key of a user or device. Point-to-Point push semantic is the most essential method in packet forwarding. When a router receives an incoming packet, it is just need to look up the FIB (Forwarding Information Base) to decide the next hop where the packet will be sent to. If no match is found in FIB, the router will drop the packet. Both ends in a point-to-point session can validate each other's identifier without any third-party certification body by using the hash value of the public key as the identity identifier. This is called the self-certified function of identifiers.

Another basic transmission semantic in MIN is the pull semantic, which is the typical transmission semantic in Information Centric Networking (ICN). Data transmission in ICN is driven by the consumer (receiver). There are two types of packets in ICN: Interest Packet and Data Packet. There are three major data structures: Forward Information Base (FIB), Content Store (CS), and Pending Interest Table (PIT).

FIB is used to forward interest packets to sources of matching the data. The FIB in the sovereignty network stores a list of outgoing faces rather than a single one [1]. Other than that, it's almost identical to The FIB in IP. ICN's FIB allows multiple data sources to be queried in parallel.

The CS is the same as the buffer memory of an IP router, but the replacement strategy is different [1]. Because each IP packet belongs to a separate point-to-point session, it has no further value after being forwarded downstream. So, the IP "forgets" the packet and recycles the cache (MRU replacement) as soon as the forwarding completes. ICN packets are idempotent, self-identifying, and self-certified, so each ICN packet may be useful to many consumers, for example, many hosts read the same news or watch the same YouTube videos. To maximize the possibility of sharing and minimize upstream bandwidth requirements and downstream latency, it is necessary for ICN nodes to remember incoming packets with LRU or LFU substitution strategies as long as possible.

PIT records the return path of the interest that is forward to upstream source of content, so the returned data packets can be sent downstream to the requester. In ICN, only interest packets are routed because they propagate upstream to possible data sources and leaving a "trace". This "trace" provides a return path to the source requester for a matching packet. Each PIT entry is a trace. Once the PIT entry is used to forward a matching data packet, the PIT entry is erased (data packet consumes interest packet). PIT entries that do not find interest packets that match the packet will eventually time out by a soft state model; the consumer sends interest packets repeatedly if they still want the packet [1].

The process of data transmission in information centric network is shown in Fig. 4.1.

The requester sends an interest packet with name of the content. The router that receives the request will record the interest packet's arrival face, and perform Longest Prefix Match Algorithm (LPM) for the content name.

Firstly, the CS is queried. If the requested content exists in the CS, the content is returned directly to the requester, and the interest packet is discarded; actually, it has been satisfied.

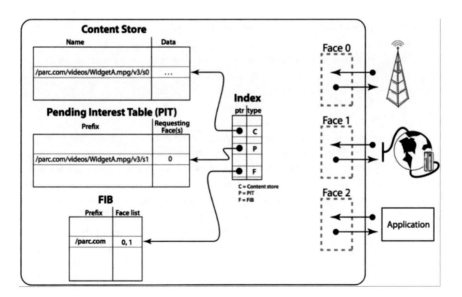

Fig. 4.1 The process of data transmission in information centric network [1]

Then, the content name of the interest packet is queried in PIT. If there are exactly matching PIT entries, the arrival face of the interest packet is added to the list of requesting faces for PIT entries. Then the interest packet is discarded because a same interest packet has already been sent to upstream nodes. Hence, the router will send a copy of the data packet to each corresponding incoming face recorded in the PIT when the data packet arrives.

Finally, the content name of the interest packet is queried in FIB. If there is a matching entry, the interest packet needs to be sent upstream to the data source. If the resulting list of querying FIBs is not empty, the interest packet is then sent out all the reserved faces, and a new PIT entry is created according to the interest packet and its arrival face.

If the interest packet does not match any entry in FIB, it is discarded. It means that this node does not have any matching data and does not know how to find the matching data.

Once the interest packet reaches the node that has the requested resource, the data packet containing the name, content and the publisher's signature is forwarded to the requester along the reverse path of the interest packet.

During the data transmission, neither interest packets nor data packets carries any host or interface address. In addition, ICN introduces the design of network cache. The router which the data packet passes through will cache the correct contents in its buffer memory, namely CS. Caches in ICN can help reduce the delay and the occupation of bandwidth in the content downloading process. If the cache has stored the request content, it can be returned to the requester without accessing to the data source when the request arrives at the router.

The process of data forwarding in the information centric network is as follows. When multiple interest packets request the same data at the same time, the router records incoming faces of these interest packets in PIT and only forwards the first received interest packet. When the data packets are returned, the router finds the matching entries in PIT and forwards the packets to those faces recorded in the entries.

4.1.3 Process of User Access

In identity centric network, the management strategies combining identity information is introduced for user access. In order to encourage users to be responsible for the published content, new contents published by users are bound with their identity information.

The process of user registration to the sovereignty network based on blockchain [2] is shown in Fig. 4.2.

Each user in the sovereignty network is a client node. Users in the sovereignty network must register with their real identities. The client generates public and private keys, then submits the public key, identity information, and information signed with the private key to any node in the blockchain. All nodes of the

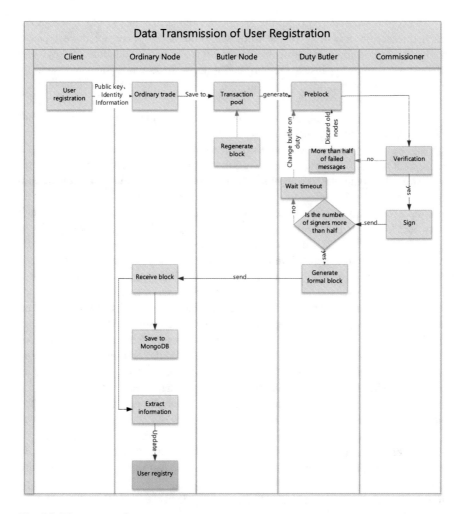

Fig. 4.2 The process of user access

blockchain open service threads. When a blockchain node receives the request sent by the client, the request format is first checked. Then the blockchain node searches the user information in the local database and simply validates some contents. If one of the above steps failed, error message is returned to the client. If all the verifications are successful, the blockchain node encapsulates the user registration request as a common transaction and sends it to all consortium nodes.

The butler that receives the ordinary transaction stores it in the transaction pool. At the beginning of each consensus round, the duty butler takes ordinary transactions from the transaction pool to generate the pre-block and sends it to all commissioners for signatures.

The commissioners receiving the pre-block shall verify the pre-block header and each transaction according to the rules set in advance. There are three types of validation: no validation, probabilistic validation, and validation of keywords against a custom filter list. If the verification fails, the commissioner will send the failure message to the duty butler. Otherwise, the signature of the block header will be returned to the duty butler.

If more than half of the commissioners is collected rejecting signature, the duty butler will delete the pre-block in the memory, take out transactions from the local pool to generate the pre-block and send it to all commissioners for signatures. If more than half of the commissioners is collected agreeing signature, the duty butler will store the signatures in the block header and calculate the number of the duty butler for the next consensus period. Then it adds the timestamp to make the pre-block be a formal block. The formal block is finally released to the blockchain network. If less than half of the signatures are received, the duty butler will wait until time out, i.e., 20 seconds. Then the duty butler will be replaced and the pre-block will be regenerated and sent to the commissioners for signatures.

In blockchain, each node receiving formal block will verify signatures of commissioners and whether the number of signatures is more than half of commissioners. If the validation is successful, the block is stored in MongoDB database. The user registration information is then extracted from the block and is stored in the user registry. User information outside the blockchain is also stored via MongoDB. Considering MongoDB is a type of NoSQL (Not Only SQL), internal data is stored in a JSON-like format called BSON, which is different from the concept of the data table in a common relational database. However, due to the fixed key of user data and no nested structure, it can be equated to a user information table in a relational database.

The above procedure implements the process from sending requests to storing in the database and the information table outside the blockchain. By adding user registration requests in the consensus process, encapsulating user registration information into ordinary transactions, verifying the transactions, retrieving user information from transactions and saving to the database, it realizes the combination of blockchain and user registration function.

The fields and their meanings contained in the user information table are shown in Table 4.1.

An example of the user information table is shown in Table 4.2.

Table 4.1 User information table

Key	Value	Description
Pubkey	String	Registered user public key
Prefix	String	ICN identifier prefix
Level	Int	User level (0/1:1 can publish content; 0 can only watch)
Timestamp	Double	Time stamp
Real_msg	String	Real identity information

Table 4.2 An example of the user information table

Pubkey	Prefix	Level	Timestamp	Real_msg
07602c1c5...	/Golden hill station	1	334505	Zhujiang, 1375..., 51222..., description
......	......	......	......	......

4.2 Large-Scale Multilateral Managed Consortium Blockchain Technology

The blockchain originates from a unique way to store data in the system of cryptocurrencies such as Bitcoin [3]. It can hold all historical data, transaction records, and other related information in the past by using a self-referencing blockchain data storage structure. Bitcoin has introduced the consensus mechanism into blockchain technology, making tampering with data almost impossible for attackers in computational difficulty [4, 5]. The consensus mechanism plays a key role in blockchain applications, which directly affects the safety and performance of products. Combining distributed storage, cryptography, consensus mechanism and peer-to-peer transmission, the blockchain technology reaches a spontaneous consensus in a decentralized environment with the core of safeguarding group interests.

Generally, the blockchain is divided into three types: public, private and consortium blockchain. Blockchain technology originates from the public blockchain. However, in practical application, the public blockchain suffers from various restrictions in different countries because of its transparency, untraceable of private information and weak controllability. As a compromise between the private and the public blockchain, the consortium blockchain has the advantage of realizing "partial decentralization" between some existing institutions, making the consortium of them efficient and fair.

The construction of the sovereignty network adopts the self-proposed efficient and novel consensus algorithm—PoV (Proof of Vote) [6–10], which is suitable for the consortium blockchain.

4.2.1 PoV Consensus Algorithm

There are four roles in PoV: commissioner, butler, butler candidate, and ordinary user. A certain degree of concurrent role is allowed, as shown in Fig. 4.3.

1. **Commissioner**

A commissioner is a member of the consortium committee. Several enterprises or institutions from different regions of the world form a consortium committee and maintain a consortium blockchain system together. A new commissioner must be

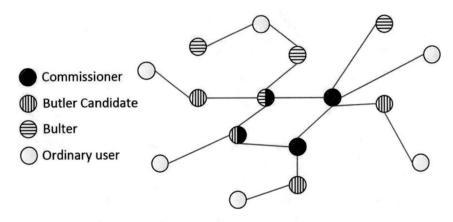

Fig. 4.3 Four roles in the PoV network

accepted through the proposed consortium law or offline consultation, and represented by a node working in the consortium blockchain network. It uses CS (Commercial Server) to provide services.

Commissioners have the following characteristics:

(1) Commissioners have the right to recommend, vote for and evaluate butlers the book keeping nodes.
(2) Commissioners are obligated to verify and forward blocks and transactions.
(3) Different consortiums can set voting weights according to the shares, which can be reflected in the proportion of the signature of the commissioners. By default, each commissioner has the same rights and obligations and is of equal standing.
(4) When a block gets majority votes, the block will be marked as valid and added to the blockchain. The result of voting represents the will of all commissioners.

2. **Butler**

Butlers specialize in producing blocks. The number of butler nodes is limited. They can be considered as representative nodes in the traditional consensus algorithm, but the difference is that the authority of butlers is supervised and voted by commissioners in the consortium. The role of butler is designed to separate the voting and bookkeeping right. Commissioners have no right to produce blocks. However, a butler should gather transactions from every commissioner via network, pack them into a block, and sign it.

To becoming a butler, one needs to take two steps:

(1) Register as a butler candidate.
(2) Participate in the election at the end of each term. The butler candidate will be voted by commissioners and the successful one will be elected as the butler.

The butlers take turns to generate blocks in random order during the tenure and accept re-election after the expiration of their term of office.

3. **Butler Candidate**

The system numbers the butlers $\{0, 1, 2, ..., n - 1\}$ which win the election in each round. As the number of butlers is limited, commissioners can elect butlers only from butler candidates through voting. If butler candidates lose the election, they can stay online, and wait for the next election.

There are three steps to apply for a butler candidate:

(1) Register a user account in the consortium system and send a request to a commissioner to be a butler candidate.

(2) Submit a recommendation letter. After verifying and ensuring that the butler candidate's identity information is correct, the commissioner signs the recommendation letter generated via calling a function of asymmetric encryption. The private and public keys are respectively used to encrypt and decrypt the recommended letter to prevent forgery.

(3) Pay the guarantee deposit to become a butler candidate. Commissioners can retain dual roles as butler candidates by recommending themselves.

(4) **Ordinary User**

All three of these nodes use cryptography to authenticate their identities and need to sign the hash values of their operational messages. In contrast, ordinary users have the following characteristics:

(1) No identification is required. The behavior of ordinary users can be arbitrary and anonymous. In the specific implementation, the user's real name may be required according to the configuration of the consortium blockchain, or the user's identity information in the transaction may be hidden by the encryption function.

(2) Ordinary users can join or exit the network at any time.

(3) Ordinary users cannot participate in the block generation, only in the block distribution and sharing.

(4) Ordinary users can see the whole consensus process while accepting the service of the system. In the process of block generation, ordinary users have the obligation to participate in the process of block forwarding.

Figure 4.4 shows the relationship between the four roles.

4.2.2 PoV Consensus Process

The overall process of PoV consensus is shown in Fig. 4.5. After initialization, each node first enters the phase of the genesis block generation, which is jointly generated by commissioners and contains the information of the initial consortium members and the first batch of butlers.

When the genesis block is created, the system will automatically enter the cycle of "generating B_W ordinary blocks +1 special block". Each cycle is a tenure, and a

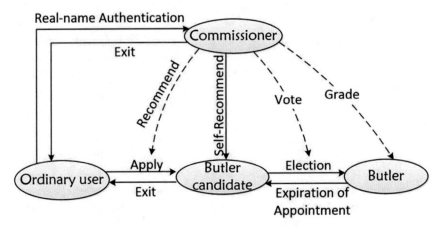

Fig. 4.4 Conversion of the four roles [8]

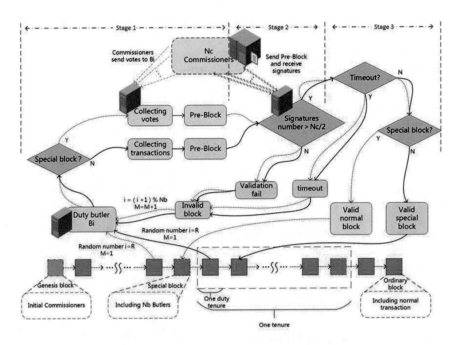

Fig. 4.5 Block generation process [8]

round of consensus may pass through *M* duty butlers to eventually generate a block. The butler circulates the work during on-duty and off-duty, and periodically applies to the vast majority of commissioners for block synchronization to ensure the latest status of itself. The generation cycle of a block is also the duty cycle of a selected butler to create a block. Each block contains a random number R generated by the random number algorithm, specifying the number of the next duty butler $i = R$.

After the genesis block is generated, the key nodes to create the block are the commissioners and the butlers. Figures 4.6 and 4.7 respectively show the flow chart of the perspective of the butler and the commissioner of ordinary blocks, where $\langle h, hs, M, time, R, sign(B) \rangle$ represents the block height, the latest special block height, the cost duty cycle, the timestamp, the random number, the butler's signature and other key attributes in the current block.

Figures 4.6 and 4.7 explain the key processes of generating ordinary blocks and special blocks only from the perspective of commissioners and butlers. On the other hand, other nodes, such as butler candidates and ordinary users are in a continuous cycle of synchronizing blocks, updating stored data, forwarding blocks, submitting and forwarding transactions. Most of these operations are in the network layer and the data layer. Submitting a common application transaction is in the application layer and usually operated by the wallet.

Algorithm 4.1 gives the pseudocode to run PoV algorithm on a node. After a series of initializations, the node determines how to run the PoV process by its own state and configuration.

Algorithm 4.1: The running process of PoV state machine

Input:
   Initial state.
Begin
1:   System_init()
2:   {*gen_com_ list*} set_commissioner_list_genesis()   // set the initial commissioner list
3:   {*Block_list*}←BLOCK_SYNC()   // synchronize the latest block and update variables and memory pools
4:   examine({*com_list*}, {*bul_list*}, {*bc_list*}, {*user_list*})
5:   *myaddr*←key_manager.get_my_public_key()   // get the address of the node, which is the public key
6:   **if** *my_addr*{*com_list*}{bc_list} **then**
7:     **if** *my_addr*{*com_list*} **then**
8:       run the commissioner's working process
9:     **end if**
10:    **if** *my_addr*{*bc_list*} **then**
11:      run the butler candidate's working process
12:    **end if**
13:   **else if** *my_addr*{*user_list*} **then**
14:    run the ordinary user's working process
15:   **else then**
16:    Forward_block_and_message()   // forward blocks and messages
17:   **end if**
End of Algorithm

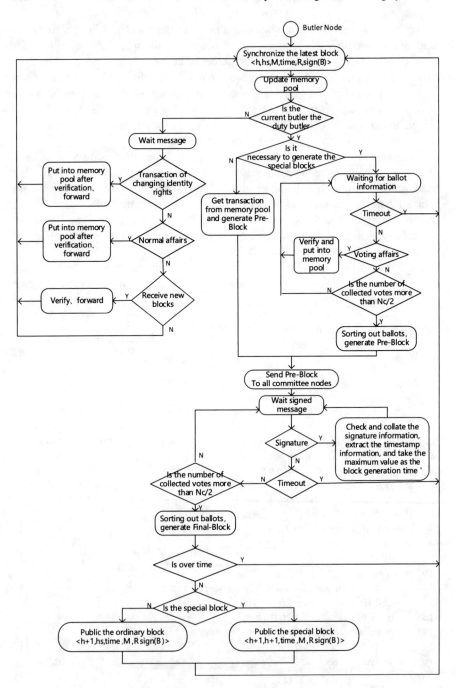

Fig. 4.6 Flow chart for generating ordinary blocks and special blocks (butler's perspective)

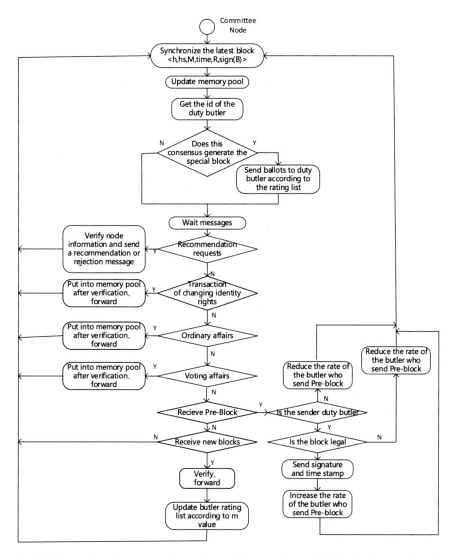

Fig. 4.7 Flow chart for generating ordinary blocks and special blocks (commissioner's perspective)

Algorithm 4.2 describes the implementation of the commissioner process, including phases of the genesis block generation and the ordinary block generation.

Algorithm 4.2: The commissioner's working process

Input:
   Initial state.
Begin
1:   **while** *is_connecting_to_network*=*true* **do**
2:      {*Block_list*}←BLOCK_SYNC()   // synchronize the latest block and update variables and memory pools
3:      *Height*←make_get_height_request_mag()   // request the latest height
4:      **if** *Height*=NULL   // there are no blocks in the network yet
5:         send Tx_PERMISSION<gen_com, com, *NULL*, *my_addr*, *sign*>
6:         **if** *is_needed_to-be_bulter*=*true* **then**
7:            send Tx_PERMISSION<com,bc,*self_recommand,my_addr, sign*>
8:         **end if**
9:         **if** *my_addr*==min(sort({*com_list*})) **then** // the initial commissioner with the smallest public key is the acting committee one
10:            generate the genesis block
11:         **end if**
12:      **else then**
13:         the commissioner process enters the phase of generating blocks
14:   **end if**
15: **end while**
End of Algorithm

Algorithm 4.3 describes the implementation of the butler candidate process.

Algorithm 4.3: The butler candidate's working process

Input:
  Initial state.
Begin
1:   **while** *is_connecting_to_network=true* **do**
2:        {*Block_list*}←BLOCK_SYNC() // synchronize the latest block and update variables and memory pools
3:        process the received voting transaction, validate and put it into the memory pool
4:        process the received identity changing transaction, validate and put it into the memory pool
5:        process the received ordinary transaction, validate and put it into the memory pool
6:        process the other message, verify its validity and forward it
7:        process the received new block, verify its validity and update the information
8:        if *my_addr*{*bc_list*} then
9:             the butler candidate process enters the phase of the butler's tenure
10:      **end if**
11:    **end while**
End of Algorithm

This PoV has been updated to highly efficient version of Parallel PoV, or shortly as PPoV.

4.2.3   PoV Hierarchical Signature Mechanism

Due to the division of labor among nodes in the identity centric network is different, the sovereignty network considers using a hierarchical group/ring signature scheme [11]. Signatures of nodes in the network form a tree structure, and each superior manages a group of subordinate nodes as its leaves. Non-leaf nodes and their leaves form a group/ring. The public key table with all public keys in the group/ring is maintained locally where the signature formats of leaf and non-leaf nodes are respectively $\sigma = (r, s)$ and $\sigma = (y_{new}, \hat{r}_1, \cdots \hat{r}_t, s), \hat{r}_i = (r_i, \sigma_i)$, as shown in Fig. 4.8.

The superior signature is generated by the combination of the subordinate signatures and contains all information of the subordinate nodes. So, the verification of the superior signature also includes that of the tree rooted by the signature. In addition, according to the security requirements of the hierarchical group signature scheme, the group manager can only track the signer identity of its leaf node and cannot open the signature generated by members in other groups. By establishing

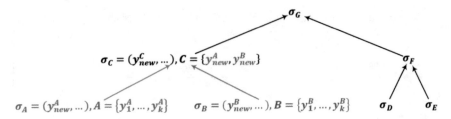

Fig. 4.8 Hierarchical group/ring signatures

groups among nodes with different levels and identities, the superior group managers can quickly locate the problem group and identify the corresponding malicious nodes.

To reduce the size of a single tree and the complexity of iterative verification, the
signature tree is divided into two types according to its ownership and purpose: ring
signature tree for voting and common group signature tree. The hierarchical signature mechanism based on group/ring signature technology with PoV blocks is
shown in Fig. 4.9.

(1) Any ordinary user in the bottom domain generates the transaction and attaches
    the signature S. It also receives intra-domain transactions and verifies the
    correctness in terms of contents and signatures. If correct, the transaction is
    forwarded to other nodes in the domain. Butlers listen for intra-domain trans-
    actions and puts valid transactions into the local pool.
(2) The duty butler regularly takes transactions from the pool and encapsulates into
    the pre-block. The ordinary users to which these transactions belong are added
    to the group of the duty butler to generate a new superior group signature S'.
    Then the duty butler sends the pre-block and S' to commissioners and butlers in
    the domain.
(3) After the commissioner receives the pre-block, it will verify the transaction and
    the butler's signature S'. If it agrees to generate the corresponding block, it will
    send back its signature P and timestamp as a ticket to the duty butler.
(4) If has collected signatures and timestamps from more than half of the
    intra-domain commissioners before the deadline, the duty butler will form a
    ring with the commissioners belonging to these signatures to generate a new
    superior ring signature P'.
(5) When the commissioner receives the final block, it verifies the signatures P' and
    S'. If valid, the transactions contained in the block will be removed from the
    local pool. If the commissioner is not in the top domain, it will extract the block
    header as a transaction, replace the attached butler signature S' with the new
    superior group signature S'', and then propose the transaction as an ordinary
    user in the superior domain. The other superior nodes continue to verify the
    signatures P' and S''. If the commissioner is in the top domain, the block will
    become legal and will been finally confirmed when more than half of the
    commissioners acknowledge were receipted.

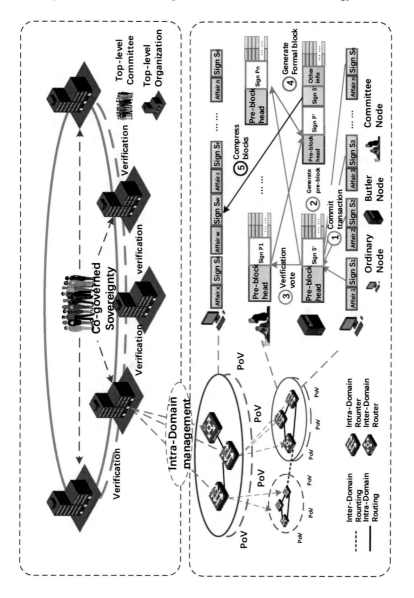

Fig. 4.9 PoV hierarchical signature mechanism

4.3 Routing Scheme for Billions of Multiple Identifiers

Traditional Routing methods based on flat Routing Protocol, such as Routing Information Protocol (RIP) and Open Shortest Path First (OSPF), are faced with the problem of Routing Information synchronization, and cannot be adapted to hierarchical network architecture. Considering the hierarchical management characteristics of the sovereignty network, the BGP protocol is adopted to synchronize the routing information between the autonomous system of the same level network. Considering the future Industrial Internet and other application scenarios, the network addressing scale will have been continued explosive growth.

In order to further improve the efficiency of routing, hyperbolic identifier and routing scheme [12, 13] is proposed for the core networks which has more stable topology and under greater routing pressure than other parts. Then the hash table with prefix tree algorithm is designed for edge networks which topology changes frequently to support a huge amount of identifiers routing problem.

4.3.1 Border Gateway Protocol

The Border Gateway Protocol (BGP) is an optimal distance vector routing protocol, which is used to connect the routes between autonomous system. BGP protocol provides an inter-domain routing system, it guarantees that the autonomous system can only exchange routing information acyclic and routers exchange information about the paths to the target network.

The BGP is modified from the Exterior Gateway Protocol (EGP), where EGP can only simply transport routing information between ASs. However, EGP does not distinguish any priority in routing and does not consider how to avoid routing loops between ASs. So BGP is generally adopted in the operator's core network.

Different with the original EGP, the BGP provides a better service due to the routing optimization, avoiding routing loops, efficiently routing, and maintain large amounts of routing information. This is a policy-based routing protocol that allows the autonomous system to transport data based on a variety of BGP attributes. The most critical factor to be considered is the BGP attributes rather than the speed, when determining the best path.

BGP forwards by maintaining three tables: (1) a neighbor relationship table that records all neighbors, (2) a forwarding database that records neighbor network, path attributes, and BGP attributes, (3) a route table that records the optimal path and the distance of the BGP route from the outside/inside.

The main message types are listed as Table 4.3.

BGP adopts different strategies to establish neighborhood relationships according to its states. In the Idle state, BGP rejects connection requests from neighbors. Only after receiving the Start event from this device, BGP tries to make TCP connection with other BGP peers and goes to the Connect state. The Start event is

Table 4.3 The message type
of BGP

Open	Negotiate BGP parameters
Keepalive	Detect BGP neighbor relationship
Update	Route to BGP
Notification	Error message
Refresh	Refresh message, send and receive again

triggered by one of these reasons: a BGP procedure is configured by an operator, an existing procedure is resettled, and the BGP procedure is resettled by a router software. Whatever the state BGP is, BGP will go to Idle state after receiving Error events such as Notification message, TCP pipe broken Notification.

If in the Connect state, TCP build the connection through three times handshake. If TCP do not complete the handshake, the BGP starts the Connect Retry timer and waits for TCP to complete the connection. If the TCP connection is successful, then BGP sends an Open message to the peer and switches to the OpenSent state. If the TCP connection fails, and the BGP switches to the Active state. If the Connect Retry timer timeouts and the BGP still does not receive a response from the BGP peer, the BGP attempts to build TCP connection with another BGP peer, and BGP remains in the Connect state.

In the Opensent state, if three times handshake is successful, and sending OPEN message to negotiate related parameters of BGP (e.g., AS, version, auth). BGP waits for the Open message of the peer, and checks the AS number, version number, authentication code and so on in the received Open message. If the received Open message is correct, the BGP sends the Keepalive message and switches to the OpenConfirm state. If any error is found in the received Open message, the BGP sends the Notification message to the peer and switches to Idle state.

When it enters the Establish state, BGP can exchange the Update, Keepalive, Route-Refresh and Notification messages with peers. If the correct Update or Keepalive message is received, then the BGP judges that the peer runs, and maintains the BGP connection. If an incorrect Update or Keepalive message is received, the BGP sends the Notification message to notify the peer of going to the Idle state. The Route-refresh message does not change the BGP state. If the Notification message is received, the BGP switches to Idle state. If the TCP chain notification is received, the BGP disconnects and switches to the Idle state. If Active TCP fails to establish three times handshake, it will attempt three times then goes back to Idle state.

Advantages of BGP:

- BGP guarantees the network security, flexibility, stability, reliability and high efficiency from various aspects.
- BGP guarantees network security through authentication and GTSM.

- BGP provides various routing policies, which can be used to select routes flexibly and instruct neighbors to publish routes according to policies.
- BGP provides the function of route aggregation and route attenuation to prevent route oscillation, which effectively improves the stability.
- TCP is used as the protocol of transport layer (port number is 179) to combines BGP, BFD, BGP Tracking, BGP GR, as well as NSR, which improves the reliability of the network.
- In the scenario with large number of neighbors and the routing scale, if most neighbors have the same exit strategy, BGP uses group packing technology improving the performance of BGP packing.

4.3.2 Hyperbolic Identifier and Routing Scheme

Sovereignty networks forward content based on the name, which suffers from the large identity scale and dynamic requests brought by many new types of identifiers and many future application scenarios such as IoT, Industrial Internet, high security private network.

Greedy geometric routing (GGR) maps the cyberspace into a metric space and assigns an address or coordinate to each node. Each segment of the network message transmitted in the network is accompanied by its destination coordinates. Each router calculates the geometric distance between each adjacent node and the destination separately after receiving the packet. The one with the smallest distance will be selected as the next hop for forwarding. In this process, since the required information of each node only includes the coordinates of its neighbors, GGR can minimize the size of FIB as much as possible. GGR is a basis for providing a routing protocol for large-scale networks.

Hyperbolic routing (HR) is based on the scale-free property of the network, which means that the degree of nodes in the network follows a power-law distribution. Through the mapping algorithm, the network is mapped to a space with negative curvature (i.e., hyperbolic space). Two-dimensional space is taken as an example. Each node is mapped into a disk with radius R and assigned a polar coordinate (r, θ). The angular coordinate θ represents the relative position of the node in the network, and the radial coordinate r indicates the central degree of the node. The smaller the radius coordinate of a node, the closer to the center of the disk. When the angular coordinates of the two nodes are constant, the hyperbolic distance between them will decrease with the decrease of radial coordinates. Therefore, greedy routing based on hyperbolic distance tends to select more centralized nodes as its next hop for forwarding.

Many networks such as the IP Internet have the scale-free property. Combining with an appropriate mapping algorithm, a simple greedy strategy based on hyperbolic range can forward the message to the destination node with a high success rate. For the few cases that forwarding fails, auxiliary intelligent forwarding strategies can be adopted to make the success rate of hyperbolic routing approach 100%.

However, HR algorithm also has some defects. Compared with the routing protocol based on the traditional shortest path algorithm, the forward path selected by HR algorithm has a larger transmission delay. It's the inherent disadvantage of the greedy strategy, and most of the existing hyperbolic mapping algorithms do not consider network delay. To avoid this disadvantage, we have proposed a hyperbolic routing algorithm that reduces the network latency and ensures the fast selection of forwarding paths to guarantee the fast forwarding of the sovereignty network.

The proposed HR algorithm maps a scale-free cyberspace to a three-dimension hyperbolic space H^3. Each node in the network is assigned a three-dimension spherical coordinates. The distance between two points (r_1, θ_1, ϕ_1) and (r_2, θ_2, ϕ_2) can be calculated based on the cosine law.

$$d_{12} = \cosh^{-1}(\cosh r_1 \cosh r_2 - \sinh r_1 \sinh r_2 \cos \Delta\theta_{12}) \tag{4.1}$$

where $\Delta\theta_{12}$ represents the central angle between the two points and the origin.

$$\Delta\theta_{12} = \cos^{-1}[\cos \theta_1 \cos \theta_2 + \sin \theta_1 \sin \theta_2 \cos(\theta_1 - \theta_2)] \tag{4.2}$$

The algorithm includes two parts: the angular coordinate mapping and the radial coordinate mapping. The specific process is described in the next part.

1. Angular Coordinate Mapping

Each node is assigned an angular coordinate, which is mapped to the sphere S^2. Sphere S^2 simulates the surface of the earth, while the angular coordinates of nodes represent their actual positions in the network as shown in Fig. 4.10.

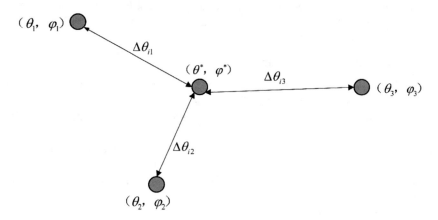

Fig. 4.10 Angle coordinate mapping

The angular coordinates of high degrees nodes are set directly as their geographic location, i.e., the latitude and longitude information. The reasons are listed as follows:

- The transmission delay between two nodes is proportional to the geographical distance between them. Hence the mapping based on geographical location can optimize effectively on the delay.
- The mapping method is convenient to calculate.
- The mapping method is independent of the topology information of the network, so it maintains strong stability in the dynamic environment of the network.

We have proposed a different approach to non-central nodes with low degrees, because their network location depends on local topology than geographic information. For node i whose degree is greater than or equal to 3, it will calculate its average delay from each central node, then select the three central nodes j_1, j_2, j_3 with the smallest delay to calculate its angular coordinate.

If the delay between i whose angular coordinate is (θ^*, φ^*) and j_k whose angular coordinate (θ_k, φ_k) is t_k, we can obtain that:

$$\min_{(\theta^*,\varphi^*)\in S^2} [|\xi| + \varepsilon(\Delta\theta_{i1} + \Delta\theta_{i2} + \Delta\theta_{i3})] \tag{4.3}$$

$$s.t. \lambda\Delta\theta_{ik} = t_k - \xi (k = 1, 2, 3) \tag{4.4}$$

$\Delta\theta_{ik}$ is the central Angle of (θ_k, φ_k) and (θ^*, φ^*), which can be obtained from Eq. 4.2. The Eq. 4.2 reflects the direct proportional relationship of the network delay and spherical distance, where the relaxation variable ξ is used to ensure a viable solution.

The former term of the objective function ensures that the value of ξ is as small as possible. The latter term $\varepsilon(\Delta\theta_{i1} + \Delta\theta_{i2} + \Delta\theta_{i3})$ is used to select the smallest sum of spherical distances when there are multiple feasible solutions.

For non-central nodes with degrees less than or equal to 2, their angular coordinates will directly copy one of the highest degrees in the neighborhood, since there is only one path to the central node.

2. Radial Coordinate Mapping

The radial coordinate r represents the central degree of a node. In a scale-free network, r follows the exponential distribution.

"Supernodes" in a network may delay the generation of suboptimal paths. For example, Shanghai has an extremely large number of Internet users, so there are several high "supernodes". If a message from the north Korean city of Incheon to the south Korean city of Busan, the forwarding path selected by HR may be attracted to the high center of Shanghai, i.e., Incheon—Shanghai—Busan causing additional delay, because these cities have a smaller population than Shanghai.

To solve this problem, the global network is divided into subgraphs. The most central node in each subgraph has similar radial coordinates. Therefore, the forwarding process is more likely to select the central node in the subgraph, which improves the locality of routing and reduces transmission delay. The m nodes $i_1, i_2, \ldots, i_m$ with the highest degrees in the network are selected, and the other nodes measure the delay between themselves and each i_*. If i_k is the one with the smallest delay, then this node belongs to the corresponding sub-graph G_k.

Radial coordinates are obtained by maximum likelihood estimation, and we have the following prior conditions:

(1) The degree of nodes follows a power distribution $\rho(k) \sim k^{-\gamma}$, where the lowest degree is k_0, and the average value is $\bar{k}$. The degree and radius coordinates satisfy the following relation:

$$r(k) = R - 2 \ln \frac{k}{k_0} \tag{4.5}$$

where R indicates the radius of the sphere.

(2) The probability of connecting two nodes with hyperbolic distance x is:

$$p(x) = \left\{ 1 + \exp \left[\frac{\zeta(x - R)}{2T} \right] \right\}^{-1} \tag{4.6}$$

T is temperature and represents the aggregation degree of control nodes. ζ is the curvature of hyperbolic space. R can be obtained by the following integral:

$$\bar{K} = \frac{N}{2\pi} \int_0^R \rho[k(r)] \int_0^R \rho[k(r')] \int_0^\pi \int_0^\pi p(x) d\varphi' d\theta' dr' dr \tag{4.7}$$

x is the hyperbolic distance between (r', θ', φ') and $(r, 0, 0)$.

On the basis of the above prior conditions, for node i with degree k_i, the maximum likelihood of its radial coordinate is estimated as:

$$r_i^* = R - 2 \ln \frac{k_i - T\gamma}{k_0} \tag{4.8}$$

If node $i \in G_j$, its diameter coordinate is:

$$r_i = \log \left\{ \beta + \exp \left[r_i^* + (r_0 - r_i^*) \left(\frac{R - r_i^*}{R - r_j^*} \right)^4 \right] \right\} \tag{4.9}$$

β is used to adjust the relative weights of radial coordinates and angle coordinates in the routing process.

Through the above formula, the diameter coordinate r_0 of the most central node in each subgraph is obtained, and only minor modification is made to the non-central node whose original radial coordinate is small.

In the angular coordinate mapping algorithm, the network delay is equivalent to the spherical distance, and the coordinates of non-central nodes are calculated accordingly. At the same time, in the radial coordinate mapping algorithm, the delay is reduced by subgraph partition. At the same time, the network delay is taken as the basis of subgraph partition.

4.3.3   Hash Table with Prefix Tree Algorithm (HPT)

Prefix Tree (Trie), also known as Dictionary Tree, is a data structure commonly found in string matches. In a dictionary tree, an edge refers to a unit composed of a name, such as bits, characters, and so on. A node refers to a specific name whose contents are the assembly of components rooted to all the edges on the path to that node. In the storage structure based on Prefix Tree, the same prefix part between names is merged into the upstream path to realizing the compression of data capacity and the preservation of the logical relationship between names.

Because the prefix tree supports LPM (Longest Prefix Matching) algorithm and has good space utilization efficiency, most network uses prefix tree for forwarding. The disadvantage of prefix tree is that the searching speed in prefix tree is slow. Firstly, the computational overhead is roughly proportional to the expected length of the name. Secondly, at each level, the searching algorithm needs to match all the outsides of the node one by one to find the child nodes for the descent. Therefore, the forwarding architecture based on the prefix tree will cause a large searching delay and affect the overall performance of network.

Compared with the prefix tree, the searching speed of the hash table is not affected by name length and entry size, so it has better adaptability in a large-scale network. However, to cope with hash collisions, the hash table also needs to store the full key value (i.e., the content name) in the table entry, which incurs a large storage overhead. At the same time, the original hash table structure does not support the longest prefix matching algorithm, and the simplest linear implementation has a large searching time. To cope with these problems, existing ICN networks usually use data compression schemes such as footprint-based Hash Table and algorithm optimization schemes such as Random Search to improve the scalability of the system.

In general, the new identifier is much longer than the IP address, so the process of a multi-identifier will face great pressure of computing and storage. To this end, we propose a hash table with prefix tree algorithm HPT, adding semi-virtual entries to the prefix tree. This scheme accelerates the backtracking process of the FIB searching algorithm and effectively improves the efficiency of multi-identifier

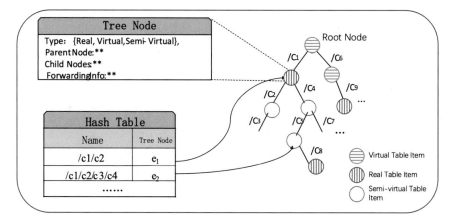

Fig. 4.11   The structure of FIB [28]

translation and addressing. Hash tables are used for quick lookups, and tree structures are used to store logical relationships between names. The main structure of FIB is shown in Fig. 4.11.

The characteristics of FIB include the following:

(1) FIB consists of hash tables and prefix trees. For any name stored in a table, all true prefixes have corresponding entries in the table. The process of checking for the existence of the prefix and adding the corresponding secondary entry is called FIB refactoring. In reconstructed FIB, table entries are divided into real entries and non-real entries, and non-real entries are divided into virtual entries and semi-virtual entries.

(2) In the hash table, the name is used as the key, and the node in the prefix tree is used as the value. In this way, we realize the fast retrieval of forwarding information.

(3) Each edge in the prefix tree represents a name component. Each node in the prefix tree represents a name that stores the forwarding information corresponding to the name and the corresponding category of table entries, as well as Pointers to maintain the prefix tree structure.

The specific definitions of real entries, non-real entries, virtual entries, and semi-virtual entries are as follows:

(1) Real entry: Names in real entries refer to actual data and are used to guide the forwarding of interest packets. Before FIB refactoring, all table entries are real.

(2) Non-real entry: Auxiliary entries used to support random searching algorithms are called non-real entries. Names in non-real entries do not refer to any actual data and do not guide the forwarding of interest packets.

(3) Virtual entry: A non-real entry is said to be virtual if it does not have any real prefix. When the random searching process ends with a virtual entry, it ends directly without generating any false-negative errors.

(4) Semi-virtual entry: If the non-real entry has a real prefix, the non-real entry is called a semi-virtual entry and requires backtracking.

When a user registers and publishes resources on MIN, multiple identifiers are bound with resources and stored in MIS. Commonly used identifiers and their inter-translation information are stored in HPT-FIB of MIR. If MIR can query corresponding information in the local HPT-FIB, it will directly forward. Otherwise, MIR will initiate a translation request to the MIS system based on the identifier provided by the user. MIS searches the other identifiers corresponding to this identifier, then selects the appropriate identifier and sends it to MIR for addressing. The usage of FIB is as follows.

1. **FIB insert**

First, we should determine whether the name to be inserted in FIB exists. If so, perform the first (1) inserting step; otherwise, perform the second (2) inserting step. The inserting steps are shown as below.

(1) The inserting steps

(1) Step 1: Determine whether the entry corresponding to the name is a real entry. If so, update its forwarding information; otherwise, perform step 2.
(2) Step 2: Judge whether the entry corresponding to the name is a virtual entry. If so, perform the modification step; otherwise, perform step 3.
(3) Step 3: Change all virtual entries in the child tree to semi-virtual entries, and then perform the step 4, Modify step.
(4) Step 4: Modify its category to be a real entry and add forward information.

To sum up, in the first inserting step, if the name to be inserted already has a corresponding entry in FIB, there is no problem with adding new entries. The case of real entries is trivial, so only non-real entries are considered. The corresponding category is modified to be real. If the entry is originally virtual, the virtual entry in the subtree needs to be modified to semi-virtual. If the entry is originally semi-virtual, the subtree does not need to be modified.

(2) The inserting steps

Firstly, search the LPM of the name to be inserted in FIB. If HIT is real, then perform the first processing step. If MISS or HIT is virtual, the second processing step is performed.

(1) Step 1: insert the real entry corresponding to the name, find all true prefixes of the name in FIB, and insert the corresponding semi-virtual entry if it does not exist.
(2) Step 2: insert the real entry corresponding to the name, find all true prefixes of the name in FIB, and insert the corresponding virtual entry if it does not exist.

Algorithm 4.4: Key inserting Algorithm

Input:
   H: HT and trie-based FIB
   n: n = "$/c1/c2/.../cN$" is the name to insert
   f: the corresponding forwarding information of n
Output:
   H: HT and trie-based FIB, with n inserted.
Begin
1:    lookup n in HT
2:    **if** n is the name of a real entry (n, e) **then**
3:          update e's forwarding information with f
4:    **else if** n is the name of a non-real entry (n, e) **then**
5:          /* as Fig. 4.13a */
6:          set e's type to real, e's forwarding information to f
7:          **for** each virtual entry $(\sim, e*)$ in e's subtree **do**
8:                set $e*$'s type to semi-virtual
9:          **end for**
10:   **else**
11:         /* as Fig. 4.13b */ create entry (n, e_N) and insert it to HT
12:         set e_N's type to real, e_N's forwarding information to f
13:         **for** $i = N - 1$ to 1 **do**
14:         lookup n_i ="$/c1/c2/.../ci$" in HT
15:               **if** n_i is the name of an entry (n_i, e) **then**
16:                     add e_{i+1} to e's child list, set e_{i+1}'s parent to e
17:                     **if** e is virtual **then**
18:                           set $e_j(i < j < N)$'s type to virtual
19:                     **else**
20:                           set $e_j(i < j < N)$'s type to semi-virtual
21:                     **end if**
22:                     **return**
23:               **else**
24:                     create entry (n_i, e_i) and insert it to HT
25:                     add e_{i+1} to e_i's child list, set e_{i+1}'s parent to e_i
26:               **end if**
27:         **end for**
28:         add e_1 to $root$'s child list, set e_1's parent to $root$
29:         set e_j $(0 < j < N)$'s type to virtual
30:   **end if**
End of Algorithm

Fig. 4.12 FIB inserting step
[28]

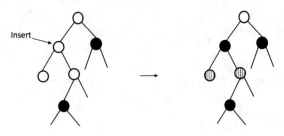

(a) Case when there exists non-virtual entry for this name in table

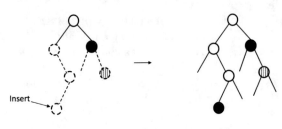

(b) Otherwise

To sum up, in the second step, if the name to be inserted does not have a corresponding entry, the corresponding real entry is inserted. At the same time, the prefixes are checked backward and forwards to ensure that they are present in the FIB. If a prefix is found not existing, the corresponding non-real entry is inserted. This process continues until the algorithm reaches the LPM or root node, and thus determines the category of non-real nodes inserted during this process (Fig. 4.12).

2. **FIB Search**

The process of lookup of FIB algorithm is shown as Algorithm 4.5 and Fig. 4.13.

The port to forward the packet is obtained by searching the name of the interest packet through the random searching algorithm. The random searching algorithm can be chosen according to the request, such as traditional binary searches.

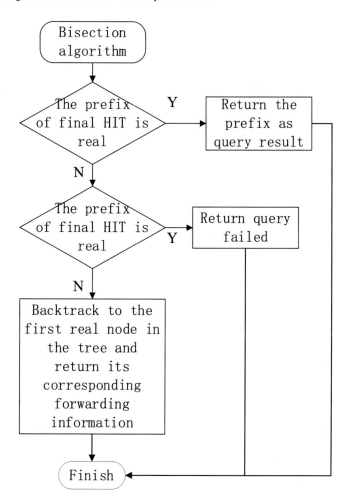

Fig. 4.13 The steps of FIB lookup

Algorithm 4.5: Searching Algorithm

Input:
  H: HT and trie-based FIB.
  n: n = "/c1/c2/.../cN" is the search key.
Output:
  f: the forwarding information of *n*'s LPM entry
Begin
1:      /* Binary Search */
2:      $L=1, H=N$
3:      $e_{LPM} = root$
4:    **while** $L \leq H$ **do**
5:        $M=(L+H)/2$
6:        lookup n_M = "/c1/c2/.../cM" in HT
7:        **if** n_M is the name of an entry (n_M, e) in table **then**
8:            $L=M+1, e_{LPM}=e$
9:        **else**
10:          $H=M-1$
11:      **end if**
12:    **end while**
13:    **if** e_{LPM} is virtual **then**
14:        **return** NO FOUND
15:    **else**
16:        /* As Fig. 4.14 */
17:        **while** e_{LPM} is not real **do**
18:            $e_{LPM} = e_{LPM}$'s parent
19:        **end while**
20:        **return** e_{LPM}'s forwarding information
21:    **end if**
End of Algorithm

There are three patterns based on the category of the last HIT entry:

(1) If it is a real entry, the search for LPM is successful, and returns the corresponding information.
(2) If it is a virtual entry, it is sure that there is no matching real prefix in the table, so return with no match.
(3) If it is a semi-virtual entry, there is at least one matching real prefix in the table. We can backtrack in the prefix tree to find the matching real prefix out and return it. Since backtracking in the prefix tree does not involve searching, this process has a minimal time overhead.

As shown in Fig. 4.14, the last HIT prefix of binary search for the name "/c1/c2/c3/c6/c7" is "/c1/c2/c3", which is a semi-virtual table entry leading to the backtrack

Fig. 4.14 The process of FIB
searching [28]

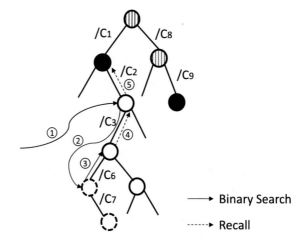

process. The algorithm starts from "/c1/c2/c3" to backtrack until it encounters the
first real entry "/c1", then returns its corresponding forward information.

So, there are two kinds of lookup results. One is HIT, which means that there is a
corresponding real entry in HPT FIB (i.e., the last HIT entry is real entry or
semi-virtual entry). The other is MISS, which means that the corresponding real
entry does not exist (i.e., the last HIT entry is virtual).

3. **Deleting FIB**

The FIB deleting step is used to discover and retrieve out-of-date non-real entries.

Firstly, determine whether there are child nodes in the corresponding entry of the
name to be deleted in FIB. If so, perform the first deleting step; otherwise, perform
the second deleting step.

(1) The first deleting step: judge whether the parent node of the corresponding
    entry is virtual. If it is virtual, then execute the first deleting sub-step. If the
    parent node of the corresponding entry is real or semi-virtual, change the entry
    category of the name to semi-virtual.

    • First deleting sub-step: Change the entry category corresponding to the
      name to virtual, and then traverse the subtree with the name as root. If one
      of the nodes satisfies the first condition (category is semi-virtual) and the
      second condition (there are no real nodes on the path from the node to its
      name), then the category of the node is changed to virtual.

(2) The second deleting step: Deletes the entry, then checks all true prefixes of the
    name upward, step by step. If the corresponding node of the prefix satisfies the
    first point (class is not real) and the second point (leaf node), then delete the
    entry.

Algorithm 4.6: Deleting Algorithm
Input:
H: HT and trie-based FIB.
n: $n = $ "/c1/c2/.../cN" is the name to delete.
Output:
H: HT and trie-based FIB, with n deleted.
Begin
1:   lookup n in HT,
2:   **if** n is not the name of a real entry **then**
3:     **return**
4:   **end if**
5:   **if** for n's entry (n, e), if e is not a leaf **then**
6:     set e's forwarding information to N/A
7:     **if** e's parent is semi-virtual or real **then**
8:       set e's type to semi-virtual
9:     **else**
10:     /* As Fig. 4.15a, here uses BFS */
11:     create an empty queue q and insert e into it
12:     **while** q is not empty **do**
13:       $e^* = q.\text{pop}()$
14:       set e^*'s type to virtual
15:       insert all e^*'s semi-virtual child nodes into q
16:     **end while**
17:     **end if**
18:   **else**
19:     /* As Fig. 4.15b */
20:     remove e from its parent's child list
21:     delete entry (n, e) in HT
22:     **for** $i = N - 1$ to 1 **do**
23:       **for** $n_i = $"/c1/c2/.../ci" and its entry (n_i, e_i)
24:       **if** e_i is non-real and e_i' is a leaf **then**
25:         remove e_i from its parent's child list
26:         delete entry (n_i, e_i) in HT
27:       **else**
28:         **return**
29:       **end if**
30:     **end for**
31:   **end if**
End of Algorithm

Through deleting steps, the categories of non-real entries can be kept correct in the dynamic environment, and out-of-date non-real entries can be found and recovered timely, so as to ensure the efficiency and stability of the forwarding plane (Fig. 4.15).

Fig. 4.15 The deleting process of FIB [28]

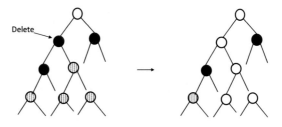

(a) Case when name to delete is not leaf and has virtual parent

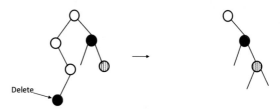

(b) Case when name to delete is leaf

Our experiments show that the FIB forwarding data structure combining prefix tree with hash algorithm could support large-scale name prefix storage and search, as shown in Table 4.4.

HPT-FIB has a significant storage overhead when the network scale further expands. Therefore, we proposed a 3D Hyperbolic Routing (HR) model instead of a forwarding table to reduce storage overhead in MIR. MIN is mapped to a 3D hyperbolic space, then MIR and all contents are given 3D spherical coordinates. In HBR, MIR only uses the greedy algorithm to select a MIR as next-hop with the smallest hyperbolic distance from the destination for forwarding. This approach significantly reduces the storage overhead of MIR.

The HPT-FIB entries of this system are more than one billion, and the lookup speed is close to log(log(N)), where N is the number of identifiers. The design completely solves the problem of false-negative errors in the existing algorithms. Besides, MIR can detect and delete obsolete table entries timely, thus improving the efficiency of memory recovery.

Table 4.4 The relationship between time and scale of FIB [31]

FIB scale	100 million	1 billion	2 billion	2.5 billion	3 billion	3.5 billion
Running time (Second)	187.58	1649.75	3723.98	4925.64	6271.49	7760.69
Actual FIB scale	100 million	1 billion	2 billion	2.5 billion	3 billion	3.5 billion

4.4 Identity Authentication Scheme Based on Real Identity and Biometric

The identity authentication of the sovereignty network users is based on human biological characteristics, and combined with blockchain technology as a decentralized identity management scheme. The user authentication function accurately identifies the user's identity, and stores the related information into blockchains, so as to ensure its integrity and consistency. Besides, combined with the identity management scheme of blockchains, it also realizes the decentralization of third-party certificate authentication and generating institutions. Through the most advanced encryption scheme, the proposed scheme effectively protects the privacy of the user's identity information.

4.4.1 Introduction of User Biological Characteristics

1. Iris

The iris is the circular region between the pupil and the white sclera on the surface of the human eye. In near-infrared light, the iris presents a rich texture, such as spots, stripes, filaments, coronae and crypts. Iris recognition technology is adopted in identity authentication by comparing the similarities between iris image features. The core step is to describe, match and classify iris features of human eyes by pattern recognition, image processing and other methods, so as to realize automatic human identity authentication.

The characteristics of iris are listed as follows.

(1) Uniqueness. According to physiological researches, the detailed texture of iris is determined by the random factors of the embryonic development environment. The random distribution of the texture details lays a physiological foundation for the uniqueness of iris. The images are significantly different even when the irises of twins or the same person's left and right eyes. Hence it is almost impossible to find two identical irises in nature.

(2) Stability. The iris begins growth in the third month of the infant's embryonic period. By the eighth month, its main texture has been formed. On the other hand, due to the protection of the cornea, the fully developed iris is less vulnerable to external damage. Therefore, it is almost impossible that the iris changes due to external physical contact. Scientists have found that the texture of the iris remains almost constant throughout life, barring surgery that can endanger the eye.

(3) Non-contact. The iris is an externally visible internal organ, whose feature collection is more hygienic and convenient than the biological features that need to be touched. This is very different from external organs such as fingerprints and face images. A qualified image of the iris can be obtained through

a contactless (or even remote) collection device. This is very convenient in practical applications.

(4) Large capacity. The acquisition of clear iris texture requires the cooperation of specialized devices and users, so it is difficult to steal iris images, compared with fingerprints and faces. In addition, eyes also have a lot of excellent optical and physiological characteristics, which can be used for detection in vivo iris.

Iris recognition process includes iris image acquisition, iris image preprocessing, feature extraction and comparison, and user identity recognition.

2. Face Recognition

Face recognition is a kind of biometric technology based on facial feature information. Images or video streams containing faces are captured with cameras to automatically detect and track the faces. The series of related technologies are commonly known as portrait recognition or face recognition.

Rapidly developing solutions include multi-light face recognition based on active near infrared image and face recognition based on machine learning.

Multi-light face recognition based on active near infrared image technology can overcome the influence of light changes and improve the recognition performance. Due to the performance of the system in accuracy, stability and speed superior to 3D image face recognition, this technology has developed rapidly in recent two or three years, which gradually makes facial recognition technology to practical application.

The face recognition technology combining machine learning is based on various theories to build the learning model and face database, which can also realize high-precision face recognition without special physical equipment.

Similar to other biological features of the human body such as fingerprints, iris, etc., the human face is innate. It is difficult to be copied with unique characteristics, which provides a necessary prerequisite for identification.

Compared with other biometrics, face recognition has the following characteristics:

(1) Non-mandatory. The process to obtain face images does not need users to cooperate with face acquisition equipment, which are almost unconsciously. Such a sampling method is not "mandatory".

(2) Non-contact. The process to obtain a face image does not need users to contact directly with the device.

(3) Concurrency. In practical application scenarios, multiple faces can be sorted, judged and recognized at the same time.

In addition, face recognition also conforms to the characteristics of "recognizing people by appearance", as well as guarantees simple operation, intuitive results, good concealment, etc.

The face recognition system mainly consists of four parts: face image acquisition and detection module, face image preprocessing module, face image feature extraction module, matching and recognition module.

3. Fingerprint

The fingerprint is lines on the skin on the front end of fingers. The lines are arranged regularly to form different patterns. Fingerprints are almost synonymous with biometric identification for their lifetime immutability, uniqueness, and convenience.

The starting point, ending point, joint point and bifurcation point of the lines are researched as the detailed feature of fingerprint. Fingerprint identification compares the detailed features of different fingerprints. Fingerprint recognition technology combines image processing technology, pattern recognition technology, computer vision technology, mathematical morphology, wavelet analysis and many other subjects. Fingerprints can be used for identification because everyone's fingerprints are different even between the fingers of the same person.

The main advantages of fingerprint identification technology are listed as follows.

(1) Fingerprints are unique features of the human body, and they are complex enough to provide features for identification.
(2) The reliability can be improved through registering and identifying more fingerprints from different fingers. Up to ten fingerprints can be taken, and each fingerprint is unique.
(3) The speed of fingerprint scanning is very fast, and it is very convenient to use.
(4) When reading a fingerprint, the user must directly touch the fingerprint sampling machine with the finger.
(5) Direct contact with a fingerprint sampling machine is the most reliable method to collect human biological characteristics.
(6) The fingerprint sampling machine is smaller and cheaper than other sampling machines.

Above all, the adoption of biometric information can greatly improve the reliability of user identification and significantly reduce the probability of user feature information being stolen.

4.4.2 Introduction of Each Module

In the sovereignty network, the authentication system based on real identity and biometric characteristics includes three modules: identity chain, Content Management (CM) module, sovereignty network client and handheld terminals.

1. Identity Chain

The identity chain uses the blockchain based on PoV consensus as the underlying storage system to store the user's identity information, public key, and part of the encrypted identity information. Identity information refers to symbols that can be individually mapped to a particular unique user, such as relevant certificates, fingerprints, iris images and face information. Depending on the requirements of scenario with the need for high security, a location map of the off-chain storage can be written on the block, which uses a secure off-chain storage scheme to store identity information that the user refuses to disclose.

The identity chain also provides a client to query identity information. The sovereignty network client or CM module obtains the corresponding identity information with this client.

2. CM Module

CM module is responsible for completing user's operations, such as adding, deleting, modifying, searching, etc., as well as specific business, such as registration, login, logout, modification and deletion of identity information. Various designs are adopted to protect the privacy and rights of the user. The addition and deletion of the user are executed without the authorization of users, while the modification and query of user information need its consent. In fact, the client needs to generate the corresponding Access Token or the intermediate key in re-encryption technology to indicate the obtained users' permission.

During the registration process, CM module approves part of the user's information. Once approved, the summary is signed and returned to the client. Meanwhile, as the verifier in the identity management scheme, CM module invokes the identity chain of the client to write and query the identity. In addition, CM encapsulates the third-party biological interface and works as the server for biological characteristics authentication. Since the variety of proposed biological authentication methods in the sovereignty network, the CM module determines which authentication method the user uses for login.

3. Sovereignty Network Client and Handheld Terminals

The client is responsible for collecting and maintaining the corresponding hardware and software information, and the handheld terminal uses the interface of the biological verification facility in the form of APP to collect the initialization data and biological information during verification. The handheld terminal adopts Android system to develop Android applications and corresponding identity authentication applications for the sovereignty network client.

In addition, during the registration, the Elliptic Curve Cryptography (ECC) is adopted in the client to generate the corresponding public and private key pairs, and then issue a request after CM approval. The approval public key, client information and identity information are written to the identity chain. Then the erasure code technology is used by the client to split the private key into n blocks, which will be stored on trusted devices respectively. While restoring the private key, m blocks are requested from the corresponding devices to decode the complete private key. In this way, MIN enhances the stability of the private key storage with low storage overhead.

4.4.3 Application Scenarios

1. **Handheld Terminal Authorization**

As shown in Fig. 4.16, the process of handheld terminal authorization is as follows.

(1) The end-host device sends a request to CM for obtaining the public key of CM.
(2) The end-host generates the public and private keys and unique information, then encrypts the information with CM's public key and sends a request to CM.
(3) CM writes the identity information of the device into the blockchain.
(4) Blockchain returns the feedback of written information.
(5) CM returns the result to the end-host.

2. **User Registration**

As shown in Fig. 4.17, the user registration process is as follows:

(1) The client first sends a request for CM's public key.
(2) The relevant information (i.e., name, account number, ID number, etc.) is provided from the client's registration screen, and iris images are input through the iris sampling device. The client then generates public and private key pairs. The private key is encoded into n pieces by erasure code (n is configurated by

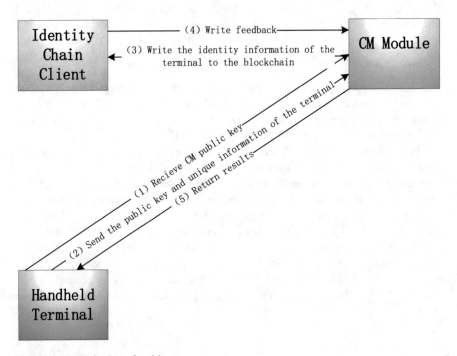

Fig. 4.16 Authorization of end-host

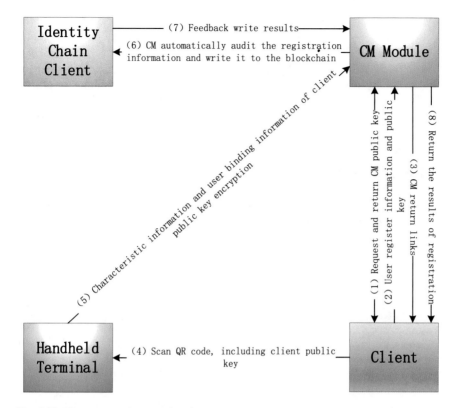

Fig. 4.17 The process of user registration

operation staff), and is stored in trusted devices. It is worth mentioning that MIN would provide a local disk to store private keys if the user does not provide any equipment.

(3) After the client encrypts iris images with its public key followed by a signature made by the private key, it uses CM's public key to encrypt the ciphertext of iris images again and sends it to CM server. After the CM server receives the registration information submitted by the client, it returns the link to submit the user's biometric information to the client.

(4) The client generates the corresponding Quick Response (QR) code and sends it to the handheld terminal. The QR code contains the client's public key which is bound with the client by the user.

(5) The user scans the QR code with a handheld terminal to log in with the identity information, and collects fingerprints, faces and other information. After all the signs are collected, then they are encrypted using the public key of CM and sent to the CM server with other encrypted information.

(6) The registration information received by CM server is automatically approved by the system. If validation passes, CM will store the identity information into the blockchain.

(7) The blockchain feeds back the results to CM.

(8) CM returns information to the client about whether the registration is successful or not.

3. User Login

As shown in Fig. 4.18, the process of user login is as follows:

(1) The user enters the user name and password. Then the client uses its private key and CM's public key to generate the re-encryption key. The re-encryption key cannot be used to invert the user's private key and CM's public key, but can be decrypted with CM's private key.

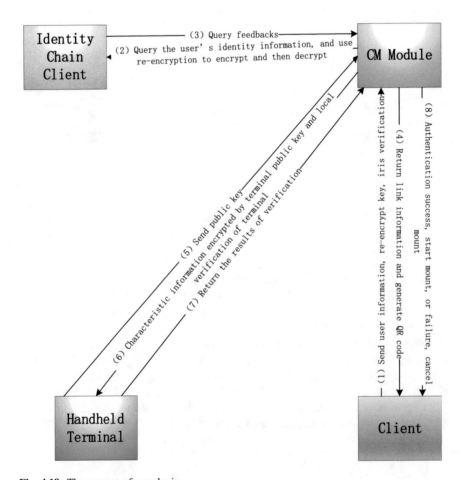

Fig. 4.18 The process of user login

(2) The client uses CM's public key to encrypt user name, password, re-encryption key and hardware and software information, and sends the ciphertext to CM.

(3) The CM module searches for the corresponding information on the blockchain according to the user ID. The query result is sent to CM and stored in the cache after being decrypted with the private key of CM.

(4) The CM module sends the link of physical verification to the client according to the policy set by administrators. Then the client generates the QR code.

(5) The handheld terminal scans the QR code and sends its public key and binding information to CM.

(6) The CM encrypts the feature information with the public key of the handheld terminal and returns it to the handheld terminal, which authenticates biometric characteristics such as fingerprint, face and iris.

(7) The handheld terminal sends the feedback result of authentication to the CM module.

(8) If the authentication is successful, CM sends a notification to allow the client to mount the file system. Otherwise, the login fails. The mount process is the same as the NFS mount process.

4. **User Identity Information Modification and Deletion**

(1) Modification of user information.

- If the user needs to re-enter biological information, the process is similar to the registration process.
- If the user needs to modify the biological information, the client would send the corresponding information to the CM module, and CM would re-write the updated identity information on the blockchain.

(2) Deletion of user information. According to the user ID, the CM module writes the information representing the deleting behavior to the blockchain.

4.5 Privacy Protection and Network Management

The broadcasting network is used as an application example of the sovereignty network, which needs to protect user privacy while managing users. Hence, the sovereignty network introduces blockchain technology, asymmetry encryption technology, privacy protection strategy and other technologies [14, 15].

In addition to the above technologies, the sovereignty network set up electronic visas. When a user of a sovereignty subnet wants to access the content of another sovereignty subnet, he or she needs to apply for an electronic visa for the target sovereignty subnet. Access to the resource in the sovereignty subnet is only possible with visa information.

4.5.1   Electronic Visas of Sovereignty Network

Each country independently builds its own sovereignty network and has full autonomy. To access the content of a country's sovereignty web, users in other countries must first apply for an electronic visa, and then carry the successfully applied visa for the visit. At the same time, the country can control visa permissions and design access rules for content, such as making it off-limits to foreign users. In this way, cyberspace corresponds to reality, just as the Internet customs. It can not only realize the mutual access between countries, but also manage and control the access behavior. See Sect. 5.4.2 for a detailed description of certificate acquisition and access to network content through certificates.

4.5.2   Asymmetric Encryptions

Existing content centric network architectures typically use "verifiable names" for data requests. In other words, each name must contain how its publisher's public key is acquired, as well as the publisher's signature of the name and content. Before the data message is cached by the routing node or received by the requester, its signature information must be verified to ensure the integrity, security and reliability of the name and content.

There are frequent public key requests in the network. In order to save bandwidth resources and reduce the transmission pressure of the network, the sovereignty network adopts the public and private key generation scheme based on the identity identification and combination matrix. The scheme is briefly described as follows:

The cryptosystem we adopt is Elliptic Curve Cryptography (ECC). In ECC, if the base point G on the elliptic curve and its order n are given, the positive integer $r < n$ is the private key, and the r times G point $rG = R$ is used as the public key. It is easy to calculate R by (R, G), but it is not computationally feasible to solve r by (R, G) because the discrete logarithm problem of elliptic curve is difficult. The private key matrix $(r_{ij})_{m \times n}$ is $m \times n$ order, where every element r_{ij} is a positive integer satisfying $r_{ij} < n$. The public key matrix $(R_{ij})_{m \times n}$ can be generated by the corresponding relation $r_{ij}G = R_{ij}$. The private key matrix is only held by the authority of key management and used for the distribution of the user's private key. The public key matrix is held by each network node and used for data signature authentication.

As shown in Fig. 4.19, the key management agency generates the user's private key r_{ID} with the user's identity ID and private key matrix (r_{ij}).

For example, the generation of the private key can be implemented in the following way. Through cryptographic chip and cryptography, each identity ID can uniquely generate a sequence, as shown below.

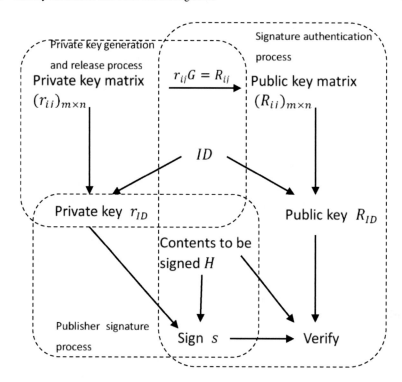

Fig. 4.19 The process of generating the private key

$$GenerateSub(ID) = \{i_1, i_2, \ldots, i_l, j_1, j_2, \ldots, j_l\} \qquad (4.10)$$

The private key corresponding to ID is the sum of the corresponding items in the private key matrix:

$$r_{ID} = r_{i_1 j_1} + r_{i_2 j_2} + \cdots + r_{i_l j_l} \qquad (4.11)$$

Similarly, the public key corresponding to the ID can be calculated by the verifier using the public key matrix and the identity ID

$$R_{ID} = R_{i_1 j_1} + R_{i_2 j_2} + \cdots + R_{i_l j_l} \qquad (4.12)$$

Because the multiple points of G form an exchange group,

$$\begin{aligned}
r_{ID}G &= \left(r_{i_1 j_1} + r_{i_2 j_2} + \ldots r_{i_l j_l}\right)G \\
&= r_{i_1 j_1}G + r_{i_2 j_2}G + \ldots r_{i_l j_l}G \\
&= R_{i_1 j_1} + R_{i_2 j_2} + \ldots R_{i_l j_l} \\
&= R_{ID}
\end{aligned} \qquad (4.13)$$

Therefore, (r_{ID}, R_{ID}) constitutes the private-public key pair relationship. In this way, the one-one mapping between the identity and the public key is completed, which ensures the superintendence and traceability of network behaviors. On the other hand, the proposed method could avoid frequent requests for public keys and improves network performance.

4.5.3   Privacy Preserving Policy

When all user terminals request the network to register an identity identifier, they need to bind the corresponding identity information to ensure the normal operation and maintenance of the network. The user generates the identity certificate with a specific hash function and the user identity information. The system sends the user's public key to the supervisor node. The user signs the identity registration request with his own identity certificate and sends it to the supervision node together with the identity registration request. After the identity registration request is received, the supervisor node first uses the same hash function to verify the user's legitimacy, and then uses the user's public key to decrypt the additional signature. The supervisor node compares the two hash values. If they are the same, then the signature can be proved to come from the user, and the identity registration request is confirmed by the supervisor node. The sovereignty network stores the user's identity certificate in a distributed database, ensuring that the identity can be traced and monitored later. At the same time, the sovereignty network requires that all identities must be registered before they can be routed through the network. In addition, the identity information of the publisher must be added when the identity is registered, which can effectively reduce the spread of illegal prohibited content in the network, including but not limited to the dark web of traditional IP networks and personal privacy data. Screening for banned content can further protect users' privacy.

The sovereignty network also introduces a permission management policy. Content posted by users will be graded. When users access network resources, access rights can be determined according to their identity information. This can help administrators implement user management, such as restricting the daily online and gaming time of students and other certain groups. Classification of Internet content can effectively protect the physical and mental health of minors and promote the reasonable and compliant development of Internet content.

4.6   Security Situation Awareness System

In addition to the internal security mechanisms of the sovereignty network, in order to further guarantee security and controllability, we come up with a security situation awareness system. This system breaks through the multi-platform security perception problem to work in a variety of networks, and adopts multiple technologies to maintain and improve the accuracy and expandability. Specifically, the proposed security situation awareness system is also deployed on MIRs, which coheres to the safety perception and routing service. In this way, the security situation awareness system is no longer just bypass detection equipment. It isolates and records the malicious packets for the first time without human intervention. After detecting, the malicious behaviors and the related user information will be automatically transmitted to the MIS system, then the MIS system will automatically intercept and submit them for manual review. In addition, the complete logging function is provided, which will be periodically audited by the system. If an abnormal condition is discovered, the system demerits the user and provides the information to the administrator for further processing. The last line of defense for security monitoring is served by the administrator.

4.6.1 Innovative Points

- **Adaptable to multiple network systems**: The proposed system can work in a variety of networks. It can not only be proposed for the existing IP network, but also can adapt to a variety of future network architectures, such as MIN.
- **Real-time packet analysis based on big data**: The proposed system based on big data technology analyzes various dimensions of massive security data to perceive existing and possible security threats at various levels.
- **Artificial intelligence-based model**: Advanced machine learning, deep learning and swarm intelligence optimization algorithm are employed to improve the efficiency and accuracy of analysis.
- **User-friendly front ends**: The proposed system can display the analysis in real-time through the front-end from multiple perspectives, so that the administrator can perceive the security situation clearly and intuitively.
- **Multi-dimension intrusion detection**: We propose a complete detection model, including three parts of detection based on network flow, host and behavior of users. Through the detection of multiple objects, the ability of continuously monitoring the network security is improved. Thus, it is easier for administrators to find network anomalies in time, and quickly speculate the attack purpose, attack means, attack path and impact range, so as to minimize network risks and losses.
- **Reliable storage technology based on blockchain**: Blockchain technology is used to store and accurately locate events to prevent attackers from tampering with attack behavior logs. Hence network administrators can make more credible risk status assessments and future development trend predictions.

4.6.2 Technical Terms

- **TF-IDF**: Term Frequency-Inverse Document Frequency, a commonly used weighting technique for information retrieval and text mining to assess the importance of a word to a document in a set of documents or a corpus.
- **ANN**: Artificial Neural Network, which has good adaptability, self-learning and nonlinear approximation ability.
- **Novelty detection**: There are no outliers in the training data, and the model is used to detect the outliers in the new sample.
- **One-class SVM**: One-Class Support Vector Machine, one type of support vector machine, which uses an unsupervised learning method and does not need to manually mark the output labels of the training set.
- **PSO**: Particle Swarm Optimization, an evolutionary calculation method derived from the behavior simulation of bird predation, which has a swarm intelligence optimization algorithm with strong global optimization ability.

4.6.3 Application Scenarios

The security situation awareness system can be applied not only in the traditional IP network, but also in the MIN architecture. The following takes MIN as an example to introduce its main application scenarios. The network topology is shown in Fig. 4.20.

If the internal MIN communicates with the external IP network, a MIN packet containing IP resource requests will be sent out, which will be translated by the Edge Multi-Identifier Router (EMIR). The corresponding IP network resources will be requested. After receiving the corresponding response, it is encapsulated by the EMIR, and forwarded as a MIN packet again. However, if the users of the external network want to access the resources of the internal MIN, they are allowed to use the client of MIN to communicate with MIN through pure MIN traffic after the authentication of the certificate layer by layer.

The security situation awareness system is applied to EMIRs. While security awareness of MIN network is carried out, IP traffic is also detected and analyzed. During this process, the security situation awareness system is applied to two core devices: the MIS servers and MIRs.

4.6.4 System Architecture

The security situation awareness system including four modules: Malicious Traffic Detection Based on BP Neural Network, Anomaly Access Behavior Detection

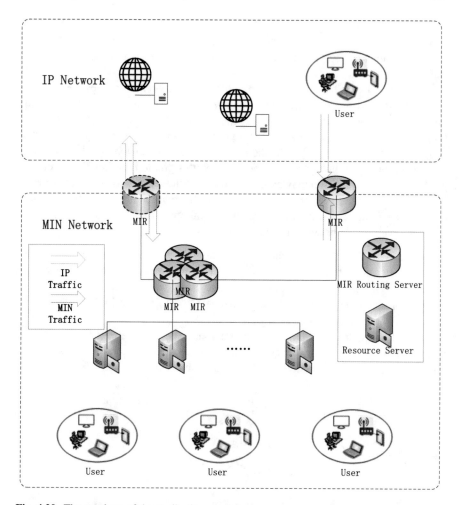

Fig. 4.20 The topology of the application scenarios

Based on One-class SVM, Security Situation Prediction Based on PSO-SVM, Quantitative Hierarchical Threat Evaluation Model for Security Situation.

1. **Malicious Traffic Detection Based on BP Neural Network**

The DDoS detection based on a neural network provides the possibility to solve the limitation of the traditional machine learning algorithms. The proposed system based on the existing neural network algorithm analyzes the DDoS attack detection theory, method and the local datasets. We build an attack traffic detection model based on six characteristics such as the packet length, the packet sending time interval, and the changing rate of packet length. Then a parameters optimization scheme for adjusting the error of neural network is proposed through a large number of experiments. The above methods effectively improve the accuracy of DDoS detection, and can be extended for other attack traffic detection, such as the port scanning attack, by combining the detection mode of neural network with statistical analysis.

For the process of feature extraction, the proposed system improves the accuracy of DDoS attack detection while ensuring low resource consumption. After tagging, normalization and feature extraction of the original data, the datasets that can be transmitted to the neural network for training are obtained. Artificial Neural network (ANN) [29] is employed as the detection model of DDoS attack detection.

When training multi-layer neural networks with sigmoid function, the traditional gradient descent algorithm may cause tiny changes in weight and deviation, or even be far away from their optimal values, because the gradient amplitude is too small. The fast algorithm can solve the problem of local error trap. The network structure of three-layer neural network is shown in Fig. 4.21.

Where N_{in}, N_{hid} and N_{out} represent the number of neurons in the input layer, hidden layer and output layer respectively. Wih_{ij} represents the connection weight between the i_{th} neuron in the input layer and the j_{th} neuron in the hidden layer. Who_{jk} represents the connection weight between the j_{th} neuron in the hidden layer and the k_{th} neuron in the output layer.

80% of the datasets obtained from previous processing are used for training neural network and 20% for attack detection. We compared the results of based and modified algorithm. The results are shown in Table 4.5.

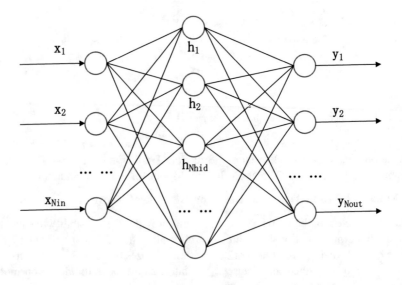

Input layer   Hidden Layer   Output Layer

Fig. 4.21 The network structure of three-layer neural network [29]

Table 4.5 The results of based and modified algorithm

Types of algorithms	Average time spent (ms)	Average number of studies	Accuracy (%)
Traditional three-layer ANN	3027	2268	97
Improved three-layer ANN	1494	919	98.4

The results show that the proposed modified algorithm reduces the average number of iterations by more than 50%. Therefore, the modified algorithm can significantly shorten the detection time and improve the efficiency of DDoS attack detection. At the same time, the modified algorithm also improves the average intrusion detection accuracy by about 1.4%.

In order to verify the generalization ability of the model, the validation datasets of the model are formed by combining the normal flow data collected and the manual DDoS flow data. The validation results are shown as follows (Table 4.6).

The results show that the multi-layer neural network combined with the statistical characteristics of network traffic in this system is accurate and efficient.

2. **Anomaly Access Behavior Detection Based on One-class SVM**

We use anomaly access behavior detection based on white samples, and sample learning is carried out through unsupervised or one-class SVM. The minimum model that can fully express white samples is constructed as Profile to realize the detection of anomaly requests.

We extract 150,000 normal requests from the network access log as the dataset for model training, which is used to train the Profile of normal samples. More than 150,000 XSS, SQL injection and other payloads are collected from threat intelligence platforms and other datasets as anomaly access requests. The frequency-Inverse Document Frequency (TF-IDF) algorithm is used to extract the

Table 4.6 The results of validation model

Dataset name	Number of abnormal traffic	The number of abnormal traffic detected	Total abnormal traffic detected	Accuracy (%)	Noise factor (%)
ddosData.csv	733	733	743	100	0.13
ddosData2.csv	1733	1733	1763	100	0.07
ddosData3.csv	2111	2111	2111	100	0%

Table 4.7 The results of detection

Dataset name	Number of abnormal traffic	The number of abnormal traffic detected	Total abnormal traffic detected	Accuracy (%)	Noise factor (%)
bad_fromE. txt	4027	4027	4027	100	0
ddosData2. csv	46,083	45,908	45,908	100	99.6

text features and output them in the form of a matrix. TF-IDF is a common weighted technology for information retrieval and text mining.

In the binary classification problem of exception request detection, we consider learning the minimum boundary of a single class of samples through a single classification model, and those outside the boundary are identified as exceptions. The One-class SVM in machine learning is used to identify the anomaly access requests in the system, which fits the business scenario and requirements.

The results of detection are shown in Table 4.7.

The results show that the one-class SVM model trained by white sample datasets is feasible and effective in detecting anomaly access behaviors.

3. Security Situation Prediction Based on PSO-SVM

The proposed system predicts the security situation based on the nonlinear time series, and comprehensively analyzes the historical law of security situation to predict the future security situation within a certain period of time or at a certain moment, which fits well the business scenarios and requirements. On this basis, a network security situation prediction model named PSO-SVM is proposed, which combines Particle Swarm Optimization (PSO) and Support Vector Machines (SVM). PSO-SVM is used to effectively on small sample data to forecast the trend of value.

When constructing the dataset, the value of security situation is regarded as a simple time sequence, in which each monitoring point corresponds to a value of network security situation. Those values constitute a nonlinear time series. In order to predict this nonlinear security situation time series, we need to find the relationship between the security situation value at the moment $i+p$ and the security situation value at the previous p moments $[x_i, x_{i+1}, \ldots, x_{i+p-1}]$. In other words, we need to explore the function $x_{i+p} = f(x_i, x_{i+1}, \ldots, x_{i+p-1})$. Function f is a nonlinear function and represents the nonlinear relationship along time series. According to the theory of SVM, the function f can be obtained by learning and training several groups of known samples of security situation time series.

The PSO-SVM prediction model dynamically generates the security situation sample set with a sliding window algorithm. The corresponding network security situation value of monitoring point $1, 2, \ldots, n$ is $a_1, a_2, \ldots, a_n$. If the size of window is set to be m, the 1st sample record is $a_1, a_2, \ldots, a_m$. Hence, the network security situation value at monitoring point $m + 1$ is a_{m+1}. Then the second sample is constructed to record $a_2, a_3, \ldots, a_{m+1}$, and the situation value of network security at monitoring point $m + 2$ is a_{m+2}, and so on. In the proposed system the m is set to be 3, and the size of sliding window is set to be 3. At the same time, in order to prevent the accumulation of errors, when the proposed model is used to predict the security situation value at a certain time point t in the future, the predicted value at time t will be covered by the actual security situation value, if the security situation value before time point $t - k$ has been calculated according to the practical situation.

The method of constructing the sample set is shown in Fig. 4.22.

The proposed model combines the SVM model based on statistical learning theory. Compared with the neural network model, this model is currently the best small sample statistical and learning scheme, which solves the problems of over-learning, nonlinear and dimensional disasters. In addition, SVM adopts the principle of structural risk minimization, and the whole solution process is transformed to a convex quadratic programming problem to obtain the global optimal and unique solution, which overcomes some shortcomings of neural network.

In the training process, Particle Swarm Optimization (PSO) is used to optimize the parameters of SVM and ensure the accuracy of predictive data. In this algorithm, each solution of the optimization problem is called a particle, and an adaptive function is defined to measure the superiority of each particle. A group of particles and the velocity of particles are randomly initialized, then each particle travels in a swarm based on its own "flight experience" with other particles to search for the optimal solution from the whole space.

The process of security situation prediction is shown in Fig. 4.23.

Lots of experiments show that the proposed model predicts the security trend in the future for a period of time providing us with a forward-looking of the network security situation, which helps us to take preventive measures in advance according to the security situation.

There are some limitations in processing small samples with neural network, such as that it is easy to fall into the local minimum point and the convergence speed is slow. Considering the above limitations and the strong linear features of network security situation values, we study the feature of the SVM method to use the mathematical advantage of processing nonlinear data, small sample data. Then a complex nonlinear fitting model is built which is more suitable for network security situation dataset. The proposed PSO-SVM combined with PSO guarantees the fast-global optimization and nonlinear fitting. Based on the periodic characteristics of network security situation, periodic grouping and prediction are carried out.

4. **Quantitative Hierarchical Threat Evaluation Model for Security Situation**

Combined with the application scenario of MIN boundary router, we adopt the hierarchical security situation quantitative awareness model of bottom-to-up, local-to-overall strategy. The security situation is evaluated from three aspects: abnormal event, host situation and network situation. Except the statistics of alarm

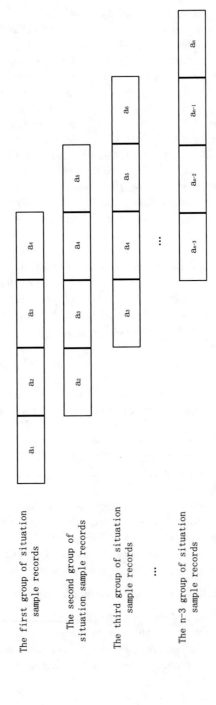

Fig. 4.22 The method of constructing the sample set [32]

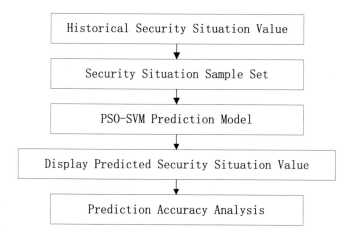

Fig. 4.23 The process of security situation prediction

frequency, alarm severity and network bandwidth consumption rate, the proposed method weights the importance factor of service and host, and calculates the threat index of service, host and the whole network to evaluate and analyze the security threat situation.

The threat index is calculated as follows:

$$R_{S_j}(t) = f\left(\vec{\theta}, \vec{C}_j(t), \vec{A}_j(t), \vec{N}(t), \vec{A}_d(t)\right) = \vec{\theta} \cdot \left(\vec{C}_j(t) \cdot 10^{\vec{A}_j(t)} + 100\vec{N}(t) \cdot 10^{\vec{A}_d(t)}\right)$$

$$(4.14)$$

where vector $\vec{\theta} = (\theta_1, \ldots, \theta_h)$ represents the normal traffic, and h is the number of time periods a day divided into. The initial element value of $\vec{\theta}$ is assigned by the system administrator according to the average normal traffic $F_i(i = 1, \ldots, h)$ of the protected network system in different time periods. After the average visits are quantified, the element value of $\vec{\theta}$ is obtained as follows:

$$\theta_i = \frac{F_i}{\sum_{t=1}^{h} F_t} \qquad (4.15)$$

Vector $\vec{A}_j(t) = \left(\vec{A}_{j1}, \ldots, \vec{A}_{jt}, \ldots, \vec{A}_{jh}\right)$ and vector $\vec{C}_j(t) = \left(\vec{C}_{j1}, \ldots, \vec{C}_{jt}, \ldots, \vec{C}_{jh}\right)$ describe the attack severity and occurrence times at time t respectively. The types and values of these elements are obtained by counting the attack event log database.

$\vec{N}(t) = \left(\vec{N}_1, \ldots, \vec{N}_t, \ldots, \vec{N}_h\right)$ represents the network bandwidth utilization and $\vec{A}_d(t) = \left(\vec{A}_{d1}, \ldots, \vec{A}_{dt}, \ldots, \vec{A}_{dh}\right)$ represents the threat level vector of DoS attack. Their elements $\vec{N}_i(v) = \left(\vec{N}_{i_1}, \vec{N}_{i_2}, \ldots, \vec{N}_{i_v}\right)$ and $\vec{A}_{di}(v) = \left(\vec{A}_{di_1}, \vec{A}_{di_2}, \ldots, \vec{A}_{di_v}\right)$

$(i = 1, \ldots, h)$ represent the network bandwidth utilization and the DoS threat level vector of each time window in the i time period respectively. v is the number of analysis event windows in the i_{th} period. The coefficient is set as 100 for converting the occupancy rate into an integer to evaluate the threat of DoS attack. Combining with Common Vulnerability Scoring System (CVSS), we set the threat level of malicious events such as DDoS and scanning behavior. CPU utilization increases more rapidly than bandwidth utilization when attack events occur. Hence, we not only take advantage of bandwidth utilization, but also add CPU utilization to the evaluation.

This scheme is more stable and efficient than the situation awareness algorithm based on machine learning, and avoids some deviation. In addition, we combine the application scenario of MIN and adopt the situation awareness consist of IP network threat situation and host threat situation including MIN network awareness. The real-time evaluation of the system security makes the evaluation results completer and more appropriate.

The results of experiments show that the proposed hierarchical network security situation quantitative awareness model can intuitively display the security threat situation of the entire server, so that network administrators can timely understand the security situation and find out the reasons for security changes to adjust security policies. In this way, the maximal security of the system is guaranteed. Moreover, the evolution rule of security situation can be obtained from the long-term curve, which evaluates the threat of common network attacks and frees administrators from the heavy task of alarm data analysis.

4.7 Security Analysis

To construct the sovereignty network, one of the main focuses is to ensure network security, especially the security of core components. This section will analyze the anti-attacking strategy and security of the sovereignty network.

4.7.1 Security Mechanisms

To guarantee security, the IP network is not included in the sovereignty network. The most obvious differences between the devices in the sovereignty network and the existing system is the addition of the ID-ICN router and Edge Multi-Identifier Router (EMIR) in the sovereignty network, which form the first two levels of the defending barriers of the sovereignty network.

An ID-ICN router is a router that supports addressing of identity and content identifiers and network data inter-translation. When a user retrieves certain content, if the content is within the sovereignty network, the content identifier and user's real address would be translated first on the ID-ICN router, and then the data would be transferred in the identity centric network.

EMIR not only has the packet forwarding function as the ordinary MIR but also works as a two-way access interface between the IP network and the sovereignty network. On the other hand, the content that arrives at the node is initially reviewed and filtered through relevant content audit procedures installed in EMIR, such as AI content audit procedures. Through these two mechanisms, the outside network attacks can be isolated to ensure the security of the sovereignty network. If the user asks for content in the external network, the content identifier and the IP address would be inter-translated on the EMIR of the sovereignty network, then the request would be transported to the content source. If the requested content is in the sovereignty network of other countries, multi-identifiers would be inter-translated at the EMIRs of the sovereignty network, and then the data would be transmitted in the identity centric network.

The third level is CMD architecture, which is the core component in the sovereignty network.

In brief, security mechanisms in the sovereignty network mainly include the protective mechanisms such as EMIR, blockchain technology, asymmetric encryption, and security gain brought by data transmission through the identify-centered network; link protection consisting of security mechanisms of ID-ICN routers such as AI detection and packet detection [16]. And security devices such as cyberspace mimic routers, firewalls, and distributed storage systems [16, 17]. These anti-attacking mechanisms provide a high secure system. The framework of security mechanisms is shown in Fig. 4.24.

4.7.2   Security Mechanism of Network Architecture

Because the sovereignty network is built based on the identity centric network, it has certain defense capability. The data transmission mode in the identity centric network is different from the existing IP network. The sovereignty network filters access information through EMIR first. Only the content is actively requested by users in the internal network can be accessed through EMIR. In other words, the attacker cannot scan, attack, or even send malicious information into the sovereignty network continuously as in the IP network.

In the sovereignty network, after real-name registration, users need to pull data from the network with their signatures. For data requested by internal users, its contents and requesters are recorded by blockchain log. In case of any abnormal circumstances, the system traces back and does accountability according to the blockchain log, so as to ensure the authenticity and reliability of the information. To a certain extent, the system avoids malicious operations by intranet users.

In Fig. 4.24, the security mechanism mainly relies on cryptography technologies such as the identity authentication. The attack difficulty of existing encryption

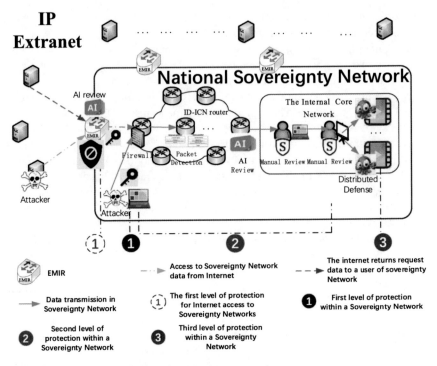

Fig. 4.24 The security mechanisms in sovereignty network

algorithms has reached exponential level. For example, it would take decades to run the most powerful supercomputers to break the common RSA algorithm [18, 19].

The difficulty of cracking the RSA algorithm is related to the length of the key. For an RSA algorithm with public key e and module n, the complexity of the brute force attack is $O(n^e)$ [20]. The most common way to break RSA is through factorization. When the key length is 256 bits or less, a high-speed computer can successfully factor it in one day. A long key length will increase the factorization time. In 1999, a Cray supercomputer took five months to factor a 512-bit key. Ten years later, on December 9, 2009, some researchers reported that they had factored 768-bit and 232-bit RSA keys, and it took thousands of times longer to factor a 768-bit RSA key than a 512-bit one. It takes 1000 times longer to factor the current commonly used 1024-bit key than a 768-bit key, so 1024-bit keys can still meet security requirements in a short period [21].

With current computing power, it takes two years to factor a 1024-bit key, and 80 years to factor a 2048-bit key. Hence, we assume that the attacking time is 50 years, then the attack success rate per second is calculated as 6.43×10^{-10}.

4.7.3 Security Mechanism of Network Links

The attack chain is formed of two°parts, including the nodes between EMIR and the content request node, and the nodes between the content request nodes to network core components the attackers need to breakthrough. The attack process at this stage is mainly the dissemination of malicious information in the internal links of the sovereignty network, which is regarded as a random walk on the attack chain [22].

After the requested content is pulled into the sovereignty network, it will go through multiple filtering mechanisms between EMIR and the content request node, such as firewall, packet detection, text, audio, image and video recognition detection, and natural language processing. Between the content request node and network core components, the transmitted content is filtered through a series of human censorship mechanisms. An attacker needs to break through levels of protection to reach the target, namely core network components.

The complete network link consists of many filters. If attackers want to attack core components along the attack chain, attackers need to attack each filter along the attack chain. The attacker advances along the attack chain, and each successful escape from a filter leads one step forward along the attack chain. If the attacker is captured by a filter, it goes back along the attack chain. If the attacker neither succeeds in the attack nor is caught by the filter, it stays on the node. This approach that next stage is only related to the present state and the range of the next move is consistent with the characteristics of Markov chains. Therefore, the Markov chain and Martingale [23] are used to model and solve this problem.

The probability of escaping from a filter is denoted as μ, and the number of the node in the attack chain is denoted as θ. The probability of capturing the attacker is ω. We assume that the attacker has escaped from k nodes, for example, he stays at the k_{th} node (Fig. 4.25).

The attack process is denoted as a matrix $M_{\theta \times \theta}$. The element $M_{i,j}$ represents the probability that the attacker has escaped from the i_{th} filter and his target changes to the j_{th} filter. During the attack, the attacker moves along the attack chain. After conquering a node, the attacker will get the information of the next node. During the attack, the single node attack can be successful only if the attack being captured. The attack has three directions: going back to the last node, going forward to the next node, and staying at the present node. The transition probability is as follows:

(1) Going back to the last node ($M_{i,i-1} = \omega$). No matter whether the attacker escapes from the device, as long as the system detects the attacker, the attack

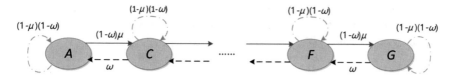

Fig. 4.25 The Markov chain

will not be able to be carried out and the attacker must fall back to the previous device.

(2) Going forward to the next node ($M_{i,i+1}=(1-\omega)\mu$). The probability of no effective detection is $(1-\omega)$. And the probability of the attacker escaping from the filter is μ. Hence, the probability that the attacker escaping from this filter without effective detection is obtained as $M_{i,i+1}=(1-\omega)\mu$.

(3) Staying at the present node ($M_{i,i}=(1-\omega)(1-\mu)$). The attacker stays at the same node in the next time slot if the attacker does not escape and be captured.

The Markov chain $X_0, X_1, X_2, \ldots, X_n$ denotes a set of random variables, in which $X_i (X_i \in [0, \theta], X_0 = 0)$ denotes the position attacker staying at the start of the i_{th} time slot. If the attacker stays at the k_{th} device, the possibility of the next stage is denoted as follows:

$$P\{X_{n+1} = k + 1 | X_n = k\} = (1 - \omega)\mu \tag{4.16}$$

$$P\{X_{n+1} = k | X_n = k\} = (1 - \omega)(1 - \mu) \tag{4.17}$$

$$P\{X_{n+1} = k - 1 | X_n = k\} = \omega \tag{4.18}$$

Hence,

$$\begin{aligned} E[X_{n+1}|X_n] &= (1 - \omega)\mu(k + 1) + (1 - \omega)(1 - \mu)k + \omega(k - 1) \\ &= k + (1 - \omega)\mu - \omega \end{aligned} \tag{4.19}$$

According to the above Markov chain, we can build another set of random variables $M_0, M_1, M_2, \cdots, M_n$, where

$$M_i = X_i - [(1 - \omega)\mu - \omega] \cdot i \tag{4.20}$$

The M_n can be proofed to be a Martingale related to $X_0, X_1, X_2, \ldots, X_n$.

If the attacker escaping from a filter with probability μ, and be captured with probability ω, for an attack chain with θ nodes, the steps before the attacker assesses the target node, for example, the production and broadcasting platform located at the θ_{th} node is:

$$E[S] = \frac{\theta}{[(1 - \omega)\mu - \omega]} \tag{4.21}$$

Therefore, the steps which the attacker assesses the production and broadcasting network is represented by $E[S]$, which can be calculated with θ, ω, and μ. In this way, the quantitative relationship between the limit probability and system parameters is obtained [22].

4.7.4 Security Mechanism of Core Components

For the core components, we adopt the CMD (Cyber Mimic Defense) security mechanism, which stores the data in a distributed system redundantly. Each independent server is regarded as an executor, and multiple heterogeneous-structure executants perform the same task independently. Their running results are sent to the arbitrator, which will output a result according to the above results. In the section, we take a system with three executors as an example [24] (Fig. 4.26).

A Generalized Stochastic Petri Net (GSPN) model is established, where all the surviving executors are under attack. The failure order of different executors can be inferred based on their attacking difficulty, but that will make the analysis complex. Ignoring the slight differences caused by different attack orders, the simplified GSPN model is shown in Fig. 4.27, assuming that the executor is successfully attacked in the order of No. 1, No. 2, and No. 3.

Places denoted as circles represent the different states of the system. Place P_{ix} consists of the element i and x, where i represents the number of compromised executors and x represents the state of attacked executors. There are five states of compromised executors, including working (W), compromising minor executors (B), compromising the most of executors without a consistent result (C), compromising the most of executors with a consistent result (D), and compromising all of the executors with a consistent result (E). The most dangerous phase is P_E, which means that all executors are tampered with the same result, namely the production and broadcasting system is destroyed.

Transitions represent the different behaviors of a defender or attacker who changes the system between different states. The transitions can be divided into the immediate transition measured by probability and the timed transition measured by the delay of behavior. Immediate transition and timed transition are represented by a solid rectangle and hollow rectangle respectively. Transition t_{ijx} indicates that the

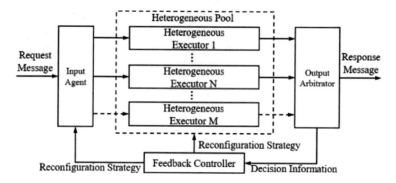

Fig. 4.26 The CMD architecture

Fig. 4.27 The GSPN model

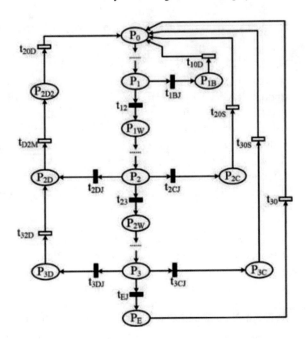

behavior x turns the system from the states with i compromised executors to the states with j compromised executors. There are six behaviors of the arbitrator, including attacking (a), driving out the compromised executors (e), mistakenly driving out the innocent executors (m), stopping and replacing all the living executors with new ones (s), random disturbance (d), and arbitration (j).

We assign values and use SPNP to simulate the proposed GSPN model. If the probability of random disturbance is set to 0.01%, the steady-state probability of breaking the CMD production and broadcasting system is calculated as 1.30×10^{-6}. The defenders can reasonably choose random disturbance frequency according to their security requirements. Different random disturbance frequency corresponds to different steady-state probability of breaking the system. The correspondence between the disturbance frequency and the probability of failure is shown in Table 4.8. In this way, the result is obtained as [25].

Table 4.8 The relationship of disturbance frequency and probability of failure

Disturbance frequency	0.001	0.0001	0.00001	0.000001	0.0000001
Failure probability	1.296×10^{-7}	1.296×10^{-6}	1.296×10^{-5}	1.296×10^{-4}	1.295×10^{-3}

4.7.5 Security Gain Brought by Sovereignty Network

We assume an attacker from the external network, whose attacking process is shown in Fig. 4.28.

For the third level, when the random disturbance probability is 0.0001, the steady-state probability of breaking the CMD production and broadcasting system is calculated as 1.30×10^{-6}.

For the second level, we assume that there are five filters with the same effectiveness (i.e., $\omega_1 = \omega_2 = \omega_3 = \omega_4 = \omega_5 = 0.137931$) and the attacker escapes from each filter with probability $\mu = 0.160$. Then we have

$$E[S] = \frac{\theta}{[(1 - \omega)\mu - \omega]} = 1.25 \times 10^8 \ (s) \tag{4.22}$$

Considering the filtering effect of the first two levels, the time of breaking the system is expected to be 1.517×10^{23} s. In other words, it takes 4.8×10^{15} years to break the system on average.

Hence, for a sovereignty network with a five-level filtering mechanism, three-redundancy of CMD production and broadcasting system and 0.0001 disturbance frequent, when the filtering failure rate of each device is 0.16 (i.e., 1.6 out of 10 malicious messages can escape on average), the failure time of production and broadcasting system reaches 4.8×10^{15} years. This calculation result is obtained under an obvious loose attack condition leading to an enlarged attack success rate.

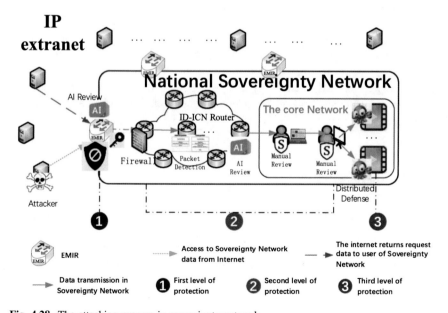

Fig. 4.28 The attacking process in sovereignty network

Table 4.9 The relationship of disturbance frequency and the failure time

Disturbance frequency	0.001	0.0001	0.00001	0.000001	0.0000001
Attack time (year)	4.8×10^{16}	4.8×10^{15}	4.8×10^{14}	4.8×10^{13}	4.8×10^{12}

However, in practical application, the success rate of each filtering operation is much higher than 14%, and the attack success rate of a single executor is far less than 100%. Hence in the sovereignty network, the failure time of the core system is also longer than 4.8×10^{15} years. The corresponding relationship between the disturbance frequency and the time to break a sovereignty network is shown in Table 4.9.

4.7.6   Conclusion

According to the above analysis, the sovereignty network can adjust its configuration to realize more effective defense.

Defenders can adopt a less costly configuration in a safe environment. In the circumstances, although an attacker could theoretically break into the system, it would cost millions of years and would not be feasible in reality. When the network environment is poor, the defending cost of the sovereignty network can be improved to exchange for higher security. In the circumstances, the successful time of the theoretical attack is longer. That is to say, the attacker can't break into the system.

By various security mechanisms, the sovereignty network has successfully reversed the imbalance between attackers and defenders. Protected by the set of proposed technologies, including identity centric network system, blockchain, EMIRs, as well as CMD technology, the production and broadcasting network and other important subnetworks of the sovereignty network can work at a high level of security.

4.8   Transmission Control

The transmission mode of the traditional TCP/IP network is defined as end-to-end communication in the push semantic. However, with the popularity of the Internet and the exponential growth of data quantity, users are more concerned about how to obtain the content, and don't care about the location of the content producers. To solve this problem, the content centric network with the pull semantic has been proposed, which makes the network transmission mode compatible with the user communication requirements.

Considering the progressive deployment of the sovereignty network and the applications under different scenarios, we propose MIT, a transmission control scheme based on MIN. MIT supports the transmission control in both the push semantic and the pull semantic, realizes reliable data communication under different business requirements of the sovereignty network. MIT detects congestion based on the active queue management mechanism, and then signals it towards clients by explicitly marking certain packets, so that clients can reduce their sending rates according to the network congestion status. Meanwhile, MIT regulates the packet forwarding rate at the output interface of the router via maintaining one virtual queue per flow to guarantee the sufficient utilization of network resources.

4.8.1 MIT Design

MIT supports the transmission control in both the push semantic and the pull semantic, which are defined as follows:

(1) Push Semantic

The push semantic is a host-oriented end-to-end transmission mode, the clients subscribe previously the information and then the servers push to the clients the available information. The whole data transmission process is dominated by the sender, and the transmitted data will not be cached in the intermediate nodes of the network. The client will check the data received from the server, if no mistake, the client confirms this by sending a packet back to the server with the ack flag set. The transmission control under the push semantic is represented by TCP, applies to the Instant Messaging services, such as the real-time video conference, online chatting, Internet telephony and other interaction scenarios.

(2) Pull Semantic

The pull semantic has emerged in recent years, as a content-oriented transmission mode driven by the consumers of data. There are two packet types, the request packet and the response packet. In this semantic, consumers pull response packets by sending out request packets to the network. One response packet matches one request packet, and both of them contain the name of the requested content. Any content source node or intermediate node that satisfies the requirements can return the requested data. The response packet returns along the opposite path of the request packet and the content can be cached at the intermediate node according to the caching strategy. The transmission control under the pull semantic has strong scalability and is often used for content distribution, which can realize the efficient reuse of network resources.

Based on the above concepts, we further define the concepts of flows in the push semantic and pull semantic respectively.

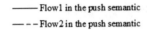

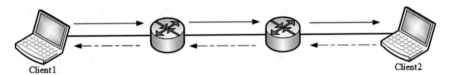

Fig. 4.29 Transmission in the push semantic

(1) Flows in Push Semantic

A flow in push semantic is composed of the one-way packets transmitted from the sender to the receiver, and uses the service identifier to identify a flow. For example, a conversation between Client1 and Client2, as shown in Fig. 4.29, one flow from Client1 to Client2 and another flow from Client2 to Client1, both of which are completely independent and unrelated. The direction of a flow is from source to destination, and the upstream and downstream are defined according to the direction of flow.

(2) Flows in Pull Semantic

A flow in pull semantic is composed of request packets and response packets for the requested content, and uses the content name to identify a flow. As the Fig. 4.30 shows, the consumer issues the content request, and it hits the cache of the content source (producer). We define the direction of the consumer as downstream, the direction of the content source as upstream, and the request packet is forwarded from the downstream to upstream. After hitting the content source, the response packet containing the requested content will be sent to the consumer.

Both the client and the router are involved in the transmission control. In order to realize the hop-by-hop shaping scheme, MIT maintains one virtual FIFO queue per flow in each output interface, identified by the name of the identifier. We use f_j^i to represent the flow j in output interface i, use q_j^i to represent the virtual queue of flow

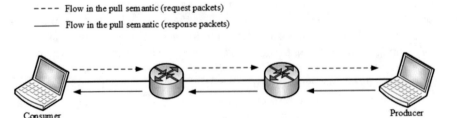

Fig. 4.30 Transmission in the pull semantic

j in output interface i. Flows in the push semantic and the pull semantic are associated with different virtual queues, identified by their identifiers.

Based on the above definition, MIT consists of four components:

(1) Active Congestion Detection: MIT directly detects congestion status in intermediate nodes via the active queue management mechanism.
(2) Explicit Congestion Notification: After congestion detection, the router signals congestion by marking packets, and the marked packets will be fed back to the client.
(3) Hop-by-Hop Rate Shaping: The router dynamically adjusts the forwarding rate according to the difference between the current transmission capacity of the uplink and the downlink to achieve the hop-by-hop rate shaping.
(4) Client Rate Adjustment: The client dynamically adjusts the size of the congestion window which is increased on unmarked packets and decreased on marked ones.

4.8.2 Active Congestion Detection

CoDel algorithm is an AQM (Active Queue Management) mechanism. It detects congestion by measuring the queuing delay ("sojourn time") of each packet on its outgoing links. If the minimum sojourn time over a time period (default: 100 ms) exceeds a threshold (default: 5 ms), it considers this link as congested. CoDel algorithm can effectively avoid the problem of queue size oscillation caused by the burst traffic and keep the queue small as long as the buffer size of the router is set in a reasonable range.

MIT uses the CoDel algorithm to actively detect congestion in intermediate routers, and detects congestion by measuring the queuing delay ("sojourn time") of each packet on its outgoing links.

4.8.3 Explicit Congestion Notification

The network congestion is mainly caused by the excessively fast transmission rate of the client, which makes the amount of data transmitted over the link exceed the capacity of the link under the current network condition. Therefore, after the router has detected network congestion, a mechanism is required to notify the client of the current network congestion status, so that the client can reduce the transmission rate to alleviate the network congestion.

Explicit Congestion Notification (ECN) is a mechanism for signaling congestion in TCP/IP network, an ECN-aware router may set a mark in the IP header instead of dropping a packet to signal impending congestion. The receiver of the packet echoes the congestion indication to the sender, which reduces its transmission rate as if it detected a dropped packet.

MIT notifies clients of the current network state via explicit congestion notification, requiring an optional congestion mark field at the header of the packet to record the congestion status of the network. When a router has detected congestion, it will set the congestion field in the packet. The client judges the network status by determining whether the received packet carries a congestion mark.

Through the explicit congestion notification, the congestion information carried in the packet will be fed back to the client. For the flows in push semantic, after the marked packet arrives at the receiver, the receiver will set the corresponding congestion field in the ACK packet header, so that the congestion information in the received packet can be fed back to the sender by the ACK packet. For the flows in pull semantic, the response packet carried the congestion mark will be forwarded to downstream nodes until it reaches the client.

4.8.4 Hop-by-Hop Rate Shaping

After congestion detection, the router will adjust the forwarding rate of the packet through the hop-by-hop rate shaping mechanism. The details are as follows:

(1) When no congestion occurs on the outgoing queue of the router, it shows that the resource utilization on the outgoing link doesn't exceed the link capability. At this moment, the router doesn't enable the rate shaping mechanism.

(2) Once the router has detected that one of its outgoing links is congested, the state of the corresponding output interface will be marked as congestion. Since MIT requires to maintain one virtual FIFO queue per flow in each output interface, the hop-by-hop rate shaping mechanism can adjust the forwarding rate of the packet at the congested interface via its virtual queue. Therefore, the router will dynamically adjust the forwarding rate according to the difference of the current transmission capacity of the uplink and the downlink to achieve the hop-by-hop rate shaping.

Notice that when the client stops sending packets, there may be some packets in the virtual queue that have not yet been forwarded. To solve this problem, when a flow stops sending packets, each router will detect whether the virtual queue of the flow is empty, and if not, forwards the remaining packets in the virtual queue at the last forwarding rate.

The above hop-by-hop rate shaping mechanism is shown in Fig. 4.31. N1 and N2 are a pair of terminal nodes which adopt the push semantic. C and P are the consumer and the producer respectively, which adopt the pull semantic. R1, R2, R3 and R4 are routers in the network. F1, F2 and F3 are interfaces on router R2. L1, L2 and L3 are links connected with interfaces F1, F2 and F3 respectively. Flow1 is a

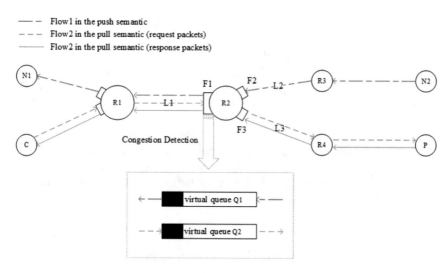

Fig. 4.31 The model of router rate shaping

flow that adopts the push semantic and Flow2 is a flow that adopts the pull semantic. Q1 is a virtual queue maintained for Flow1 at the interface F1 of router R2, and Q2 is a virtual queue maintained for Flow2 at the interface F1 of router R2.

Assuming L1, L2 and L3 have the same capability, so the network congestion may occur at bottleneck link L1. If router R2 has detected the link L1 is congested, it will mark the status of interface F1 as congestion and maintain a virtual queue for each flow passing through interface F1. For the Flow1 in the push semantic and through the interface F1, packets will be queued in its virtual FIFO queue Q1 served at the shaping rate. For the Flow2 in the pull semantic and through the interface F1, request packets will be queued in its virtual FIFO queue Q2 served at the shaping rate. The congestion on the link L1 will be alleviate quickly through the rate shaping on the interface F1 of router R2 and the client rate adjustment based on received marked packets.

4.8.5   Client Rate Adjustment

The client maintains a congestion window (specifying the maximum number of inflight packets) for each flow, which is increased on unmarked packets and decreased on marked ones. Through this rate adjustment mechanism, the client can achieve the optimal sending rate and adjust it dynamically to adapt to the changing network status. MIT can implement many classic loss-based TCP algorithms like Reno, New Reno, HTCP, HSTCP, BIC, and CUBIC. The only difference to traditional TCP is that a window decrease is triggered not only by timeouts, but also by marked packets. After experimenting with them, the CUBIC algorithm is selected for the client rate adjustment mechanism in MIT.

Besides, to avoid the sharp reduction of the congestion window caused by the burst traffic, the classic TCP SACK-based conservative loss recovery algorithm were introduced in the client. When the client timer is timed out, MIT adopts the conservative loss recovery algorithm to limit the decrease of the window: the client performs at most one window decrease per RTT, so that MIT can prevent the network oscillation caused by the burst traffic. When the client receives the marked packet, the mechanism in Sect. 4.8.2 can effectively avoid too many packets are marked. MIT doesn't adopt the conservative loss recovery algorithm to restrict the adjustment of the window for marked packets, so that the client can quickly response to the network congestion.

4.9 Addressing Model for Space-Terrestrial Integrated Networks

Although the terrestrial communication system has been developed rapidly in recent years, its quality of service is subject to the surface morphology and natural disasters. Satellite communication, which is not affected by time, place or environment, has gradually attracted people's attention, and the Space-Terrestrial Integrated Networks (FSTINs) has been formed to provide communication services with high capacity and seamless coverage. In order to improve the performance of the sovereignty network, we aim at constructing the Space-Terrestrial Integrated Networks based on MIN. However, due to the multi-level construction of the Space-Terrestrial Integrated Networks, as well as the particularity of satellite network, it is subject to exposure of satellite nodes, openness of channels, interconnection of heterogeneous networks, dynamic change of the topology height, large delay of transmission, large variance of delay, limited capacity of on-board processing, and so on.

The Space-Terrestrial Multi-Identifier Network-Virtual Private Network (ST-MIN-VPN) is proposed based on MIN. The greedy routing strategy based on hyperbolic routing technology is designed for terrestrial network, and the lightweight distributed self-adaptive satellite routing algorithm based on delay is designed for satellite networks with intersatellite links. Different routing schemes and forwarding strategies are designed for different application scenarios. The routing strategy and mobility management scheme of ST-MIN is shown in Fig. 4.32.

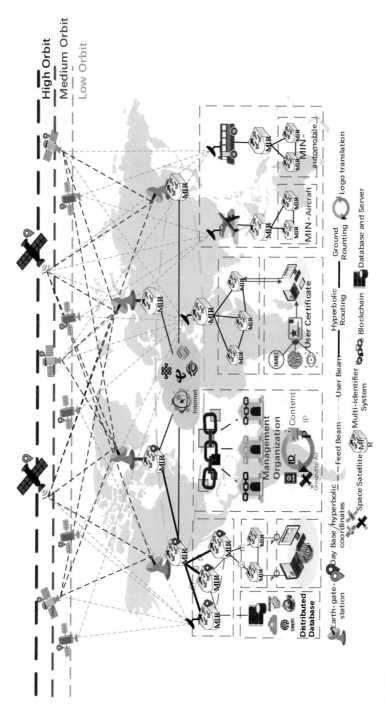

Fig. 4.32 The routing architecture in ST-MIN

4.9.1   Hyperbolic Routing Algorithm in Terrestrial Networks

The identifier space of ST-MIN adopts the idea of hierarchy. The network domain is divided into k levels, and the network topology of each level domain is mapped to hyperbolic space respectively. MIS allocates the hyperbolic coordinate for each edge router of domain, and uses each hyperbolic coordinate as the hyperbolic identifier of each domain. Each node records its own hyperbolic identifier and its neighbor nodes' hyperbolic identifiers. We assume that the whole network domain is divided into k levels, which is determined by actual requirements and stability of topology. In each level, routers can support N network identifiers. MIS embeds each level domain of terrestrial network into the hyperbolic space in order, so the hyperbolic coordinate set (R_i, Θ_i), $i = 1, 2, \ldots, k$ of each level domain can be obtained. The divided network supports the network identifier space with N^k orders of magnitude.

Take a three-level network as an example. Level-1 domain contains multiple domain nodes. The network topology constituted by all nodes in the level-1 domain is embedded into the hyperbolic space to obtain level-1 domain's hyperbolic coordinate set (R_1, Θ_1). As the hyperbolic identifier of nodes in the level-1 domain, (R_1, Θ_1) directs inter-domain routing between the level-1 domains. Each level-1 domain is divided into multiple level-2 domains, the network topology constituted by the nodes in the level-2 domain is embedded into the hyperbolic space to obtain the level-2 domain's hyperbolic coordinate set (R_2, Θ_2), which directs inter-domain routing in the level-2 domain. Because each level-2 domain belongs to a level-1 domain, its complete hyperbolic identifier is "$(R_1, \Theta_1) : (R_2, \Theta_2)$". Similarly, each level-2 domain can be further divided into several level-3 domains. Users are included in the level-3 domain.

At present, the mainstream algorithm of hyperbolic embedding is HyperMap proposed by Papadopoulos [26]. It can embed a given real network topology G (V, E) into the hyperbolic space and calculate the hyperbolic coordinates (r, θ) of the embedded nodes. The procedure of HyperMap Algorithm is shown in Algorithm 4.7.

Algorithm 4.7: HyperMap Embedding Algorithm

Input:
  Undirected connected Graph $G = (V, E)$
Output:
  Hyperbolic coordinates $(r_i, \theta_i)_{i=1}^{t}$ $(t = |V|)$
Begin
1:    Sort node degrees in decreasing order $k_1 > k_2 > \cdots > k_t$ with ties broken arbitrarily.
2:    Call node $i, i = 1, 2, \ldots, t$, the node with degree k_i.
3:    Node $i = 1$ is born, assign to its initial radial coordinate $r_1 = 0$ and random angular coordinate $\theta_1 \in [0, 2\pi]$
4:    **for** $i = 2$ to t **do**
5:        node i is born, assign to its initial radial coordinate $r_i = \frac{2}{\zeta} \ln i$.
6:        Increase the radial coordinate of every existing node $j < i$ according to $r_j(i) = \beta r_j + (1 - \beta) r_i$
7:        Assign to node i angular coordinate θ_i maximizing the likelihood $L = \prod p(x_{ij})^{\alpha_{ij}} [1 - p(x_{ij})]^{1 - \alpha_{ij}}$.
8:    **end for**
End of Algorithm

Hyperbolic embedding computation complexity of HyperMap algorithm is $O(n^3)$. In recent years, Bläsius [27] proposed the Fast Embedding algorithm to improve the hyperbolic embedding method and reduce the computational complexity to $O(n)$. The pseudocode of the fast embedding Algorithm is shown in Algorithm 4.8:

Algorithm 4.8: Fast Embedding Algorithm

Input: Undirected connected Graph $G = (V, E)$
Output: Hyperbolic coordinates $(r_i, \theta_i)_{i=1}^n$ $(n = |V|)$
Begin
32:   Estimate global parameters n, R, α, T
33:   Estimate radial coordinates r_i
34:   **for** all nodes v $\in$ V **do**
35:        Place v in layer L_i *if* $\deg(v) \in [2^i, 2^{i+1} - 1]$.
36:   Embed all nodes in layers$\geq \frac{\log n}{2}$
37:   **for** i $= \frac{\log n}{2} - 1 \dots 0$ **do**
38:        **for** $\log n$ times **do**
39:             **for all** v $\in \bigcup_{j \geq i} L_j$ **do**
40:                  Embed v by optimizing its loglikelihood
41:             **end for**
42:        **end for**
43:   **end for**
End of Algorithm

In the proposed scheme, the Fast Embedding algorithm is used to do hyperbolic embedding for each level's domain. Take the three-level domain as an example, the specific process is as follows:

(1) Firstly, MIS uses the Fast Embedding algorithm to embed the network topology of level-1 domain nodes into the hyperbolic space and obtain level-1 domain nodes' hyperbolic coordinate set (R_1, Θ_1). The hyperbolic coordinates are used as the level-1 domain nodes' hyperbolic identifiers. Because the topology of the level-1 domain is stable, the hyperbolic coordinates of the domain nodes will not change in a period of time.

(2) Secondly, MIS uses the Fast Embedding algorithm to embed each network topology of level-2 domain nodes into the hyperbolic space, to obtain the level-2 domain nodes' hyperbolic coordinate set (R_2, Θ_2). In order to keep the uniqueness of identifiers in the entire network and support cross domain communication, complete hyperbolic identifier of level-2 domain node is defined as "$(R_1, \Theta_1) : (R_2, \Theta_2)$", and the edge routers of each domain provide cross domain identity transformation.

The Greedy Routing process between domains based on hyperbolic identifiers is as follows:

(1) We assume that the hyperbolic coordinate of the source node is (r_s, θ_s), and the hyperbolic coordinate of the destination node is (r_d, θ_d). The hyperbolic coordinate of the destination node is encapsulated in the packet and the source

node sends the packet to the destination node through the forwarding of intermediate nodes.

(2) When an intermediate node receives the packet, it will compute the hyperbolic distance of each neighbor node (r_i, θ_i) to the destination node (r_d, θ_d) according to the hyperbolic distance formula $x_{id} = \text{arccosh}(\cosh r_i \cosh r_j - \sinh r_i \sinh r_j \cos \theta_{id})$, $\theta_{id} = \pi - |\pi - |\theta_i - \theta_d||$, then it chooses the nearest neighbor node as the next hop to forward the packet.

(3) Through the process in 2), the packet finally reaches the destination node (r_d, θ_d).

Algorithm 4.9 shows the Greedy Routing algorithm executed by each node in the network with the above routing strategy.

Algorithm 4.9: Greedy Routing Algorithm
Input:
G: network topology, v: current node, d: destination node
Output:
next: the nearest neighbor node
Begin
1:    **function** GR(G, v, d) //
2:        $d_v \leftarrow hyperbolic\_distance(G, v, d)$
3:        **for** all $v_n \in$ neighbors(G, v) **do**
4:            $D_n[n] \leftarrow hyperbolic\_distance(G, v_n, d)$
5:        **end for**
6:        $v_{n\_min}, d_{n\_min} \leftarrow key(\min D_n), \min D_n$
7:        **if** $d_{n\_min} < d_v$ **then**
8:            $next \leftarrow v_n$
9:            **return** $next$
10:     **end if**
11: **end function**
End of Algorithm

In case of a short-term failure of some nodes, an alternative path can be found by adding a backtracking mechanism to the simple greedy routing algorithm. In this case, the hyperbolic coordinates of the nodes do not need to be changed.

4.9.2 Delay-Based Distributed Self-adaptive Routing Algorithm in Satellite Networks

The delay-based distributed self-adaptive satellite routing algorithm is suitable for satellite networks with inter-satellite links. The algorithm calculates the propagation delay and queue delay of each candidate to the next hop to obtain the probability of selecting the next hop. Then the packet is forwarded according to the probability. In addition, when the load of satellite network is low, the data transmission between satellite network devices should be carried out through the satellite network first. When the satellite network is overload or the link fails, the data will be sent to the ground station and relayed by the terrestrial network.

The algorithm requires each satellite to establish the Access Information Table and Status Information Table. In the Access Information Table, entry AIT_s records the information of users and ground stations connected to the current satellite, and the entry AIT_u, AIT_d, AIT_l, and AIT_r records the information of users and ground stations connected to the satellite in the upper, lower, left and right direction, respectively. In the Status Information Table, the entry SIT_u, SIT_d, SIT_l, and SIT_r record the link status, size of packets in the buffer queue, load of buffer queue and channel attenuation coefficient of the satellites in the upper, lower, left and right direction, respectively.

The algorithm is designed with a notification mechanism. Each satellite node regularly sends notification messages to its neighbors, including the current satellite access information table AIT_s, packet size q_i in the buffer queue, load L_i of the buffer queue, and channel attenuation coefficient ε.

When the satellite node receives a packet, it needs to obtain the candidate node of the next hop according to the destination's address and location information in the packet header. If the destination address is in AIT_s, the satellite node will direct forward the packet to the user in the terrestrial network. If the destination address is in AIT_u, AIT_d, AIT_l, or AIT_r, the satellite node will forward the packet to the corresponding satellite. Otherwise, the candidate next hop is obtained according to the destination's location information and the SIT table.

Depending on the orbit and in-orbit position of the current satellite node and the destination satellite node, the number of candidates for the next hop is usually one or two. If there is only one candidate for the next hop, the probability that this node to be the next hop is 100%. If there are two candidates for the next hop, we should calculate the probability of which to be the next. Assuming based on current node, it faces the choice of the next hop in the vertical direction and the horizontal direction, and the paths after two hops completely coincide, which means the probability of calculation only considers the delay of the next two hops. If the next hop in the vertical direction is N_h and the next hop in the horizontal direction is N_h, then the probability of the next hop is inversely proportional to the total delay of the two paths from the current node to the second hop via N_v and N_h, respectively. The total delay is the sum of propagation delay and queue delay, which is obtained as follows:

$$T_{total} = T_{propagation} + T_{queue} \qquad (4.23)$$

As a distributed algorithm, the probability calculation ignores the queue delay on other satellite nodes. The probability P_v of choosing the next hop in the vertical direction and the probability P_h of choosing the next hop in the horizontal direction can be obtained by the following equation:

$$\frac{P_v}{P_h} = \frac{T_p(intra) + T_p(inter_h) + T_q(h)}{T_p(intra) + T_p(inter_v) + T_q(v)} \tag{4.24}$$

where T_p is the propagation delay and T_q is the queue delay. We use R, H, and c to represent the radius of the earth, the orbital altitude, and the velocity of light, respectively. N represents the number of satellites in an orbit, and M represents the number of satellite orbits. The propagation delay between adjacent satellites in the same orbit is calculated as follows:

$$T_p(intra) = \frac{2\pi * (R + H)}{N * c} \tag{4.25}$$

Assume the latitude of N_h is lat_h and the latitude of N_v is lat_v, then the propagation delay between the current node to N_h, and N_v to the node of the second hop is:

$$T_p(inter_h) = \frac{2\pi * (R + H) * \cos(lat_h)}{2 * M * c} \tag{4.26}$$

$$T_p(inter_v) = \frac{2\pi * (R + H) * \cos(lat_v)}{2 * M * c} \tag{4.27}$$

Assume the packet size of N_h's and

$$T_q(h) = \frac{q_h}{C * \varepsilon_h} \tag{4.28}$$

$$T_q(v) = \frac{q_v}{C * \varepsilon_v} \tag{4.29}$$

Finally, according to the ratio of P_v and P_h, the probability of the next hop in the vertical direction and the horizontal direction can be calculated. Hence the node can forward the packet according to the calculated probability.

The complete process of the delay-based distributed adaptive satellite routing algorithm is as follows:

When the satellite node receives a packet, ① if it is an interest packet with a content identifier, then the satellite node will check CS and return a copy if cache hits. Otherwise, the satellite node will check PIT to verify if an entry for the same content name already exists, if so, appends the incoming interface information to the entry and discards the interest packet, if not, creates a new PIT entry, and then follow the normal routing process. If it is a data packet with a content identifier, it will be forwarded according to the interface information in PIT entry. If the name of the data packet cannot be found in PIT, it will be discarded. ② If the received packet with an identity identifier or a service identifier, it will be processed directly according to the normal routing process. The specific routing process is shown in Algorithm 4.10.

Algorithm 4.10: Satellite Routing Algorithm

Input:
    Packet input from an input port's lower layer
Output:
    Specific neighbor satellite or destination ground node
Begin
1:      **if** des_id include in AIT_s **then**
2:              forward packet to the destination through satellite to ground interface.
3:      **else if** des_id include in either of AIT_u, AIT_d, AIT_l, AIT_r **then**
4:              forward packet to that direction's satellite which advertise this user information.
5:      **end if**
6:      **if** packet flag $LOAD = 1$ **then**
7:              **if** any ground station include in AIT_s **then**
8:                      forward packet to the ground station.
9:              **else if** any ground station includes in either of AIT_u, AIT_d, AIT_l, AIT_r **then**
10:                     forward packet to that direction's satellite.
11:             **else**
12:                     choose one node with the lowest load from the neighbors except packet's incoming direction's satellite and forward packet to it.
13:             **end if**
14:     **end if**
15:     **if** the number of next hops N = 1 **then**
16:             **if** the load of the next hop L_i > $the\ threshold\ L$ **then**
17:                             set packet flag $LOAD \leftarrow 1$;
18:                     go to 6.
19:             **else**
20:                     forward packet to the next hop.
21:             **end if**
22:     **else**
23:             let the load of the next hops be L_{max} and L_{min}
24:             **if** $L_{min} > L$ **then**
25:                     set packet flag $LOAD \leftarrow 1$;
26:                     go to 6.
27:             **else if** $L_{max} > L > L_{min}$ **then**
28:                     forward packet to the next hop with lower load.
29:             **else**
30:                     forward packet to the next hop with probability P_v and P_h.
31:             **end if**
32:     **end if**
    End of Algorithm

The integrated routing of ST-MIN can be divided into space-to-space routing, space-to-terrestrial routing, terrestrial-to-space routing, terrestrial-to-terrestrial routing. ① Space-to-space routing refers to the routing of packets transmitted between communication devices both connect to the satellite network. ② Space-to-terrestrial routing refers to the routing that satellite network device sends packets to the terrestrial network device. ③ Terrestrial-to-space routing refers to the routing that the terrestrial network device sends data packet to the satellite network device. ④ Terrestrial-to-terrestrial routing refers to the routing of packets transmitted between terrestrial devices.

In space-to-space routing, the communication process is established as follows. The sender searches the receiver's GPS identifier according to the receiver's identity identifier in the MIS. The GPS identifier is used as the destination of the packet. Then the packet is forwarded in the ST-MIN. when the condition of the satellite network is good, the packet can arrive the receiver by transmission in the satellite network, otherwise, it is sent to the terrestrial network to relay. Finally, the packet will arrive the receiver. The routing process is shown as route ① in Fig. 4.33.

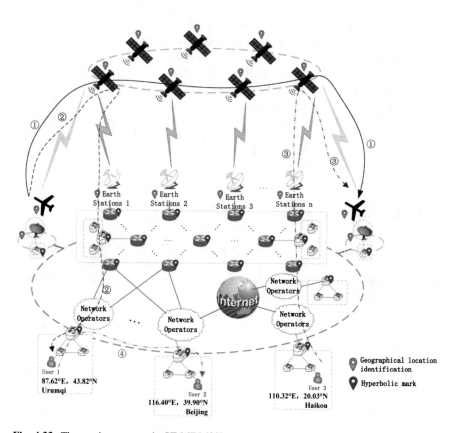

Fig. 4.33 The routing process in ST-MIN [30]

In space-to-terrestrial routing, the communication process is established as follows. The sender searches the receiver's hyperbolic coordinate according to the receiver's identity identifier in MIS. The sender calculates locally the hyperbolic distance from several nearby ground stations to the receiver, and chooses the ground station with the shortest distance as the destination to send the packet. After arriving the terrestrial network, each intermediate node selects the nearest neighbor node to the destination as the next hop by calculating the hyperbolic distance between the neighbor and the destination. After arriving at the lowest level autonomous domain, the packet arrives at the receiver through the intradomain routing. The routing process is shown as route ② in Fig. 4.33.

In terrestrial-to-space routing, the communication process is established as follows. The sender searches in MIS to obtain the receiver's GPS identifier according to the receiver's identity identifier, and one or more hyperbolic coordinates of the ground station which is responsible for the receiver's area. Then through local calculation, the ground station with the smallest distance is selected as the destination of data uploading. After arriving at the ground station by hyperbolic routing, the packet is uploaded to the satellite network. Then the network routes the packet through receiver's GPS identifier, and finally sends packets to receiver. The routing process is shown as route ③ in Fig. 4.33.

In terrestrial-to-terrestrial routing, the communication process is established as follows. The sender searches the hyperbolic coordinate of the receiver in MIS through the identity of the receiver. For cross domain communication, the packet will be routed to the edge router of its domain, and then it will be routed to the edge router of the receiver's lowest level autonomous domain through hyperbolic routing. Finally, it will arrive at the receiver through intra-domain routing. For intra-domain communication, the packet will be routed directly through the intra-domain routing protocol. This process is shown as route ④ in Fig. 4.33.

4.10   Identifier Extension Technology

In order to meet the needs of various communication scenarios, there are multiple identities coexisting equally in MIN. Further, in the view of new communication modes and scenarios that will appear in the future, we propose a model to support the evolution of MIN. The evolution of MIN architecture is the continuous extension of routing identifier in network layer. Therefore, in order to guarantee endogenous evolution ability of MIN, we designed an identifier extension mechanism that allows the gradual extension of MIN identifiers.

Firstly, we classify the identifiers of MIN and define the identifier space. Then, we propose a network packet format to support network evolution, and the network identifier generation, management and resolution mechanism. Based on the proposed network packet format and identifier management system, a mechanism supporting identifiers fallback and the routing mechanism that supports handling packet are designed to provide the endogenous support for network identifier extension of MIN.

4.10.1 Basic Formats for Network Packet

MIT supports the transmission control in the push semantic and the pull semantic. The network packet encoding method uses a specific TLV (Type-Length-Value) format for encoding. TLV encoding divides a binary data block into three fields. The Type field represents the type of the current data block. The Length field, indicates the Length of the Value field. The Value field is used to store the data or to nest one or more TLV blocks. The basic data structure in TLV encoding mode is shown in Table 4.10.

The length of the Type field and Length field should comply with the regulation of Table 4.11. The value of the first byte indicates the length of the field, and reserve twelve values for the expansion of the Type field and the Length field in the future. Given a Type field or a Length field, the first byte of the field will be read first, this byte represents an 8-bit unsigned integer. If the first 8-bit unsigned integer's value is in the range [0,240], it means that this filed has only one byte. If the first 8-bit unsigned integer's value is 241, it means that this filed has three byte, and the next two bytes represent a 16-bit unsigned integer which is used to store the value of Type filed. If the first 8-bit unsigned integer's value is 242, it means that this filed has five bytes, and the next four bytes represent a 32-bit unsigned integer which is used to store the value of the Type field or the Length field.

According to the regulation in Table 4.11, when we want to represent a Type field with a value of 98, one byte is used to represent the Type value, and this byte represents an 8-bit unsigned integer with a value of 98. When we want to represent a Type field with a value of 890, three bytes are needed to represent the Type field. The first byte of these three bytes is an 8-bit unsigned integer with a value of 241, and the next two bytes are a 16-bit unsigned integer with a value of 890, as shown in Fig. 4.34. And so on, the length of the Type field can be 5, 9, or longer. The Length field is represented in the same way as the Type field.

Table 4.10 The packet structure with TLV format

Type	Length	Value

Table 4.11 The length of Type and Length field

Value	Length/Byte	Scope
0 ~ 240	1	0–240
241	3	$241 \sim 2^{16} - 1$
242	5	$2^{16} \sim 2^{32} - 1$
243	9	$2^{32} \sim 2^{64} - 1$

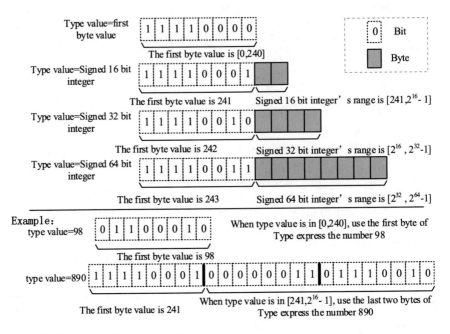

Fig. 4.34 The type and length encoding structure

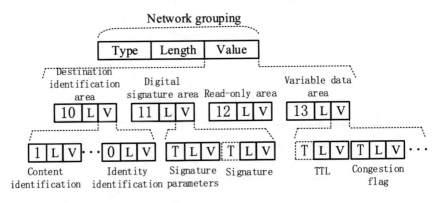

Fig. 4.35 The packet structure after TLV encoding

The packet structure in TLV encoding is shown in Fig. 4.35. Each field of network packet is encapsulated in the Value field of the top-level TLV structure, and different areas in each field are recursively encapsulated into the Value field of the field's TLV structure. The basic fields that must be included in the packet and the assignment of corresponding Type values are given in the Table 4.12. The identifier of packet including the source address and destination address are also organized as a TLV structure, which uses the Type field to represent the type of

Table 4.12 The basic fields of a packet

Type value	Field name	Function
10	Destination identifier field	Store all destination identifier
11	Signature field	Store a source identifier and the digital signature of packet
12	Read only field	Store payload data
13	Variable field	Store the information which can be modify by intermediate routers, such as TTL, congestion mark, forwarding hints and so on

identifier. Considering different semantics of the same forms of identifiers, another Type field is added at the beginning of Value field of the TLV structure to represent the transmission semantics. Therefore, a data structure used to store an identifier in a network packet can be represented as "{Type | Length | Semantic-Type | Value}". In addition, in order to distinguish the priority of the identifiers, rather than adding additional fields, we use the location of the identifier in the data packet to indicate the priority. The closer the location of the identity is to the network packet's head, the higher its priority will be.

The destination identifier area can store multiple destination identifiers for identifier fallback, but only one of them represents the intent of the sender, which is referred to the original identifier. The more identifiers stored in a destination identifier area, the higher the transmission overhead will be. Considering the above trade-off, up to six different destination identifiers can be stored in a data packet, which can be adjusted in the future when computing ability is improved. The size of the identifier can be defined by the user. In general, the destination identifier area size should not exceed 7.5% of the maximum network packet size. In the first implementation version of the proposed method, the maximum length of network packet is defined to 8000 bytes, in which the identifier area's size can be up to 600 bytes. The average identifier length can support a maximum of 100 bytes, which is far beyond the IPv6 address length to meet the current network communication requirements. In the future, the length of an identifier can be configured for longer as the network packet length grows.

Finally, for describing the identity fallback mechanism later, we present five typical identifiers with their names, Type values, semantics and specific examples as shown in Table 4.13.

4.10.2   Identifiers Binding in MIS

The function of the MIS is to provide a unified identifier registration, query, management and resolution service for devices in the network. Each user in the

Table 4.13 Five typical identifiers

Type value of identifier	Identifier	Type value of semantic	Semantic descriptions	Examples
0	Identity	0	Point-to-point push communication semantics	e98a32e6175bbd375
1	Content	1	Point-to-point push communication semantics, intermediate router cache	/min/pkusz/002.txt
2	Service	2	Pull communication semantics, request packets can carry data, no router cache	/min/pkusz/OA
3	Geographic information	0	Point-to-point push communication semantics	(113.97, 22.59)
4	IP address	0	Point-to-point push communication semantics	127.0.0.1

network is bound to a unique identity identifier in the network, and the identity identifier of a user will also be bound to other identifiers, including content, service, geographic information, IP address. At the same time, considering the mobility, the user also needs to be bound to the identifier of the access router.

The users can request a human readable string as its name of identifier set, similar to a domain name address. For example, a user can request a name of "Alice" so that others can find her communication ID. In this case, the acquisition of a communication identifier is equivalent to a DNS resolution, and the specific identifier resolution process is described in the section about MIS.

4.10.3 Identifier Extension Mechanism

Identifier extension is achieved by carrying an alternate destination identity in the network packet. The identity identifier (or other basic identifiers) of the destination must be carried in each packet to ensure that all routers in the network support packet forwarding. With the support of router processing mechanism, the basic process that a user sends a packet with a new network identifier contains the steps shown as follows.

(1) The user queries all identifiers of the communication entity in the MIS with the new destination identifier X or the user name.
(2) The user encapsulates the new identifier X, X's corresponding identity identifier, and corresponding identifier which has the same transmission semantic with X into the destination identifier field of the packet. All the identifiers are sorted according to the addressing priority desired by the user;

(3) When an intermediate router receives the packet and reads the identifier type from the Type field in the destination identifier area. Then according to the priority of the various identifiers in the destination identifier area, the identifier with the highest priority and supported by the current router is selected for subsequent forwarding. When the router selects an old identifier (i.e., not the identifier X) for forwarding and the forwarding is successful, the process is called identifier fallback;

(4) If the router selects the identifier with high priority for forwarding, but the forwarding is unsuccessful, the router will continue to select the identifier with lower priority for forwarding. When all the identifiers in the destination identifier area have been tried but none of them can be used to forward the packet successfully, the packet will be discarded.

(5) When the packet arrives at the destination, if there is a principal wait for the packet with the new identifier X, the X will be used by the destination host to forward the packet. Finally, the new identifier X is used for local forwarding to the corresponding process or receiver. This process can be referred to as the recovery of the new identifier X.

Before the network packet is sent out, it is the suitable time to select alternate identifiers. If all the identifiers with the same semantic are loaded into the destination identifier, there may be the problem that the number of identifiers exceeds the upper limit, and some identifiers will not be used in the whole network communication process causing unnecessary communication overhead. Identifier space detection mechanism is introduced to solve this problem. Similar to the ICMP protocol in an IP network, according to the detection mechanism the user sends a probe packet, which carries only an identity identifier as the alternate identifier. The intermediate router records the identifier type that it supports and has the same semantic as the new identifier X in the variable data area of the probe packet. The destination host records the source address, which can be acquired in the signature information of the packet, and its corresponding sequences of identifier space, then returns the reply packet. The reply packet returns the identifier space information recorded in the probe packet to the sender. According to the identifier type recorded in the variable data area of the reply packet, the user selects the appropriate alternate identifiers and loads them in the destination identifier area.

Identifier extension achieved by identifier fallback mechanism is based on one or several fundamental identifiers existing in MIN. As long as an identifier follows simple point-to-point push semantic, the identifier can be used as a fundamental identifier, and can be used as the anchor for the fallback process of other identifiers. Therefore, the proposed method allows that there can be a variety of basic identifiers in MIN as the anchor of fallback. For example, we can use the identity identifier, geographic information identifier, and hyperbolic identifier as fundamental identifiers. With the development of the network, when all routers do not support some obsolete fundamental identifiers, these obsolete fundamental identifiers can also be replaced gradually to support network evolution.

4.10.4   *Procedure of the Packet Processing*

When the router receives a packet, it firstly decreases the TTL value in the packet by one. Then If the TTL value is less than 0, the packet is dropped. If the TTL value is greater than 0, the next operation is performed. Next, determining whether the network packet is an identifier space probe packet, if so, a specific area in the packet is set to record the identifier type number which is supported by the current router and has the same identity semantic as the packet's first identifier. When the router processes a packet with multiple destination identifiers, the intention of the sender, identifier priority and its own ability to support the identifier should be considered. The procedure of the packet processing is shown as follows:

(1) Step 1: The router reads each identifier in the destination identifier area from front to back;
(2) Step 2: For each identifier, the router judges whether the current router supports the addressing, forwarding and processing of the identifier;
(3) Step 3: If the router supports this identifier, it will try to use this identifier to transmit the packet. If the forwarding process of the packet is successful, the procedure of the packet processing will end; otherwise, return to Step 1;
(4) Step 4: If the router does not support the identity, return to Step 1;
(5) Step 5: After all identifiers have been traversed, if the packet still cannot be forwarded, it will be discarded.

Algorithm 4.11: Packet Processing Algorithm

Input:
   The packet from an incoming face
Output:
   The specific neighbor router or drops the packet
Global: Support Id Type Set
Begin
1:      var i = 0
2:      **while** i < packet. getIDNum **do**
3:            var id = packet.getID(i)
4:               **if** id's type in SupportIdTypeSet **then**
5:                                 process packet with id
6:                                 **if** forward success **then**
7:   end this process
8:                                 **end if**
9:               **end if**
10:            i++
11:   **Done**
12:   Drop this packet
End of Algorithm

References

1. Jacobson V, Smetters DK, Thornton JD et al (2009) Networking named content. In: Proceedings of the 5th international conference on emerging networking experiments and technologies-CoNEXT, pp 1–12
2. Li H, Ma H, Li HP et al (2017) Blockchain based domain name resolution system. US Patent. App. No. 15768833, 2018.04.16
3. Nakamoto S (2008) Bitcoin: a peer-to-peer electronic cash system. https://bitcoin.org/bitcoin.pdf. Accessed 14 Jan 2020
4. Eyal I, Gencer AE, Sirer EG et al (2016) Bitcoin-NG: a scalable blockchain protocol. In: Proceedings of the 13th usenix conference on networked systems design and implementation, Berkeley, CA, pp 45–59
5. Kiayias A, Russell A, David B et al (2017) Ouroboros: a provably secure proof-of-stake blockchain protocol. In: Proceedings of annual international cryptology conference. Springer, Cham, pp 357–388
6. Li KJ, Li H, Hou H et al (2017) Proof of vote: a high-performance consensus protocol based on vote mechanism & consortium blockchain. In: Proceedings of 19th IEEE international conference on high performance computing and communications (HPCC). IEEE, pp 466–473
7. Li KJ (2017) Research on the new consensus mechanism of consortium blockchain. Peking University, Beijing, p 2017
8. Li KJ, Li H, Wang H et al (2020) PoV: An efficient voting-based consensus algorithm for consortium block-chains. Front Blockchain 3(11):1–16
9. Li H, Li KJ, Chen YL et al (2017) Determining consensus in a decentralized domain name system. US Patent. US.10382388 B2, 2019.08.13
10. Wang XG, Li KD, Li H (2017) Consortium DNS: a distributed domain name service based on consortium chain. In: Proceedings of the 19th IEEE international conference on high performance computing and communications (HPCC). IEEE, pp 617–620
11. Li H, Li HP, Ma HJ et al (2017) Indexing a multi-layer blockchain system. US Patent. App. No. 15997726, 2018.06.05
12. Wei GH, Li H, Bai YJ, Li GX, Xing KX (2020) Space-terrestrial integrated multi-identifier network with endogenous security. Space-Integrated-Ground Inf Netw 1(02):66–73
13. Lv S, Li H, Wu JX et al (2020) Routing strategy of integrated satellite-terrestrial network based on hyperbolic geometry. IEEE Access 8:113003–113010
14. Xu L, Li H, Hu JW et al (2017) An autonomous system based security mechanism for network coding applications in CCN. In: Proceedings of international conference on mobile, secure, and programmable networking. Springer, pp 34–48
15. Li H, Wang H, Wu JX et al (2018) A method and system for multi-identifier network privacy protection and identity management. PCT Patent. PCT: CN2018/119724, 2018.12.07
16. Li WJ, Li XF, Li H et al (2018) CutSplit: a decision-tree combining cutting and splitting for scalable packet classification. In: Proceedings of IEEE international conference on computer communications (INFOCOM), 2018, May, Honolulu, USA
17. Yu HY, Li H, Yang X et al (2020) On chord in distributed storage system. In: Proceedings of IEEE international conference on Big Data (Big Data). IEEE, pp 1–6
18. Boneh D (1999) Twenty years of attacks on the RSA cryptosystem. Not Am Math Soc (AMS) 46(2):203–213
19. Mumtaz M, Ping L (2019) Forty years of attacks on the RSA cryptosystem: a brief survey. J Discrete Math Sci Crypt 22(1):9–29
20. Kocher PC (1996) Timing attacks on implementations of Diffie-Hellman, RSA, DSS, and other systems. In: Proceedings of the 16th annual international cryptology conference on advances in cryptology. Springer, Berlin Heidelberg
21. Members of loria (2006) Integer factoring records. https://members.loria.fr/PZimmermann/records/factor.html. Accessed 14 Jan 2020

22. Yang X, Li H, Wang H (2018) NPM: An anti-attacking analysis model of the MTD system based on Martingale theory. In: Proceedings of 2018 IEEE symposium on computers and communications (ISCC), p 1–7
23. Ross SM (1983) Stochastic processes
24. Li H, Wu JX, Yang X, Bob LI et al (2019) Anti-attacking modelling for CMD systems based on GSPN and Martingale theory. US Patent. US10440048B1, 2019.10.08
25. Yang X, Li H, Wu JX (2019) A two-dimension security assessing model for CMDs combined with generalized stochastic Petri net. SCIENTIA SINICA Informationisnis 50(12):1–17. https://doi.org/10.1360/SSI-2019-0224
26. Papadopoulos F, Psomas C, Krioukov D (2014) Network mapping by replaying hyperbolic growth. IEEE/ACM Trans Netw 23(1):198–211
27. Bläsius T, Friedrich T, Krohmer A et al (2018) Efficient embedding of scale-free graphs in the hyperbolic plane. IEEE/ACM Trans Netw 26(2):920–933
28. Hu JW, Li H (2019) A composite structure for fast name prefix lookup. Front Blockchain 6 (15):1–9. https://doi.org/10.3389/fict.2019.00015
29. Yang KX, Sang YS (2017) Research on DDoS detection based on BP neural network. J Sichuan Univ (Nat Sci Ed) 54(1):71–75
30. Wei GH, Li H, Bai YJ, Li GX, Xing KX (2020) Space-terrestrial integrated multi-identifier network with endogenous security. Space Integr Ground Inf Netw 1(02):66–73
31. Li H, Wu JX, Xing KX et al (2019) Prototype and testing report of a multi-identifier system for reconfigurable network architecture under co-governing. SCIENTIA SINICA Informationisnis 49:1186–1204
32. Meng J (2012) Research on key techniques in network security situation assessment and prediction. Doctoral dissertation, Nanjing Univ Sci Technol 1–114. https://doi.org/10.7666/d.Y2276837

Chapter 5
Prototype of Sovereignty Network and Application of Private Network Based on MIN

Multi-Identifier Network (MIN) is compatible with IP network, and supports naturally and gradually de-IP, which will be promoted by users and the market for its performance gains rather than by compulsively. It is a predictable circumstance that the IP network may still be mainstream at United States of American in the future. But other countries will move away from IP to MIN in order to safeguard their sovereignty over cyberspace, and the connectivity between them and IP network are guaranteed through MIN. In other words, IP network will become the internal network of the United States, while other countries will constitute a multilateral governance network system based on MIN.

MIN integrates theories and technologies such as various network architecture, corresponding protocols, network defending mechanisms, artificial intelligence, blockchain consensus algorithm, and intelligent contract security.

MIN is based on the co-governing multi-identifier network architecture, which integrates various security control technologies. The primary application scenarios of MIN are the private network of government, military, financial industries and other large enterprises with high-security requirements. As a unified serving platform, MIN can also be applied to Industrial Internet, Internet of Things, and Internet of Vehicles. MIN can provide co-governing for international entities, such as the Shanghai Cooperation Organization and the "One Belt and One Road" states. It also supports top-level identification registration generation, full-cycle management, and analysis services. Starting from conducting networking experiments from a few states, MIN aims at forming a multinational public network to guarantee the cyberspace sovereignty of each states. The wide deployment of MIN will constitute the United Nations of Cyberspace with independent sovereignty and constitute a global public network system.

We have developed a sovereignty network testbed based on MIN architecture in operators' network environment. The theory experiment and related applications of the sovereignty network have been carried out in this testbed.

The sovereignty network testbed covers Beijing, Guangzhou, Shenzhen, Hong Kong and Macao. The topology of this testbed, which is shown in Fig. 5.1, includes

H. Li and X. Yang, *Co-governed Sovereignty Network*,
https://doi.org/10.1007/978-981-16-2670-8_5

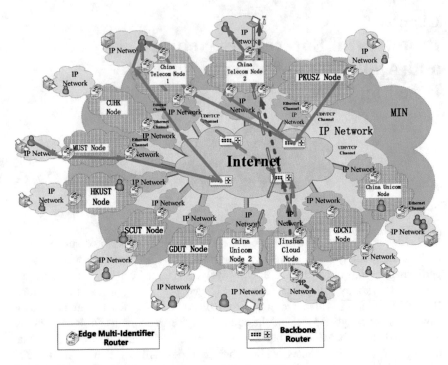

Fig. 5.1 The topology of the prototype network testbed [17]

China Telecom, China Unicom, Peking University Shenzhen Graduate School, Kingsoft Cloud, South China University of Technology, The Hong Kong University of Science and Technology, The Chinese University of Hong Kong, Macau University of Science and Technology, as well as Guangdong Communications and Networks Institute etc.

5.1 Experiments of the Prototype System

Functions of the sovereignty network are tested in Operators' network. The experimental environment is shown as follows:

1. IDC Nodes

The operating system of servers in the Internet Data Center (IDC) is Ubuntu 16.04.

2. Mainframes Used in Testing

The experiments use two type of mainframes, one with Ubuntu 16.04 and the other with Windows 10 Pro 64-bit. The former is used to demonstrate blockchain voting, process of group signing and ring signing, while the latter is used to demonstrate other processes.

5.1.1 User Registration and Resource Publishing

Environment Description

This functional experiment is carried out within the sovereignty network. Users on the Kingsoft Cloud node, conduct the registration and resource publishing.

1. User Registration

The users register in the client with their real identity information, such as ID numbers, telephone numbers, and so on. The registration interface is shown in Fig. 5.2.

Fig. 5.2 The registration interface [18]

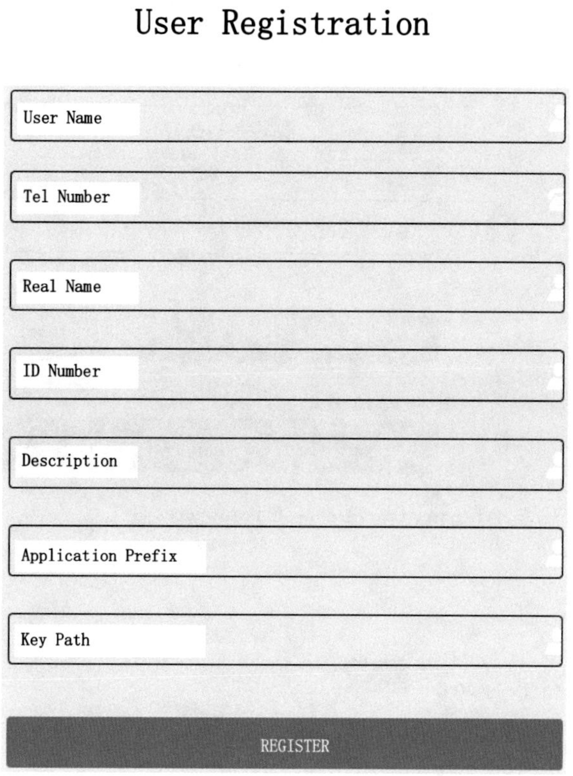

User Registration

- User Name
- Tel Number
- Real Name
- ID Number
- Description
- Application Prefix
- Key Path

REGISTER

2. **Resource Publishing**

  (1) User who has registered in the system successfully can log in the system with fingerprint and iris.

  (2) After logging in the system successfully, user can publish their resources which will be displayed on the client interface.

The interface of publishing resources is shown in Fig. 5.3. The interface of publishing resources successfully is shown in Fig. 5.4. The published resources can be accessed with users' certificate, as shown in Fig. 5.5.

Resource Publishing

Resource identification

Mapping address

Resource hash code

Resource description

Key path

Publishing

Living Certification

Fig. 5.3 The interface of publishing resources [18]

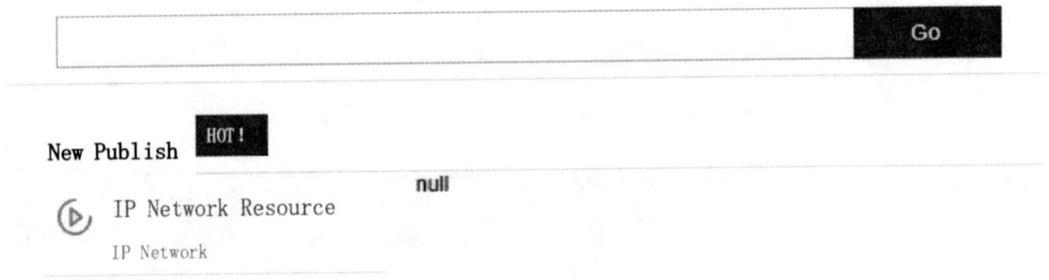

Go

New Publish   HOT!

null

(▷) IP Network Resource

IP Network

Fig. 5.4 The interface after publishing resources successfully

Internet access certificate   ✕

Enter the path or certificate name

> misiyu

[Confirm]   [Application]

Fig. 5.5 Using the certificate to access published resources

5.1.2 Accessing to IP Internal Network Resource

Environment Description

To demonstrate accessing function of the sovereignty network, a VoD video transmission testing have been conducted between the nodes of Kingsoft Cloud and the nodes of Peking University Shenzhen Graduate School.

Demonstration Details

Users Located on Kingsoft Cloud, visit the video resources of the National Digital Library and the National Cultural Database, which are located on Peking University Shenzhen Graduate School. The results show that these video resources could play normally on the screen of the remote client.

(1) Video resources: HD, 1080P
(2) Number of ways: 2 (limited by bandwidth)

Demonstration Results

In actuality, the video pulling result was shown in Fig. 5.6.

Fig. 5.6 The actual video pulling effect

5.1.3 Accessing to External IP Resources

Environment Description

The users Located at Kingsoft Cloud ask for IP resources, which are located on the node of South China University of Technology. The demonstration shows that the system gets the file from South China University of Technology.

Fig. 5.7   The system prompts the user to apply for the group signature

Demonstration Details

(1) When a user tries to get the file at IP network for the first time, the system will
    prompt user to apply for the group signature. Only users who have passed the
    group signature can access external IP resources.
(2) User access information is recorded on the blockchain node.
(3) After all this, the user successfully gets the file from the external IP node.

Demonstration Results

The group signature is shown in Figs. 5.7 and 5.8.
    Relevant information is locked in the blockchain, as shown in Fig. 5.9.
    The user successfully gets the file at the external IP node, as shown in Fig. 5.10.

5.1.4   Certification Between Sovereignty Networks

Environment Description

Files with .txt suffixes are transferred between users of China Telecom and users of
Peking University Shenzhen Graduate School.

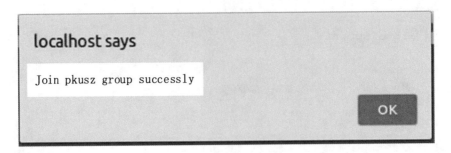

Fig. 5.8 The system prompts that the user has successfully joined the group

Fig. 5.9 Group signature information is locked in the blockchain

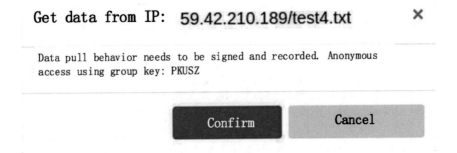

Fig. 5.10 The user successfully gets the file at the external IP node

Demonstration Details

(1) A user of Peking University Shenzhen Graduate School applies for the certificate of the node at China Telecom.

(2) If applying for the certificate successfully, user downloads the files of sovereignty network from the node at China Telecom.

(3) If user doesn't successfully apply for the certificate, user will have no right to obtain files in the sovereignty network, which are located on the China Telecom node.

Demonstration Results

The interface of applying for the certificate is shown in Fig. 5.11.

Users ask for other content with their certificates in the sovereignty network, as shown in Fig. 5.12.

The certificate information is recorded in the blockchain, as shown in Fig. 5.13.

Fig. 5.11 The interface of applying for the certificate

Fig. 5.12 A user asks for other content with the certificates in the sovereignty network

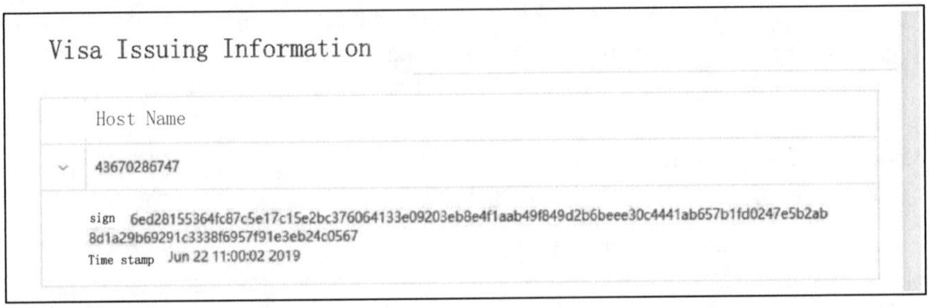

```
Visa Issuing Information

    Host Name

 ⌄  43670286747

      sign  6ed28155364fc87c5e17c15e2bc376064133e09203eb8e4f1aab49f849d2b6beee30c4441ab657b1fd0247e5b2ab
      8d1a29b69291c3338f6957f91e3eb24c0567
      Time stamp  Jun 22 11:00:02 2019
```

Fig. 5.13 The certificate information

5.1.5 Data Filtering Function of EMIR

Environment Description

When a sovereignty network user accesses the .txt file in IP network, sensitive words in the file will be filtered. A user of Kingsoft Cloud visits the file, which is an IP resource and located on the node of South China University of Technology.

Demonstration Details

(1) The Kingsoft Cloud node audits the received packets.
(2) If the packet contains harmful information, the harmful character is replaced with "**".
(3) The Kingsoft Cloud node sends the filtered file to the client.
(4) When the client detects the character "**" contained by the file, the interface displays that "this file contains sensitive words".

Demonstration Results

The result of using a signature to get the external IP text content is shown in Fig. 5.14.

The system will give a prompt when it has detected sensitive information in the text, as shown in Fig. 5.15.

The final version of the file that user gets has been filtered out for harmful information, as shown in Fig. 5.16.

5.1.6 E-Mail Transmission in Sovereignty Network

The two sovereignty subnetworks of Kingsoft Cloud and Peking University Shenzhen Graduate School form a large sovereignty network. A user of Kingsoft Cloud, sends an email to another user of Peking University Shenzhen Graduate

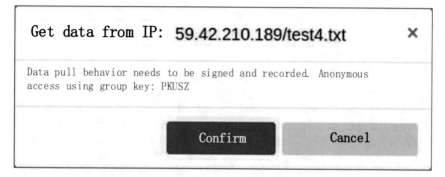

Fig. 5.14 Getting external IP text content

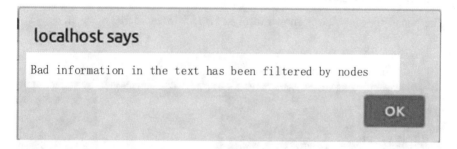

Fig. 5.15 The system filters sensitive information in the text

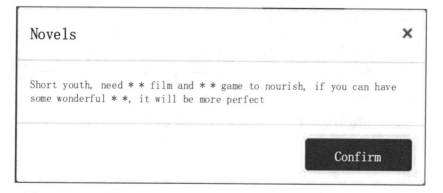

Fig. 5.16 Text content after filtering out harmful information

School through the sovereignty network. User of Peking University Shenzhen Graduate School will receive this email successfully.

Demonstration Details

(1) Firstly, a user of the sovereignty network is located on the node of Kingsoft Cloud. Another user of the sovereignty network is located on the node of Peking University Shenzhen Graduate School.
(2) Then the user of Kingsoft Cloud sends an email to another user of Peking University Shenzhen Graduate School. The system interface shows that the mail has been sent successfully.
(3) Finally, the system interface of Peking University Shenzhen Graduate School shows that the user mailbox receives a new email.

Demonstration Results

The e-mail transmission is shown in Figs. 5.17, 5.18 and 5.19.

Fig. 5.17 The interface of mailbox login

Fig. 5.18 The interface of the inbox

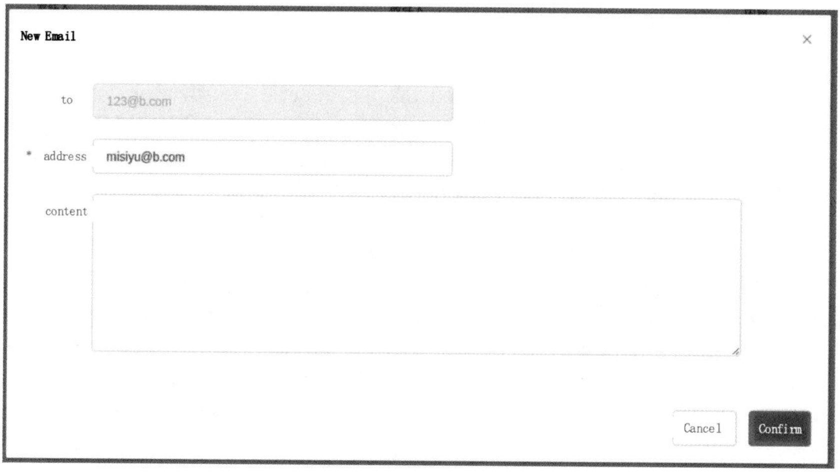

Fig. 5.19 The interface of writing a new email

5.1.7   Voting Through Blockchain

The blockchain voting process is displayed in real-time by the administrator end deployed on the host with the operating system of Windows ver.10, and the interface information is shown in Fig. 5.20.

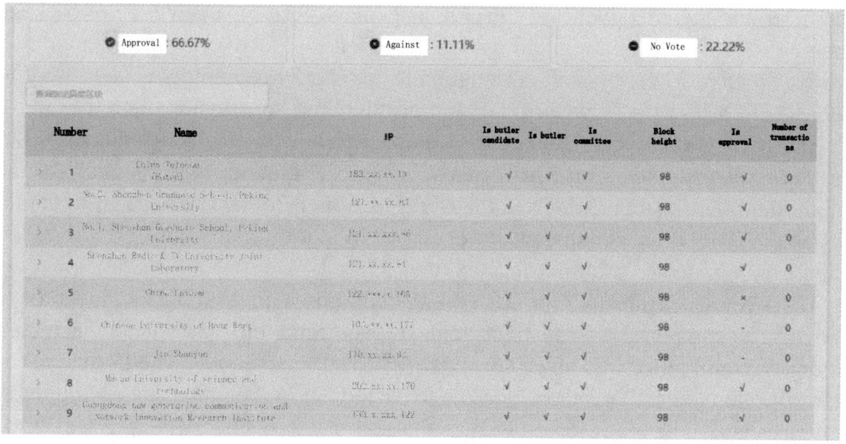

Fig. 5.20 The process of blockchain voting

5.2   MIN-Security Reliable Private Network

On March, 22, 2019, MIN has realized the multilateral co-governing and sovereignty autonomy in cyberspace for the first time. On, Nov. 2019, MIN and its prototype system were awarded as the leading technological achievements of the sixth World Internet Conference hold in Wuzhen, China [1]. However,the size of existing IP networks is so large, it is difficult to replace IP network architecture with the revolutionary MIN architecture in one day.

In 2020, considering the primary application scenarios of MIN are virtual private network of government, military, financial industries and other large enterprises with high-security requirements, we developed a MIN-Security Reliable Private Network (MIN-SRPN) based on the existing IP environment, which allowed both IP network and MIN to coexist. MIN-SRPN can meet the practical needs of mobile office, identity management, authority management, log storage, behavior detection, identity authentication, and network security.

5.2.1   MIN-SRPN

Multiple innovations have been adopted in MIN-SRPN to achieve efficient network access and orderly regulation. Firstly, blockchain technology guarantees the credibility of log records. Secondly, Cyber Mimic Defense [16] technology ensures theendogenous security of the core system. Thirdly, AI technology is used to detect, ser behavior and aware of security situations to ensure network security. Fourthly, real identity and biological characteristics are used to assures the reliability of user identifier and the effectiveness of user management. Fifthly, a new type of package binding identity information and data is proposed to effectively supervise the network. Finally, a variety of cryptographic signature technologies are used to achieve198 a balance between privacy protection and supervision.

The MIN-SRPN v1.1 has been developed completely, which includes background systems and front-end systems. The background systems include the Multi-identifier System (MIS) and the Multi-identifier Router (MIR). The front-end systems include the administrator's client on Windows and four kinds of users' clients on Windows, Android, macOS, and iOS.

The overall architecture of MIN-SRPN is shown in Fig. 5.21. This private network is composed of the management plane and the data plane, including storage system, office PC, office software, MIR, MIS server, etc. The IP network is used for interconnection and free access to each other in the office area. Multiple IP entrances and exits are reserved to help that internal network users access external resources freely. At the same time, only one MIN entry is reserved to help that external network users access internal resources.

The management plane is composed of MIS servers shown in the dashed box on the top of Fig. 5.21. These MIS servers communicate with routers on the data

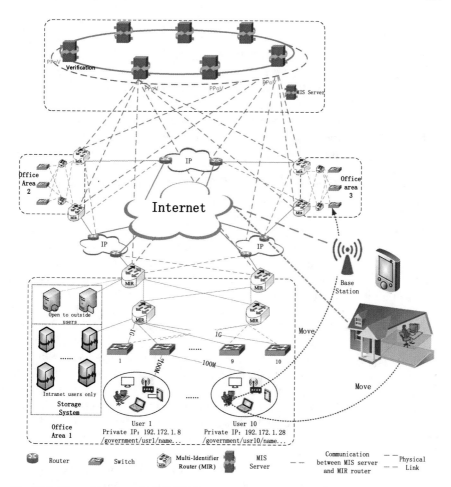

Fig. 5.21 The architecture of MIN-SRPN

plane. MIS is deployed on blockchain nodes to record the identity and behavior log of users to ensure that the content of the whole network is unified, tamper-resistant, and traceable. The identity management module is responsible for the functions including user registration, user login, and certificate issuance. The behavior detection module is responsible for storing and analyzing access records of users to guarantee the security of information.

The data plane is mainly composed by user terminals, switches and MIRs. As the core equipment of data plane, MIR is mainly used for identifier inter-translation, routing, content filtering, data protecting, and other functions. MIR in MIN-SRPN is mainly used for traffic entry, that is, the external network users use MIN-SRPN to visit internal resources, and it is also used for forwarding MIN resources.

The storage system is mainly for storing resources, which are divided into internal IP resources and internal MIN resources. The internal Private IP (P-IP) resources refer to the resource located in an internal IP network. Users in the internal network can freely access P-IP resources in the traditional way, while users in the external network have to use MIN-SRPN to access P-IP resources. When the access traffic passes through MIN, MIS is responsible for identity management and behavior recording, and MIR is responsible for forwarding and identity authentication.

MIN-SRPN is a network without IP. All attack methods and weapons against TCP/IP protocol do not affect MIN-SRPN. After a long period of penetration testing by several professional teams, the results demonstrate that MIN-SRPN can effectively be immune to all attacks in IP-MIN and MIN-MIN network scenarios. MIN-SRPN can effectively protect industries with high-security requirements. Interesting potential users could visit the web[1] for more messages.

For large and medium-sized enterprises, we provide customized security products and solutions based on MIN-SRPN, according to the requirements of target customers. For small businesses, we plan to provide cloud services based on MIN-SRPN. As technical exporting, the underlying technologies can be encapsulated and provided to information technology companies in the downstream.

Industrial Internet Working Group of the Ministry of Industry and Information Technology of the People's Republic of China has adopted MIN as a reference architecture for China's independent supervision root service system. Shenzhen Media Group of China, as the first customer and user, has deployed MIN-SRPN as its media resources management system for China United Television (CUTV). In cooperation with Some Smart City Technology Development Group Co., Ltd., Peking University Shenzhen Graduate School is planning to build a hierarchical security private network for over 1,000 state-owned key enterprises. In the future, MIN-SRPN will be adopted to build the Internet of vehicles, 5G private network and government-private network.

MIN-SRPN is a small scenario application of MIN. The scale effect brought by incremental deployment of MIN-SRPN will increase the proportion of MIN traffic and gradually replace the IP system. Furthermore, MIN will become the global public Internet system.

5.2.2 Water Utilities System Based on MIN-SRPN

In order to improve its network security level, One of the Top Water Supply Groups in China, denoted as OT-WSG, was adopted this MIN-SRPN to replace its current IP-VPN scheme. After a long period of penetration testing by several professional

---

[1]www.cogmin.net or www.cogmin.cn.

teams, the results demonstrate that the MIN-SRPN can effectively be immune to all attacks in IP-MIN and MIN-MIN network scenarios.

According to the management levels, the water utilities system based on MIN-SRPN of this Water Group is mainly divided into four levels, including the group's internal network, the area's internal network, the water utilities company's internal network, and the waterworks' internal network. All terminal nodes within the business scope have wired connected to MIN-SRPN.

OT-WSG is planning to adapt MIN-SRPN to achieve the aims listed as follows. The network penetration attack based on TCP/IP system defects can be prevented to ensure that the anti-attack permeability is significantly improved compared to the existing IP-VPN network, including but not limited to TCP Trojan, UPD Trojan, ICMP Trojan implantation and other classic attack methods. The number of leased special lines is decreased to reduce the group's rental cost of communication cables.

1. Requirement Analysis

The safety of drinking water is related to the health of millions of households, and safe water supply must rely on a complete information system to assist management.

Its information systems are vulnerable to cyberattack. In addition, the criminals intend to destroy the application system and industrial control equipment to achieve their purposes. In order to ensure the security of information system, computer network as the medium of information exchange is the key protection target of MIN-SRPN.

(1) **Consistency of Network Architecture**

Through continuously improving the existing network architecture of the water company, the underlying facilities of the system (such as optical fiber and physical lines) have covered all the business nodes, and the water departments and water plants have completed the deployment of facilities at all levels of the water utilities network in accordance with the existing management architecture. The water company's business system and data backup system have been relatively complete. Given the need for water companies to provide essential services to the public in their daily lives, the business systems involved cannot be disrupted for a long time. Therefore, for the replacement of the existing network, it is necessary to keep the consistency with the original network infrastructure as much as possible and be compatible with the existing business system. At the same time, we need to eliminate redundant construction in order to reduce the upgrading cost of network system.

2. Function Definition

MIN-SRPN consists of two parts: the management plane and the data plane, named MIS and MIRs respectively. All users and devices in MIN-SRPN are required to register in real identity. MIS is deployed on blockchain nodes to record the identity and behavior log of users to ensure that the content of the whole network is unified, tamper-resistant, and traceable. The identity management module is responsible for functions including user registration, user login, and certificate issuance. The behavior detection module is responsible for storing and analyzing access records of users to guarantee high-security information management. The data plane is mainly composed of switches and MIRs. As the core equipment of data plane, MIRs are mainly used for identifier inter-translation, routing, content filtering, data protection, and other functions.

The functions of MIN-SRPN are defined as follows:

(1) Progressive de-IP: MIN are compatible to IP network, so MIN-SRPN can be directly deployed on the worldwide IP network. The existing application layer software needs not to be changed, and the conversion of network protocol can be completed with the help of MIN client software.

(2) Mobile office: MIN-SRPN enables office staff to get rid of the constraints of time and space improving the efficiency of working and strengthening the remote collaboration. No matter on business trip or on the way to work, users of external network can timely approve documents, browse announcements, handle personal affairs, access internal network resources, and so on.

(3) Identity management: Identity management includes user registration, user login and certificate issuance. New users have to registrant with their real identities to access the sovereignty network. They need to authenticate and register with real information such as ID number, mobile phone number, and face when they register a MIN account. The system uploads and stores user information in the blockchain. After the MIS receives the user's login information and authenticates the user, it issues the user's certificate to the EMIR for authentication in routing.

(4) Authority management: Users can access and only access their own authorized resources according to security policies set by the system, and unauthorized resources cannot be accessed illegally.

(5) Log storage: The servers in MIN-SRPN will extract destination address, destination port, HTTP URL and other information of each packet, which will be combined with user's identity information to form user access record and sent to MIS.

(6) Behavior detection: The system should effectively manage the identity of legal users, and be able to detect illegal behaviors of legal users. The behavior detection function of MIS will analyze and review user's access records according to the user requirements and security policies.

(7) Endogenous security: The multi-signature technology enables traceability of network packet, including signatures of user and first-hop router. All routers in MIN can verify the validity of network packet by checking the signature. Illegal data packet can be traced back to individual and user accessing location.

(8) Situational awareness: The security situational awareness system can realize the real-time monitoring of the dual stack network and the security detection of the target host, as well as the real-time evaluation and prediction of the overall security of the current system.

(9) Resisting the traditional IP attack: MIN can be immune to the traditional TCP/IP-based attacks, including ARP attack, DNS hijacking, port sniffing, vulnerability scanning, RAT Trojan attack, etc. Those attacks under IP network cannot play a role in MIN-SRPN environment after testing.

3. The Architecture of MIN-SRPN

As shown in Fig. 5.22, a MIN VPN environment will be built between the head-quarters of OT-WSG and every water company of OT-WSG on China. It is a two-layer network structure. The top-level or first-level blockchain is consisted by the MIS note on the general headquarter and the MIS nodes on branch headquarter at each city. There are total tens of node on the top-level blockchain, and usually the same amount of second-level blockchain. Each MIS node of branch headquarter on each water company located at each city together with other MIS nodes being deployed on its water plants, water pump stations and etc. at the same city, to form each second-level blockchains respectively.

According to the security level of the application systems, the network for serving can be divided into general application area and core application area. The servers in general application area are open to authorized management users and authorized terminals. The servers in core application area are open to authorized management users only who login with designated bastion host. After building the MIN-SRPN, the network structure will be shown as in Fig. 5.23. MIRs are added to the dedicated line of the water group and each water company, which makes the network of the water group and company become a MIN-SRPN.

The topology is mainly composed of switches, MIRs, MIS servers and other devices, which are all in the MIN environment. MIRs are deployed at the exit of each location, and blockchain nodes are deployed on these servers to form identifier management system of the network. At the same time, these MIRs are also the exit of accessing IP network.

Within each water plant and pump station, MIRs are used to form the MIN-SRPN. MIRs connect directly to each other using network cables. The MIN packets are transmitted directly using MIN protocols, but rather the protocol for IP communication. MIRs of MIN subnet in multiple sites uses IP extranet as communication tunnel, which makes them logically form a unified MIN-SRPN.

The two-level network architecture of MIN-SRPN is shown in Fig. 5.24. The top-level chain consists of seven early network nodes, which are connected via the Internet. The secondary blockchain network consists of MIR for each node

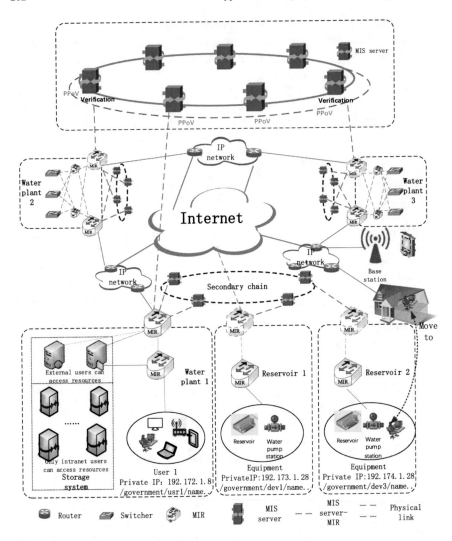

Fig. 5.22 The architecture of MIN-SRPN

connection and other water company or subordinate institutions including water plants and water pumping stations within the node area. Secondary blockchain network is used to authenticate the identity of its users, manage the authority of its users, as well as alleviate the network load of top-level blockchain network.

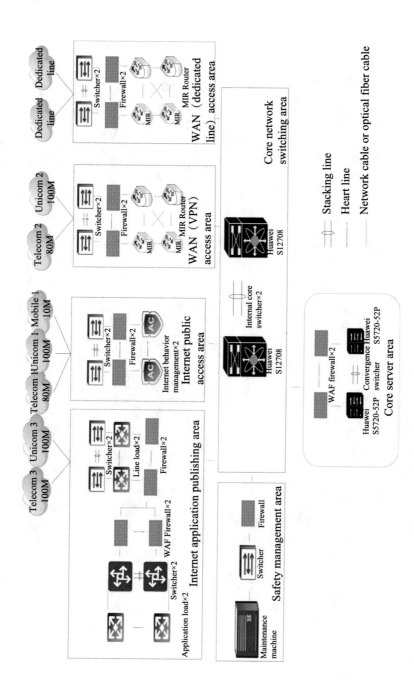

Fig. 5.23 The network structure of MIN-SRPN

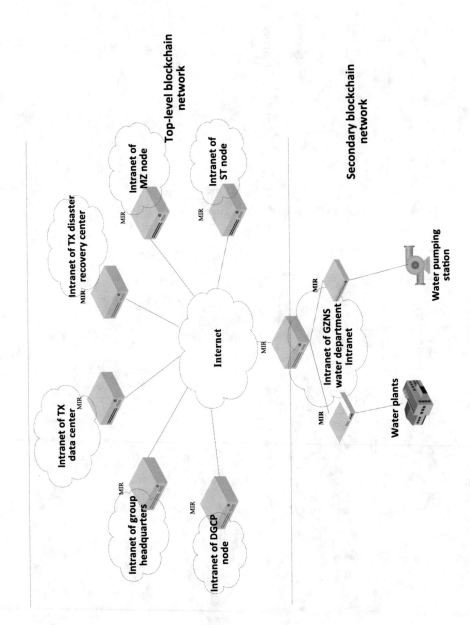

Fig. 5.24 The two-level network architecture of MIN-SRPN

The deployment of the first-level blockchain network in the early stage is designed as in Fig. 5.24. Considering that each internal network of the water group is an independent IP network, in order to facilitate the initial deployment of the MIN-SRPN, IP tunnel is adopted to realize the connection between the separate subnetworks of MIN. This approach enables progressive deployment. If a new regional company or water company called new node subsequently joins the top-level blockchain MIN, it can be gradually added to the top-level MIN in this manner.

When new node joins the first-level MIN-SRPN, the corresponding second-level blockchain network is created according to the scale of water plants and water pump stations in the region. In principle, the second-level network nodes take prefecture-level cities as the units for deploying. Secondary MIN servers are deployed in all water plants and water pump stations in the region to form a secondary MIN-SRPN. If there are more than one water company in an area, it is recommended to assign one water company as the primary node of the area to join the first-level MIN-SRPN.

There are two ways to form the secondary MIN-SRPN:

(1) If the new node and the secondary node have deployed the private wired network, only a MIR server needs to be deployed on each secondary node in the region.
(2) If there is no private wired network between the new node and secondary nodes, it needs to be connected through the Internet public network. The deployment between the secondary chain node and the regional master node is required in the way as shown in Fig. 5.25.

According to the requirement of OT-WSG to build a safety and reliable network, the proposed scheme adopts MIN-SRPN with OT-WSG in XYZ Province as a pilot program. The scheme constructs a secure and reliable network environment without changing the basic topology of the existing network.

5.2.3 The Human Resources Digital Intelligent Service Platform Based MIN

Another typical application of MIN-SRPN is the human resources digital intelligent service platform, which is collaborated with ShenZhen Zeneyes Digital Technology Co., Ltd.[2] ShenZhen Zeneyes Digital Technology Co., Ltd. is an innovative research and development company based in Shenzhen with cutting-edge block-chain technology, and focuses on the application of human resources digital

---

[2]www.zeneyesdt.com.

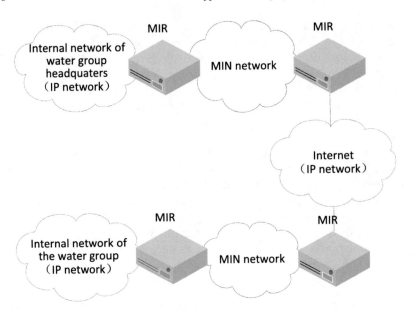

Fig. 5.25 The logic structure of network

industry. Their Smart Eye Digital Human Resource Project is an innovative human resource digital intelligent service platform with independent intellectual property rights which is deeply developed by using big data and blockchain technology. It provides a career credit system for professionals in the whole ecological field, redefines the career dynamic credit evaluation system, and reconstructs the digital ecology of career credit value by innovating "multilateral dynamic career credit certification system", "big database of career credit traceability", "full life cycle digital occupational chip", and so on.

The core function of the MIN-based human resource digital intelligent service platform is to objectively define and record the whole life cycle credit certification system of professionals and form a large professional credit database through distributed storage, traceability and tamper-resistant encryption technology of blockchain. Based on building the professional credit database, a digital occupational chip is developed.

On the premise of respecting and protecting individual privacy, the intelligent algorithm is used to realize the efficient and accurate matching of talents with almost zero cost, and intelligent contract is used to form a rapid multilateral coordination mechanism of talent transaction and management. Meanwhile, ecological tokens are used to encourage multilateral participation in building long-term value of talent credit and contribute to ecological community.

The MIN-based human resource digital intelligent service platform advocates "people-oriented, and taking credit as principle" to create a credible, transparent, professional digital environment. By this way, the whole world of integrity laborers

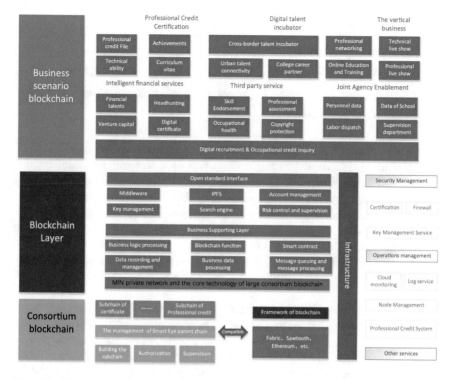

Fig. 5.26 The structure of the smart eye chain

get better returns and more fair opportunity, and the cost and risk of industrial human resources are reduced, thus improving the talent value and liquidity.

Combined with the MIN private network and the core technology of large consortium blockchain, super large digital human resource vertical industrial hierarchical consortium blockchain named Smart Eye Chain with high security can be established. The structure of the Smart Eye Chain is shown in Fig. 5.26.

In the future, the throughput of Smart Eye Chain can achieve 1 million TPS. As one of the human resources digital infrastructure in the Industry 4.0 era, it will develop into a shared, transparent, controllable, universal, and secure professional digital environment and collaboration center.

5.3   MIN Adopted in the Industrial Internet

Internet of Things (IoT) [2] describes the Internet of Everything (IoE), which is a network expanded from the Internet. The IoT can combine various information sensing devices with the Internet to realize the interconnection of people, machines and things at any time and any place. There are two key technologies in the application of the IoT, sensor technology and embedded technology.

5.3.1 National Industrial Internet Identifier Resolution System with MIN

The existing National Industrial Internet Identifier System is as shown in Fig. 5.27. The MIN has been adapted as the Architecture of a National Industrial Internet identifier resolution system of China named MIN-II [19], which is designed into four levels: national top-level nodes, international root nodes connected to national top-level nodes, secondary nodes, and recursive service nodes.

By the end of 2018, five national top-level nodes of identifier resolution in Beijing, Shanghai, Guangzhou, Wuhan, and Chongqing were put into operation, fully supporting various identifier resolution systems. As of November 15, 2020, the number of registered identifiers has been more than 915 million, with 785 pertinent enterprises.

Based on the national top-level nodes, the system functions and capabilities are continuously improved according to the established plan, and the network infrastructure of the identifier resolution system are gradually built for open integration, unified management, interconnection, security, and reliability. On the other hand, secondary nodes are auxiliary, and a number of secondary nodes have been playing

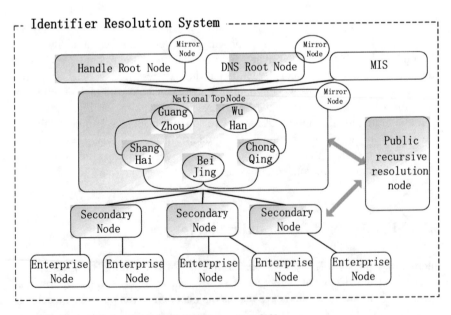

Fig. 5.27 National industrial internet identifier system [19]

their roles in researching new approaches [3]. The secondary Internet nodes are built to promote the integrated innovation application of Industrial Internet identifier resolution. Lastly, identifier resolution systems are built for Industrial applications. Identifier resolution industry ecology can be gradually built from encourage the application demonstration in many industries such as aviation and machinery vehicles.

The system security of the Internet of Things is very important [4, 5]. Not all nodes have to run at a global level, such as the TCP/IP layer. For example, many terminal sensors and actuators cannot run the TCP/IP protocol stack. Computing power of Industrial Internet devices is always low, which only provides some simple application services. The security of them rely entirely on built-in encryption mechanisms because it is difficult to install defense software. If the user keeps the default password, the hacker can easily break into the Internet of Things. After hacking into the Internet of Things, hackers will turn to attack other systems on the Internet of Things, even gain access to users' data, which is known as the Stepping Attack.

Some groups of hackers can post fake or malicious apps on Google Play to steal users' data escaping from being aware of users. Besides, they can launch blockage-style attacks through botnets comprised of the Internet of Things devices, such as printers, cameras, baby monitors, home routers and so on.

On October 21st, 2016, many denial-of-service attacks occurred at the major DNS providers, and the target of all attacks was the servers of Dyn who is the domain name system provider. Network security officials believed that it was a botnet comprised of many Internet of Things devices, which infected the Mirai malicious software. BBS, a British media, was also hit by a record 602 Gbps traffic attack.

5.3.2 National Industrial Internet with MIN

In order to solve these problems, the Internet of Things are combined with the sovereignty network.

Firstly, the sovereignty network is a secure autonomous network.

Secondly, the sovereignty network makes the Internet of Things devices use their identifiers within a domain. Only when these devices need to communicate with devices outside the domain, the identifier translation will be carried out. In this way, the devices are connected to the Internet in a limited way to compensate for the lack of access capability.

Thirdly, in the IoT system of the sovereignty network, nodes can use interest packets to manage devices with some tasks, such as turning on a household appliance. Data can be used to confirm the execution of task and report the results of operation, such as success or failure. The pull mode is used to manage detection devices, while the push mode is used for IoT application devices to transmit data.

Fourthly, there are many caches in the transmission paths of the sovereignty network. Although the resources of IoT devices are limited, the introduction of caches enhances energy efficiency, transmission rate and timeliness.

MIN architecture can be used in the existing Internet of Things and Industrial Internet. In the Industrial Internet, the identifier resolution system is not only an important part of the network architecture, but also a neural hub supporting interconnection and interworking of the Industrial Internet [6]. By giving the unique identity identifier to each product, component, machine or digital intellectual property rights copyright, network resources can be flexibly distinguished and effectively managed.

1. Identifiers System

The root service system, based on the MIN architecture, provides many functions, such as generation, management and resolution of identity, content, service, IP address, and geographic identifiers. At the same time, it is compatible with the existing TCP/IP protocol cluster, provides the traditional Internet DNS domain name resolution service, and provides the mutual translation function between multiple identifiers. MIN-II speeds up the process of "Internet of everything", ensure data traceability and privacy protection in the network, and correct the disordered and difficult supervision problems of the existing IP Internet.

In the digital space of MIN-II, digital objects should have corresponding identifiers, resolve and use identifiers dynamically on demand. In the future, the separation of digital object and position will be realized, and IP semantic overload can decouple, to realize the separation mechanism of digital object and position. However, the existing mainstream identifier systems, such as the Handle system based on the reform route, and the Ecode and OID identifier system based on the DNS technology improvement route, have not yet got rid of the IP system. The multi-identifier tunnel mechanism is used in multi-identifier root service system to complete various tunnel transmission and exchange of visits scenarios, such as IP-Content-IP, IP-Identity-IP, Content-Identity-Content and so on.

The MIN-II supporting Industrial Internet focuses on the redefinition of the existing network layer to support Industrial Internet identifiers, based on other identifiers that have already been supported, including identity, content, service, IP address, and geographic identifiers.

At the network layer of MIN, multiple identifier packets, system management packets, control packets should co-exist and be supported for routing. The specific implementation method is distinguishing different types of identifier packets by the TLV message header. At the network layer of MIN, the identifier information is encapsulated into transmissible TLV messages by MIRs and forwarded to the next MIR according to the Forwarding Information Base (FIB). Then, the scheme of the multi-identifier message format based on TLV structure is designed as follows. The tag of the interest packet is used to represent the identity information, which realizes the multi-identifier network space. Specifically, the type of the tag in the TLV structure is used to distinguish the different kinds of identifiers. Industrial Internet

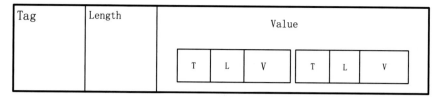

Fig. 5.28 Recursive encoding means of the identifier

identifiers are used to uniformly manage and assign different types of identifiers to their subordinates, which are also nested under Industrial Internet identifiers in TLV format. According to the requirements of the ASNI standard, the value range of Tag is 1 to 2 bytes. In order to meet the needs of various Industrial Internet identifiers at home and abroad, as well as customized identifiers for different industries and enterprises, the multi-identifier root service system adopts 2-byte scheme (Fig. 5.28).

Various packets in the network layer of MIN are distinguished by the tag of the top-level TLV. A network layer is added to the system carrying packets of multi-identifier space. According to the design requirements, the added packets used to represent identity classes in multi-identifier network space includes the following categories:

(1) MIN Interest Packet
(2) MIN Data Packet
(3) Identity Identifier
(4) Service Identifier
(5) Geographic Identifier
(6) Industrial Internet Identifier
(7) Management Packet
(8) Control Packet

In the production environment of the Industrial Internet, data transmission runs independently of the IP network environment. In this case, the data is transmitted with the network transmission mode similar to that in the Named Data Network (NDN) [7]. A receiver asks for content by issuing an Interest packet, then the corresponding Data packet is returned in response to that Interest. The different types of identifiers rely on the TLV of tag to finish the corresponding process, or relies directly on the encapsulation mode of the Industrial Internet for data packaging and transmission.

For Industrial Internet identifiers, tag values in the TLV structure are divided into four kinds according to certain rules, as shown in Table 5.1.

For domestic and foreign identifier systems, the system uniformly allocates identifiers. If different industries and enterprises need to define their identifiers autonomously, they need to apply to MIS, which is the management plane of MIN. When a user registers its identity identifier in MIS for the first time, the user needs

Table 5.1 The range and description of tag value in the TLV structure

Range	Description
0x01-0xFF	The reserved field
0x100-0x1FF	Allocate to the existing domestic and foreign identifier system, such as Handle, GS1
0x200-0xFFF	Allocate to different industries
0x1000-0xFFFF	The customized field

to provide basic information and a public key to MIS. Once the MIS passes its registration request, it issues a certificate to the user and saves it on the blockchain. After that, all the interaction information between the user and MIS requires that the user signs with its private key. MIS validates the information before further operations. When a user applies for the customized identifier, MIS first verifies the certificate, then MIS allocates the tag value in the system to ensure the uniqueness of the tag value, and according to the corresponding specifications, ensure that the customized identifier conforms to the requirements of MIN.

2. **Identifiers Registration and Request**

The network supports routing with multiple types of identifiers, including identity identifier, content identifier, spatial location identifier, and IP address identifier etc. The content identifiers of all resources in the network are bound to an identity identifier of the publisher. After a user logs into the network, the spatial location identifier and the accessed network resources will be recorded at blockchain supervision node of network for security supervision and data protection (Figs. 5.29 and 5.30).

The procedure of identifier registration includes following steps:

(1) **Step 1**: Registering a resource: Network node receives the resource content registered by the user. At the same time, it adds the identity identifier of the content publisher and the spatial location identifier according to where the content is stored;

(2) **Step 2**: Network node authentication: After receiving the identifier registration request from the user, the node will review the content and the user information, as well as the resource identifier, then registers the generated identifier to the upper-level domain and add the local identifier prefix;

(3) **Step 3**: Identifier registration request transmission: After receiving the identifier registration request, the upper-level network node sends its identifier to the controller of the located domain for subsequent authentication and registration operations based on predefined data transmission protocol;

(4) **Step 4**: Identifier verification: Once receiving the identifier registration request from the subordinate network domain, a node on the top-level domain will verify the request and return the corresponding confirmation message to the original application node. The distributed storage scheme ensures that all

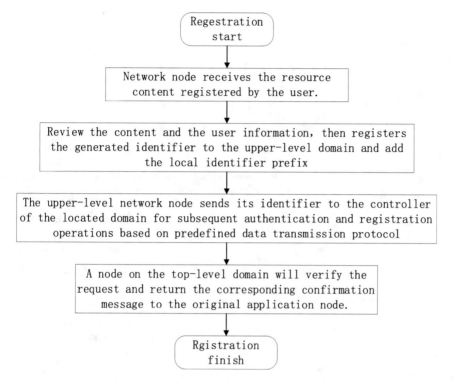

Fig. 5.29 The procedure of identifier registration

registered identifiers cannot be tampered with. The original identifier will be stored on the distributed database of top-level domain. After a predefined time, corresponding database synchronization will be carried out within the entire network to guarantee that the resource identifier information between the respective top-level domains is equivalent and unified.

The procedure of network resource requesting includes steps:

(1) **Step 1**: Inquiry request: A query request is transmitted to the nearest network node;

(2) **Step 2**: Local identifier data query: When the nearest MIN node receives the request, it will discern the identifier type firstly. If it is an IP address, it will go on with the traditional DNS query process. If it is an identity or content identifier, it will be queried on the forwarding table. If the identifier content recorded in the forwarding table already exists in the local database, the corresponding identifier content will be returned; otherwise, step 3 will be executed;

(3) **Step 3**: Requesting query transmission: When there is no corresponding identifier stored in the local database, the query request will be uploaded to node on the upper-level network. After receiving the query request, the

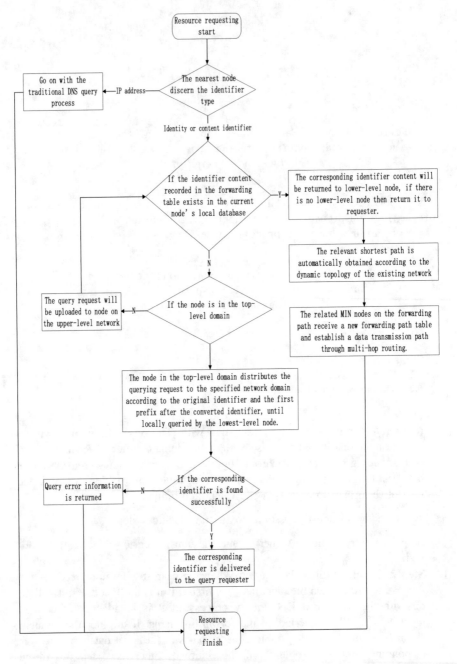

Fig. 5.30 The procedure of network resource requesting

upper-level node will query the identifier following step 1 to step 2. If the corresponding identifier content is found, it will be returned to the low-level node; otherwise, the query request is subsequently transmitted to the upper-level node recursively until the top-level domain network node;

(4) **Step 4**: Identifier query, verification, and interworking: After the relevant registered identifier is found, the relevant shortest path is automatically obtained according to the dynamic topology of the existing network. Then the related MIN nodes on the forwarding path receive a new forwarding path table and establish a data transmission path through multi-hop routing. If even the nodes in the top-level domain do not find the corresponding identifier, other network identifier information corresponding to that identifier is queried in the database proceeding as step 5;

(5) **Step 5**: The identifier request distribution: A Node at the top-level domain will distribute the querying request to the specified network domain according to the original identifier and the first prefix from the converted identifier, until locally queried by the lowest-level node. If the corresponding identifier is found successfully, it is delivered to the query requester; otherwise, the query error information is returned.

5.3.3 Inter-translation of Multiple Network Identifiers

When a piece of content is registered and published on a multi-identifier network, the identity identifier is bound with multiple identifiers, such as identity, content, location information, and IP address. Therefore, there is a need for multiple identifiers to be commonly addressed. In addition, the identifiers in the Industrial Internet should be application-oriented and record the product information. On the other hand, it should support addressing and routing. Due to the diversity of the applications, it is difficult to establish a global hierarchical naming scheme that is suitable for all applications.

Therefore, in the multi-identifier-based Industrial Internet service platform, it is inevitable that multiple network identifiers and multiple identifiers resolution standard system coexist. A globally unique namespace needs to be established, as well as a unique namespace for each application. The multi-identifier translation table is utilized to establish an inter translation table (IFB) and interoperability mechanism with existing common identifiers.

1. The Translation Process Between Name and Identity

In order to maintain a secure network environment, we bind the name of a content to the identity of its original publisher, and use a valid extension to identify network resources in the following mode:

$$/UniqueID_A/SubID_A/Name/Sig(Name, PrK_A)$$

UniqueIDA is the globally unique identifier of the publisher A, and no collision occurs. It will generate the public-private key pair of the user; SubIDA is the secondary identifier when the content is published, because the same user in the network may have multiple identities. Name is the hierarchical content name; Sig (Name, PrKA) is the signature of the content name signed by A. Before the content is received by the user or cached at the intermediate routing node, its signature must be verified to ensure its legitimacy based on the security mechanism described above. As a result, any resource in the network can be traced back to its original publisher, which guarantees the regulatory nature of the publishing behavior and the security of network transmission. Under this representation, an identifier is regarded as a particular form of extension names, that is, those with empty content names. Therefore, we use the prefix tree data structure to support storage and query operations on names and identities.

Under this representation method, identity is regarded as a special form of extension name; that is, when the content name is empty, so we use the prefix tree as a data structure to support the storage and query operations of names and identities as shown in Fig. 5.31.

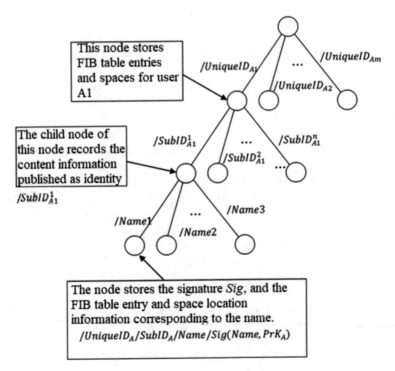

Fig. 5.31 Multiple identifiers forwarding architecture using prefix tree structure [19]

2. The Translation Between Location, Name, and Identity

As mentioned above, each user corresponds to a unique real or virtual spatial location identifier. For a name in the network, in order to reduce the routing delay, we set its location identifier to the nearest node location holding the corresponding content of the name, which is calculated and distributed by the upper control node. The transformation sequence is shown as Fig. 5.32.

(1) **Step 1**: A resource request is issued with a particular identifier.
(2) **Step 2**: Multi-identifier system performs queries based on the type of the identifier: (1) If the request is issued with traditional domain names, then DNS is queried directly. (2) If it is an IP address, and exists as entry of the identifier inter translation forwarding table (IFB), mutual translation is performed; otherwise, the agent accesses traditional IP networks; (3) If it is other type of identifiers such as an NDN identifier, or an identity identifier, the content identifier is first queried in the CS, PIT and inter translation forwarding table. If it exists, an inter translation is performed; otherwise, go to step 3.
(3) **Step 3**: If the identifier does not exist in the current domain, the multi-identifier system will recursively query up to the top domain.
(4) **Step 4**: If there is no such identifier information in the top-level domain, the query will be performed according to the specific lower-level domain of the identifier information, until the bottom-level domain specified by the identifier, and the corresponding result will be returned once it exists. Otherwise, a query error message is returned.

Besides, we use the trusted access and transmission, trusted storage and management of Industrial Internet identifier technologies, and data analysis and mining technologies of identifier routing. The root service system of basic industrial Internet is established to support multiple identifiers registration, analysis and management services of network recursive nodes and blockchain nodes. It is compatible with the existing TCP/IP protocol system and supports the non-aware transition of current IP network to future MIN network.

After the multi-identifier root service system is completed in the future, it connects with national nodes. The identifier registration and resolution services will cover the whole state, and support transnational services. Along with national top-level nodes, it provides access and resolution services for national second-level nodes, recursive nodes, top-level domain name resolution nodes, and blockchain infrastructure nodes. The development of the system requires the formation of the identifier registration, resolution, data management, identity information storage, application demonstration systems and scalable solutions. The identifier root service system provides all kinds of identifier resolution services, and overcome the weak foundation and coordination difficulties in China's industrial design, manufacturing and application fields, provides the information sharing and application across enterprises, regions and industries, cover all process and industry chains. It

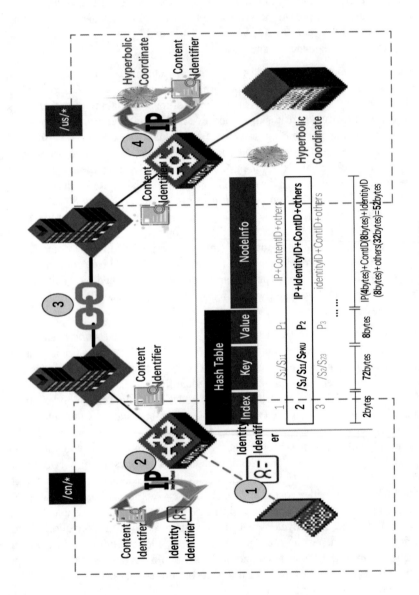

Fig. 5.32 The translation process between location, name, and identity [18]

will effectively support government regulation, build a new pattern of symbiosis and win-win industrial chains, and open up new prospects for independent, controllable and sustainable development.

5.3.4 Identifier Resolution in Automotive Industrial Internet

The Industrial Internet identifier of automotive industry is a key basic resource for identifying and managing complete vehicles, parts and equipment. It is similar to the domain name in the Internet, which gives the target object an "ID" that recognizes and manages the resources by switching identifier between physical world and virtual cyber world freely. The resolution of identifier in automobile Industrial Internet is to query the server address storing product information via product's unique "ID" (identification code), or query the information and related services of product. Therefore, the resolution of the identifier in automobile Industrial Internet is an important basis for realizing the revolution of connecting services and the automobile Industrial Internet.

The MIN-II is not only an important part of the architecture of automobile Industrial Internet, but also a neural hub that supports the interconnection of the Industrial Internet [20]. In the process of exploring the construction of secondary node for MIN-II, the construction of identifier resolution system with MIN is divided into eight steps:

(1) identification of identifier object;
(2) formulation of identifier code;
(3) selection of identifier terminal;
(4) maintenance of identifier data;
(5) assurance of identifier security;
(6) secondary node construction of identifier resolution;
(7) compilation of the standard identifier resolution system;
(8) development of identifier-based application software.

1. Identifier Object and Encoding

The automobile Industrial Internet identifier cover all aspects of the automobile industry value chain. In combination with the current status of China's automobile industry management and related standards, vehicles, parts, organizations, equipment are mainly used to construct an identifier resolution system.

(1) Vehicle Identifier

Vehicle identifier is mainly related to vehicle R&D (Research and Development), production, sales and maintenance, including: vehicle model identifier, vehicle announcement identifier, vehicle identification number (VIN) identifier, vehicle configuration list identifier, vehicle production order identifier, sales order identifier, vehicle maintenance order identifier and so on.

(2) **Parts Identifier**

The identifier of parts is used to vehicles production and vehicles maintenance, including: parts classification identifier, single or batch parts identifier, parts purchase order identifier, parts production order identifier, parts logistics order identifier, parts storage order identifier and parts maintenance order identifier.

(3) **Equipment Category Identifier**

The equipment category identifier is mainly applied to automobile during production, transportation and sales. It includes: equipment classification identifier, equipment identifier, equipment failure identifier, equipment function identifier and equipment location identifier.

(4) **Institution Identifiers**

Institution identifiers refer to various types of objects in the ecological value chain of automotive industry. Generally speaking, institution identifiers include company vehicle manufacturing identifiers, company component manufacturing identifiers, sales enterprise identifiers and company aftermarket service identifiers. In enterprise, institution identifiers also denote factory identifiers and workshop identifiers and internal management department identifiers.

(5) **Quality Category Identifiers**

Quality category identifiers express the standards and grades of products inspected by automobile industry, including: product inspection standard identifiers, quality grade identifiers, defect cause identifiers and defect level identifiers.

Code is a basic technical means for people to unify their views and exchange information. The purpose of encoding is to improve the efficiency of information processing. The establishment of identifier encoding is a technology for defining, assigning and managing the data structure of encoding format of Industrial Internet identifiers. At present, the mainstream encoding technology systems include GS1 encoding, EPC, Handle, OID, Ecode and so on [8].

The proposed encoding method of automotive Industrial Internet identifier consists of a prefix and a suffix. The prefix is assigned by the primary node and the secondary node while the suffix is mainly composed of an application identifier and a unique code. The application identifier is used to distinguish between different identifier objects in identifiers resolution of automotive Industrial Internet. For instance, a secondary node in constructing MIN-II, uses "V" to represent the vehicle and "91" to represent the automotive parts. For a vehicle, the encoding of identifier is like (Table 5.2).

Table 5.2 The encoding of identifier

88.107.00001	/	(V)	LRDXXXXXXXXXXXXXXX
88.107.00001	/	(91)	XXXXXXXX
Prefix	Component	Application identifier	Unique code

The identifiers terminal includes the carrying methods and the carrier. Existing carriers generally include bar codes, QR codes, RFID tags and sensors [9]. The carrying methods generally include nameplates, tags, labels, laser etching and mechanical stamping. Automotive industry prefers direct marking of identifiers at present. If the direct marking is not suitable, label and list is used for this case. External packing is used for making identifiers when direct marking and label and list is not appropriate. Thanks to the development of QR code, the automotive Industrial Internet identifiers terminals currently adopt engraving with QR code and bar code. Laser etching is generally used on key components to ensure long-term identifiable of identifiers. In addition, with the development of the Industrial Internet, RFID is valued for the automotive industry.

2. **Identifier Management**

Identifier is the key parameter information expressed by an identifier. There are a large number of OEMs, component manufacturers, distributors and service providers on automobile Industrial Internet, all of them have their own identifier based on their data standards. On the one hand, the owner of each identifier needs to register key information with MIN-II based on the demands of looking up by other people and therefore the system needs to perform corresponding registration, review and update operations on the identifier. On the other hand, because of the diversity of identifier data environment, the identifier data needs to integrate heterogeneous Industrial Internet application system data. In order to strengthen the interoperability of Industrial Internet resources in automotive industry and facilitate the search and discovery of Industrial Internet resources between different Industrial Internet systems, it is necessary to maintain and map identifier data in various types.

The Industrial Internet identifier resolution system is an important network infrastructure of the automotive Industrial Internet. The identifier data is important information generated during the production and operation of an enterprise, which should be protected because it may involve the company's trade secrets and is also the core asset of the enterprise. During the construction of MIN-II, it is necessary to display different information according to the user level and time, and support the secure channel function to prevent sensitive information from being intercepted at the same time.

The construction of MIN-II in the automotive industry is separated into three steps at the security level:

(1) Software level security. The rationality of software architecture and the completeness of relevant protocols are all issues for overall consideration of identifiers security.
(2) Data-level security, including security guarantees for the exchange and storage of massive data, optimized management of multi-source heterogeneous data aggregation and countermeasures against illegal data use.
(3) Operational security. It would avoid misuse of registration and illegal registration, allocate reasonable identifier resources and improve the security of environment for identifier management.

The secondary node of identifier resolution for automotive Industrial Internet is the core system that implements registration, query and analysis of identifiers by various application subjects in automotive industry. MIN constructs a secondary node for the resolution of the automotive Industrial Internet. It is used to support the registration and analysis of physical resources such as vehicles, equipment and parts in automotive industry, as well as virtual resources such as algorithms and processes. As an industry public service platform, the secondary node in MIN-II is linked up to the national primary nodes, which queries the network location of the Industrial Internet identifiers resolution from secondary nodes and linked down to the local data or local resolution system of each company on the automotive industry value chain, which queries the enterprise data storage location from secondary node.

Due to the complexity and diversity of Industrial Internet environment [15], the construction of secondary nodes for identifier resolution will face a large number of different hosts, different places and heterogeneous systems. The simple analysis of storage location can no longer meet the increasingly sophisticated requirements of automobile industry for Industrial Internet data. Therefore, when constructing the secondary node for Industrial Internet identifiers resolution, it builds the identifiers resolution secondary node based on the industry master data system, a-piece-a-code system and a public data center, as shown in Fig. 5.33.

The industry master data system, as a data standard management system, will unify the classification and description of vehicles, parts and accessories in the automotive industry, or solve the problem of "same things with different names" between different enterprises through background data mapping. An a-piece-a-code system is used for the unique code management of single pieces or single batches in the industry, providing the entire network with unique codes for the entire vehicle and auto parts. The public data center serves as a shared data storage center that stores the identifier data registered to secondary node from enterprises node so that it supports association and mapping of identifiers. The identifiers resolution secondary node built on this basis analyzes the network storage location on the one hand and analyzes the associated information of the same identity object on the other hand. It provides data support for the development of new business forms and new ecology in automotive industry.

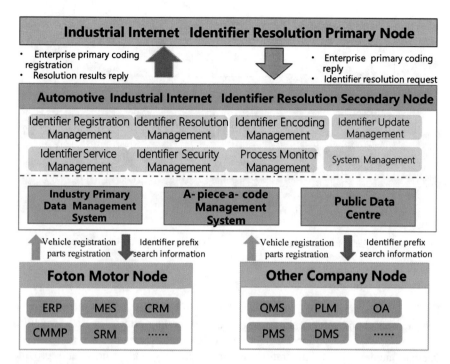

Fig. 5.33 Integration diagram of secondary node of identifier resolution in automotive industrial internet [20]

3. Standard of MIN-II

At present, the mainstream identifier standard systems include Handle, OID (Object Identifier), Ecode (Entity Code for IoT), Epc, UCode and so on, which have been proposed by different organizations. These systems are used to uniquely mark and provide information query for item objects and digital objects at the first time and they have developed into a low-level information architecture now, similar to DNS in the Internet.

The identifiers resolution standard system of automobile Industrial Internet is prepared with full consideration of industry needs and draws on and absorbs the research results of other industries. It takes technology standards as the main line and identifiers and resolution as the core. At present, it is initially composed of three parts: basic standards, technical standards and platform standards structure, as shown in Fig. 5.34.

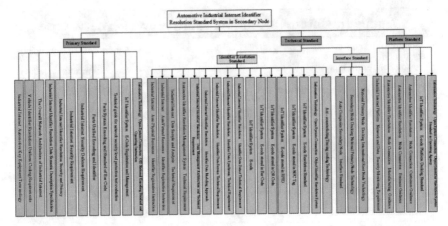

Fig. 5.34 Identifier resolution standard system of automotive industrial internet [20]

(1) **Primary Standard**

The basic standard mainly defines the definition of terms for automobile production lines, electrical and safety equipment and defines coding principles, data structures and symbolic representation methods for vehicles, auto parts and accessories. The standard achieves data integration across enterprises and regions and provide standard coding rules for OEMs, component manufacturers and distributors.

(2) **Technical Standard**

The technical standards mainly cover three parts. The first is to standardize the registration and resolution principles of identifiers in physical resources including complete vehicles, equipment, parts and components and in virtual resources including algorithms and processes. Secondly, it standardizes the technical requirements of the sources of automotive Industrial Internet identifier data, analytical methods and storage specification. Thirdly, it standardizes interface technical requirements including data transmission method and interface method to ensure the intelligence, feasibility, advancement and reliability of multi-platform interconnection after the platform is connected.

(3) **Platform Standard**

The platform standard mainly specifies the technical for network data security monitoring and privacy protection of the Industrial Internet in automotive industry. It also standardizes operating guidelines for OEMs, component manufacturers, dealers and other participants in the construction of the identifier resolution in Industrial Internet.

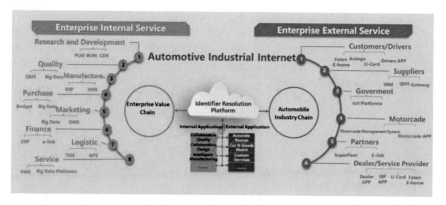

Fig. 5.35 Exploration on the innovative application of automotive industrial internet identifier [20]

4. Exploration of Identifier Applications

The construction of MIN-II in automotive industry is an important basis for the application of automotive Industrial Internet. On the one hand, by standardizing the identifier resolution standards for automotive Industrial Internet, an identifier database for products, parts and accessories in the automotive industry is established and used as the entrance to the Internet identifier query of automobile industry. On the other hand, through the implementation of the Industrial Internet, IT new technologies and the implementation of key equipment, the entrance to the Industrial Internet resource management of the automobile industry is established, national automobile manufacturers and suppliers, companies, service providers, dealers, customers and other industry agencies are established in the service platform of industrial big data for automotive industry based on this (Fig. 5.35).

5. Supply Chain Collaboration Based on Identifier

Collaborative management of the supply chain is not the management of a certain information system, but an interconnected ecosystem covering the entire value chain of planning, procurement, supply, logistics, warehousing, quality, transportation, sales and service. With the help of the identifier resolution platform for automotive Industrial Internet, the entire vehicle, parts, suppliers, equipment and tooling equipment are assigned network storage location codes, which combined with their own unique codes in their respective systems to ensure that each participating interconnected data has unique identifier information in the entire network with a good basic environment for supply chain collaboration.

In terms of implementation, taking customer needs as the starting point and basing on a unified identifier resolution service, management of the supply chain would not only link physical objects such as complete vehicles, production parts and spare parts in the supply chain, but also exam the weak points of supply chain management of the company. It also plans and gradually build a collaborative and efficient supply chain collaborative management system with formulate a collaborative supply chain management.

In the automotive industry and supply chain collaborative application scenario, the specific application process of using identifier resolution is shown in Fig. 5.36:

(1) **Step 1**: Encoding identifier of collaborative resources;
(2) **Step 2**: Register the above resources in MIN-II;
(3) **Step 3**: In the product design phase, the R&D department designs products based on the same identifier;
(4) **Step 4**: The procurement department's design requirements for R&D are communicated to the supplier in time;
(5) **Step 5**: The supplier obtains R&D requirements based on the unified identifiers and promptly feedbacks production requirements;
(6) **Step 6**: The logistics company timely feedbacks the logistics status of the product based on the unified identifiers;
(7) **Step 7**: Based on the unified identifiers, the quality department feedbacks the quality inspection information to the R&D department and suppliers;

Compared with traditional supply chain management, supply chain management based on identifier resolution has been improved in the following five areas:

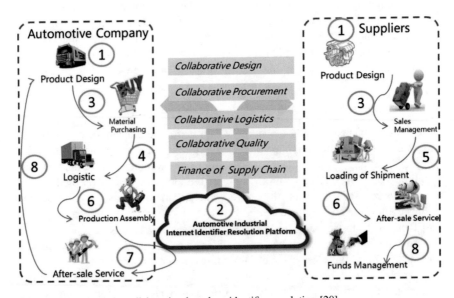

Fig. 5.36 Supply chain collaboration based on identifier resolution [20]

(1) Collaborative Design, Shorten Development Cycle

Through the identifier resolution technology, the R&D resources are fully shared in the Industrial Internet field and it becomes possible for suppliers and dealers to participate in the design and evaluation of vehicle products, form a synchronous and collaborative development situation and greatly shorten the development cycle.

(2) Collaborative Procurement to Reduce the Risk of Material Shortage

Through the Industrial Internet identifier resolution technology, OEMs and suppliers can obtain real-time dynamic information of customer orders, inventory levels and purchase orders, which will reduce the risk of material shortage.

(3) Logistics Collaboration to Reduce Logistics Costs

With Registration of logistics vehicle information and cargo information to MIN-II, the OEM and supplier can obtain the logistics information in time, as well as improve the vehicle efficiency by collecting the cargo flow and reduce the transportation cost.

(4) Quality Collaboration to Improve Supplier Capabilities

During the use of the vehicle, service providers and customers can register the collected quality problems to MIN-II and suppliers can not only obtain quality feedback in a timely manner, but also optimize the design and improve the quality of supplier parts.

(5) Finance of Supply Chain

By combining with the Internet of Vehicle, the identifier resolution technology can obtain the real-time location and maintenance information of the vehicle, provide financial guarantees for partners and expand the business of assistant partners.

6. Quality Traceability Based on Identifier Resolution

With the help of identifier resolution standard for automotive Industrial Internet and its application platform, a quality traceability coding standard that complies with the automotive industry standards is established. It makes coding rules for raw materials, semi-finished products and finished products traceable. On the one hand, in order to improve the readability of the code and reduce the cost pressure of parts traceability on the automotive industry supply chain, automobile companies use the same traceability code rules to implement quality traceability management. The analyzing system collects quality data for the entire life cycle of core components from manufacturing, transportation, quality inspection, and storage, assembly to complete vehicles, terminal sales, maintenance services, replacement, retirement and recycling, so that the product quality of companies is optimized and improved.

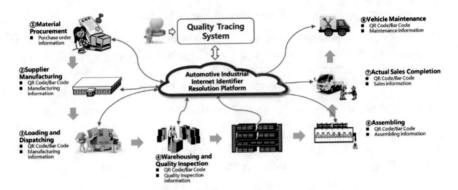

Fig. 5.37 Quality tracing based on identifier resolution [20]

From the perspective of implementation, the quality traceability of key components in automotive industry needs to accurately record the correspondence between vehicles and components during the assembly process of a vehicle. It has to accurately record the corresponding information, such as the vehicle dealer information, customers during the vehicle sales process, replacement records of parts and components in the after-sales service. By this way, when something wrong, the vehicle manufacturer can quickly determine which vehicles the problematic parts are installed on, which areas these vehicles are sent to and which end users are sold to. If these end users need to be replaced and repaired, where is the nearest service outlet should be considered.

In the application scenario of quality tracing of automotive key component, the specific application process of using identifier resolution is shown in the following Fig. 5.37:

(1) **Step 1**: Suppliers encode the key components of the car with QR code, bar code and RFID, and register them in MIN-II.
(2) **Step 2**: According to the coding identifier, the OEM records product information such as storage, quality inspection, warehousing and assembling and registers related information in MIN-II.
(3) **Step 3**: The OEM marks the entire vehicle with an identifier, then records the correspondence between the vehicle and the components and finally registers the vehicle identifier to MIN-II.
(4) **Step 4**: When a vehicle is sold to end customer, the dealer service personnel bind the customer's information such as name, age, occupation, purpose, etc. with the vehicle information and registers the sales information to MIN-II.
(5) **Step 5**: The service provider records the replacement information of the old and new parts by scanning the QR code of the parts during the maintenance link and obtains the production, logistics, quality inspection and other information of the parts.

7. Intelligent Production Based on Identifier Resolution

In the entire vehicle manufacturing process, customer needs, product resources, production materials, logistics transportation and other information related to production are registered in the Industrial Internet ecology of automotive industry through the identifier resolution system, so that intelligent production can lay the foundation. Its process mainly includes the following steps (Fig. 5.38):

(1) **Step 1**: Registration of customer identifier order. Customers complete product customization in the DMS (Dealer Management System) and get an order number, then the system automatically registers the order information to MIN-II.

(2) **Step 2**: The product design department obtains the information about the specific model and configuration involved in the order according to the order identifier and registers the designed product BOM, parts and other identifiers to the identifier resolution system.

(3) **Step 3**: Purchasing and production management departments formulate purchase requisitions and production orders according to purchase requisitions and production plans and register the purchase order and production plan information to MIN-II.

(4) **Step 4**: The supplier obtains the material specific information and demand date required by the purchase order through MIN-II and starts the production order.

(5) **Step 5**: The logistics company obtains information such as the specific delivery date and quantity of parts according to the production order identifier and purchase order identifier and transports the materials to the warehouse where the production is located.

(6) **Step 6**: According to the order identifier, material identifier and equipment identifier, the production department obtains the resource information required by customers and production and translates it into job instructions to guide the equipment to execute accurately. At the same time, the equipment feedbacks the processing results in time and the execution result is registered to MIN-II.

(7) **Step 7**: Through the identity resolution system, customers can get the specific production process of their customized products in time.

8. Service Innovation Based on Identifier Resolution

By creating an intelligent and differentiated customer service system, an intelligent service system based on the MIN-II is established. It not only promotes information interconnection between the product terminal and the client, but also upgrades the traditional after-sales service to active services, remote online services and intelligent services transformation.

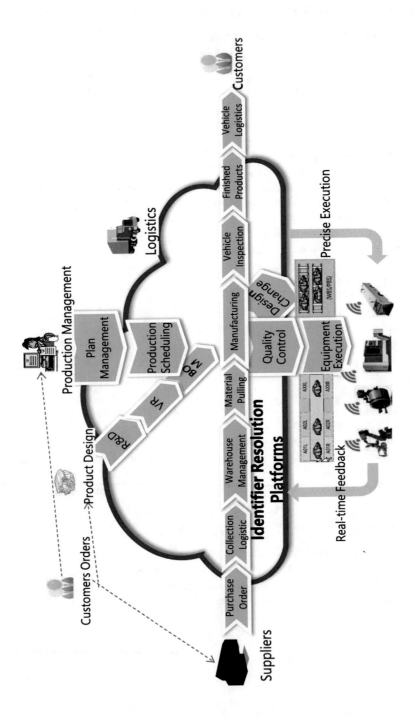

Fig. 5.38 Intelligent manufacturing based on identifier resolution [20]

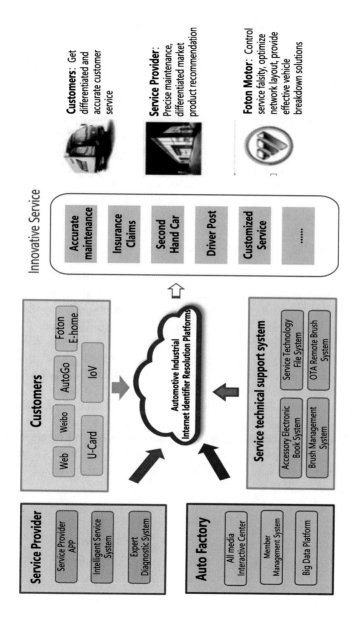

Fig. 5.39 Service innovation based on identifier resolution [20]

In the traditional vehicle after-sales service, the vehicle's operating status data cannot be grasped immediately. When the vehicle has some problems, such as limp home or even broke down to wait for rescue, the service engineer is difficult to get the fault information at the first time and always only diagnose and maintain on the spot. This situation makes the vehicle service passive. Based on the Industrial Internet big data platform, the vehicle production data, product data and customer data are registered to MIN-II, which grasps the running status of the vehicle at any time, predicts the possible faults of the vehicle, as well as timely detect the damaged parts of the vehicle for customers. Fault reminder, maintenance reminder and driving behavior guidance are provided based on the above technology, as shown in Fig. 5.39.

Fault Reminder: Through the MIN-II, vehicle production and assembly data, customer sales data and real-time data during product operation are connected to establish a big data analyzing model, so that the performance indicators and damage levels of key vehicle components are monitored effectively. Besides, SMS, APP and cars are used to push message reminders automatically and to communicate with customers on the phone in time according to the fault level. We should ask him if there is a problem with the vehicle on the phone. If the customer raises a problem, related staff is immediately sent to solve the problem, in order to avoid the expansion of the fault which makes the vehicle operation more economic and safety.

Maintenance Reminder: Through the combination with the Internet of Vehicles, the vehicle mileage and vehicle operating condition information are registered in the MIN-II. When the maintenance time or mileage is approaching, the maintenance invitation will be sent through APP and SMS in order to avoid affecting the service life of the vehicle due to improper maintenance. This will not only enable customers to save maintenance costs, improve driver safety, but also bring profit to service stations. And it will reduce the failure rate and increase the company's brand reputation at the same time.

Driving Behavior Guidance: In the operation of the vehicle, by monitoring the vehicle's gear, speed, fuel consumption and other operating data, we analyze the customer's driving behavior through the analysis and modeling of big data back end, in order to provide driving behavior guidance to customers. Good driving habits to a certain extent will prolong the service life of the vehicle and reduce the failure rate of the vehicle.

5.4 Multinational Interconnected Public Network with Co-governing and Sovereignty Autonomy

Cyberspace has become a state's fifth frontier, besides the four frontiers of land, sea, air and space. Moreover, the security of cyberspace affects and determines the security of other territories.

Each state should develop its sovereignty network, in which identifiers are defined independently to ensure that cyberspace is fully autonomous, manageable and controllable. The development of a global sovereignty network can start with the participation of a few states to form a multinational interconnected public network with co-governing and sovereignty autonomy. In this section, we will introduce the architecture, communication, and examples of the multinational interconnected public network.

5.4.1   Network Topology

The multinational interconnected public network connects multiple sovereignty subnetworks of states to develop a co-governing cyberspace. The topology of the multinational interconnected public network is shown in Fig. 5.40.

As shown in Fig. 5.40, sovereignty networks between neighboring states are connected directly via optical fibers, rather than via IP Internet. The information between remote sovereignty networks is transmitted through the Internet or other sovereignty networks. The identifiers of sovereignty network in various state are defined independently. For the content that is accessible to other sovereignty networks, its identity identifier needs to be publicized through a dynamic routing protocol, so that all the EMIRs in the sovereignty network of multinational interconnected public network know the forwarding path to access the content. When other sovereignty network users want to access the content, they first need to apply for a digital certificate to the target sovereignty network, then transmit the request to the EMIR of their sovereignty network. Finally, the identifiers are mutual translated at EMIR and are forwarded. For the content that the states prohibit other sovereignty network users to access, the EMIR in the sovereignty network directly reject the accessing requests. Besides, the scope of legitimate behaviors of users within the sovereignty network are also limited through the certificates, so as to ensure the manageability and controllability of the sovereignty network. The content providers can also mirror some or all of their content on the Internet for the convenience of sovereignty networks users in other states.

5.4.2   Network Communications

The communication of the multinational interconnected public network, mainly includes three types: (1) a user of the sovereignty network obtains the content on the Internet, (2) a user of the sovereignty network obtains the content on the other sovereignty network, (3) the point-to-point transmission such as E-mail.

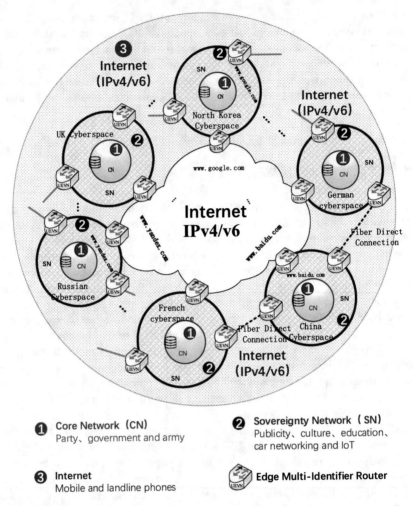

Fig. 5.40 The topology of multinational interconnected public network

1. A User of the Sovereignty Network Obtains the Content on the Internet

Users of the sovereignty network freely access the content on the Internet within their permission. Content on the Internet including two kinds, the content on the existing IP network and the content provided by other users of the sovereignty network. Sovereignty content providers publish content resources on the Internet, and other users access the content directly instead of obtaining them from another sovereignty network. This approach reduces processes of the certificate application and the certificate verification. For example, Baidu, a Chinese search engine, places part of the open content on the IP Internet in a mirroring manner. These open content does not require a high level of management and is freely accessible to

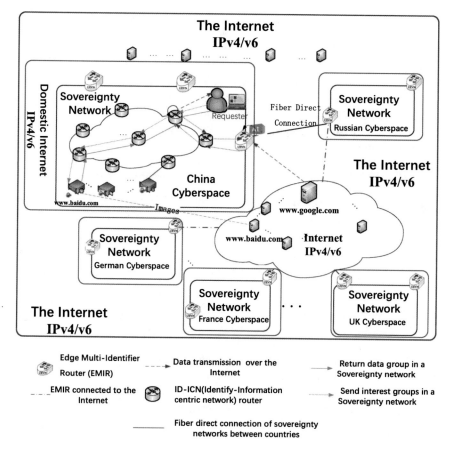

Fig. 5.41 The user of the sovereignty network obtains content from the sovereignty network and IP internet

other sovereignty network users within their permissions. The user permission verification is carried out by EMIRs of sovereignty network. The user permission management is referred to Table 3.1. Figure 5.41 shows the processes indicating that a user of the sovereignty network obtains content, including the process of obtaining content from the sovereignty network and the process of obtaining content from IP Internet.

(1) Users of the Chinese sovereignty network requests content without location of the content.

(2) The content request is sent to the ID-ICN router. If the content request hits the cache of the ID-ICN router, the corresponding content will be returned to the user. Otherwise, the content will be searched on the sovereignty network or on IP Internet.

(3) If the content is on the sovereignty network, the request will be routed to the content source, then the source will return the content.
(4) If the content is on IP Internet, the ID-ICN router sends the content request to EMIR of sovereignty network.
(5) The sovereignty network EMIR will audit the user permission. If the request conforms to the scope of the permission, the content will be obtained following the traditional IP network data transmission mode.
(6) The EMIR of sovereignty network audits the returned data content with the artificial intelligence technologies to filter out harmful data, then returns the data directly to the content requester along the opposite direction of request path.

2. **Users of the Sovereignty Network Obtain the Content on the Other Sovereignty Network**

If a user of a sovereignty network plan to obtain the content on the other sovereignty network, the user needs to apply for a certificate from the sovereignty network where the content is located. The process of applying for a certificate is shown in Fig. 5.42.

(1) A user host requests a certificate from an EMIR of its sovereignty network.
(2) The EMIR of the domestic sovereignty network sends the certificate request to the destination country through the Overlay IP network.
(3) The EMIR of the destination country audits the incoming request.
(4) The approved certificate request is sent to blockchain nodes for voting.
(5) For the request achieving consensus, the certificate is returned to the requester along the opposite direction of the request path.

The user who has obtained a certificate is demanded to put the certificate message into the signature of the interest packet when the user accesses the content on the corresponding sovereignty network. Then the EMIR of destination country will verify the certificate message. If passing the verification, the user can successfully obtain the content, as shown in Fig. 5.43.

(1) The content requester sends interest packets that carry the certificate message.
(2) The EMIR of the domestic sovereignty network sends the certificate request to the destination country through the Overlay IP network.
(3) The EMIR of the destination country verifies the certificate.
(4) For the request achieving consensus, the EMIR of the sovereignty network sends interest packets to the content source.
(5) The content source returns the content to the content requester.

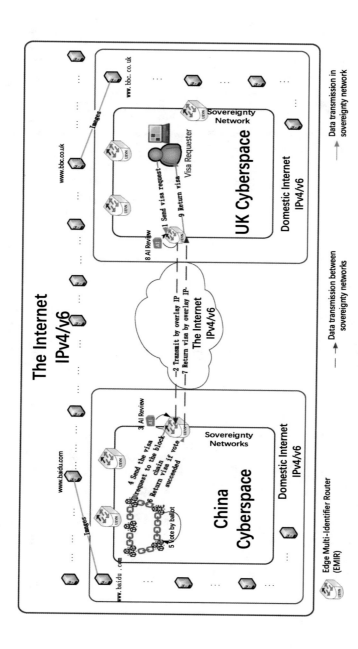

Fig. 5.42 The process of applying for a certificate

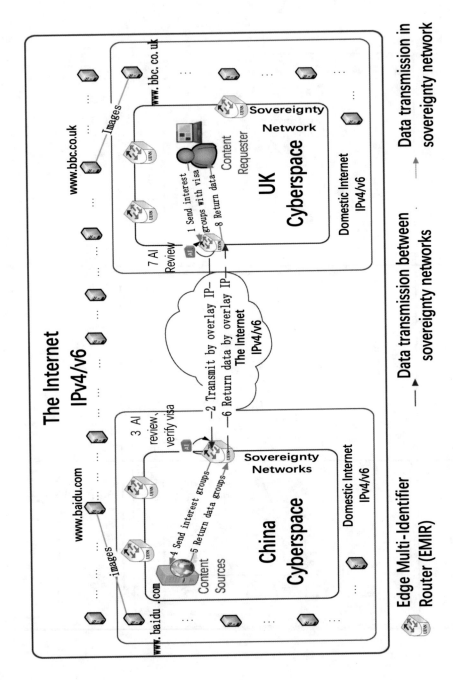

Fig. 5.43 Access transnational content with the certificate

3. Point-to-Point Transmission Such as E-Mail

For individual users, the majority of web application are occupied by scenarios peer-to-peer network communications, such as instant messaging, online shopping, E-mail and so on. By now, the sovereignty network system has realized the transmission of E-mail, and its transmission process is shown in Fig. 5.44.

(1) The content sender sends the data to the EMIR of a sovereignty network following the data transmission mode in the sovereignty network.
(2) The EMIR transmits the data content to the server in IP network through TCP/IP.
(3) This server transmits the content to the EMIR in the target country through TCP/IP.
(4) The EMIR in the target country verifies the content, then sends the approved content to the receiver through the data transmission mode in the sovereignty network.

4. Security of the Multinational Interconnected Public Network

The security mechanisms of the multinational interconnected public network are shown in Fig. 5.45. The specific process has been introduced in Sect. 4.8.

5.4.3   An Example of the Multinational Interconnected Public Network

The testbed of the system covers Beijing, Guangzhou, Shenzhen and Hong Kong, Macao, so that the Guangdong-Hong Kong-Macao Greater Bay Area is covered totally. Hong Kong is on behalf of an English-speaking region, while Macao is on behalf of a Portuguese-speaking region. The topological structure of the Guangdong-Hong Kong-Macao Greater Bay Area is shown in Fig. 5.46.

5.4.4   The United Nations of Cyberspace

Based on building multinational interconnected public network, the sovereignty network will attract more countries to participate and attract the transition of traffic from the IP network to the MIN due to its advantages, such as multilateral co-management, security and credibility, flexible autonomy, forward compatibility, backward extensibility and so on. With the development of the multinational interconnected public network, the United Nations of cyberspace will be eventually built.

During developing the United Nations of Cyberspace, we accelerates the building of global Internet infrastructure for greater connectivity, build an online

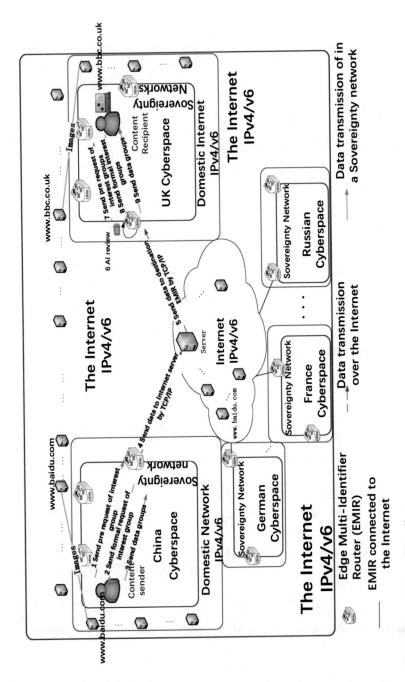

Fig. 5.44 The transmission of E-mail

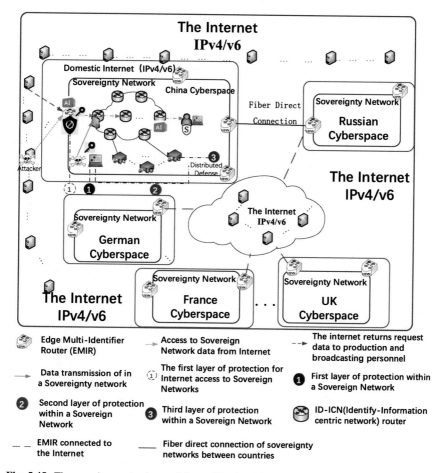

Fig. 5.45 The security mechanisms of the multinational interconnected public network

platform for cultural exchanges and mutual learning, promote innovative development of the digital economy for common prosperity, maintain cybersecurity to promote orderly development, build a system of global governance in cyberspace to promote equity and justice, as well as provide the most effective and powerful guarantee for technology and product.

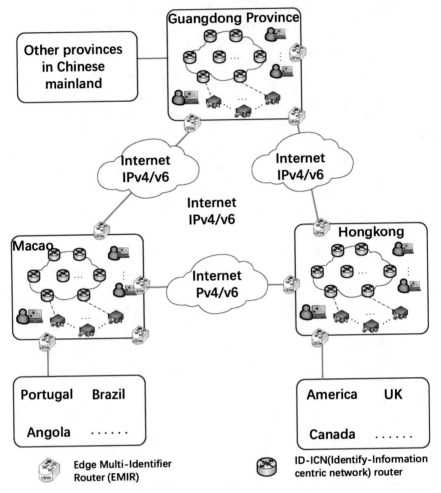

Fig. 5.46 The development of the sovereignty network in the Guangdong-Hong Kong-Macao Greater Bay Area

5.5   Current Work Basis and Future Expansion: Space-Terrestrial Multi-identifier Network

With the unceasing technical progress and the developing demand for user services, the ground communication system has developed rapidly in recent years. However, the quality of its services is limited by surface morphology and natural disasters. Satellite communication, which is not limited by time, place or environment, has gradually attracted people's attention. A Space-terrestrial Multi-identifier Network (ST-MIN) [10] with three heterogeneous layers including satellite network, space-based network and land-based network has been formed to provide communication services with high capacity and seamless coverage. To improve the performance of the sovereignty network, ultimate goal of sovereignty network is to build an ST-MIN.

Based on the Multi-Identifier Network (MIN) architecture and the space-terrestrial routing strategy proposed in Sect. 4.8, we further come up with many technologies, such as ST-MIN mobility management scheme, 5G business and 6G-based space-terrestrial networking [11]. Furthermore, we have proposed ST-MIN, as well as the corresponding architecture and protocols. We are developing key technologies of ST-MIN and verify its functions through network simulation. In the future, prototype verification of ST-MIN will be conducted in real satellite network scenarios and application demonstration systems are developed for certain industries.

5.5.1   Current Work Basis

Since January 2019, Sovereign Network has been verified, tested and applied in different scenarios in cooperation with several units.

Starting from January 2019, Peking University, China Telecom, China Unicom, Jinshan Cloud and other units began to deploy and verify the prototype of the MIN network on the operator network, which is shown in Fig. 5.47.

From January 2019 to March 2019, we have employed nodes based on the consensus of the alliance chain in Beijing, Guangzhou, Shenzhen, Hong Kong, Macao and other places to carry out the data transmission of MIN. The results showed that the project was feasible, which is a world first work as far as we know.

On March 22nd 2019, the shenzhen graduate school of Peking University and GuangDong Communications & Networks Institute jointly launched a strategic planning, the joint institute of China unicom, China telecom and innovation research institute, south China university of technology, guangdong university of technology, dongguan institute of technology, the Chinese university of Hong Kong, the Chinese university of Hong Kong, macau university of science and technology (shenzhen), Hong Kong and Macao to launch a big bay multilateral joint laboratory work network technology, world debut this prototype for verification.

On March 22 2019, the Guangdong Greater Bay Area Co-Governed Network Technology Laboratory jointly sponsored by Peking University and Guangdong Communications & Networks Institute was established and the MIN prototype was first verified worldwide (Fig. 5.48). Its co-sponsors include China Unicom, China Telecom, South China University of Technology, Guangdong University of Technology, Dongguan University of Technology, Chinese University of Hong Kong, Macau University of Science and Technology, and the Chinese University of Hong Kong (Shenzhen).

From April to July 2019, the prototype of sovereignty radio and television network based on MIN passed the test and acceptance of metrology and test center

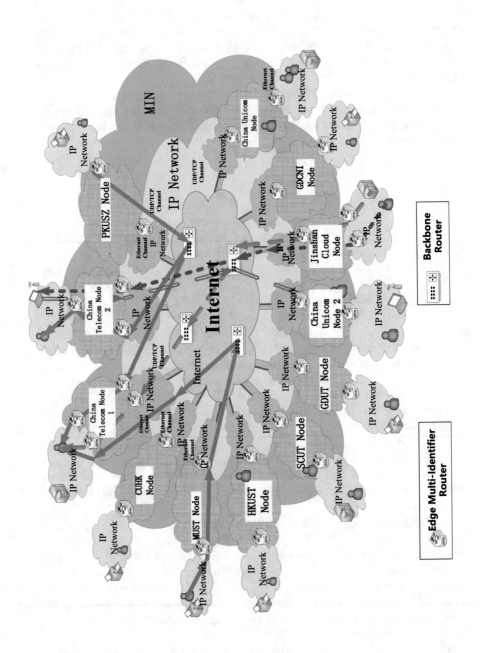

Fig. 5.47 The topology of the prototype network testbed [17]

Fig. 5.48 The Guangdong greater bay area co-governed network technology laboratory

of radio and TV, academy of broadcasting planning. Then the prototype of sovereignty radio and television network based on MIN was applied for capital investment by the National radio and Television Administration (Fig. 5.49).

At the March 2020, in combination with the current situation of the epidemic COVID-19, in order to achieve high security work at home, a high security private

Fig. 5.49 The prototype of sovereignty radio and television network

Fig. 5.50 MIN-VPN

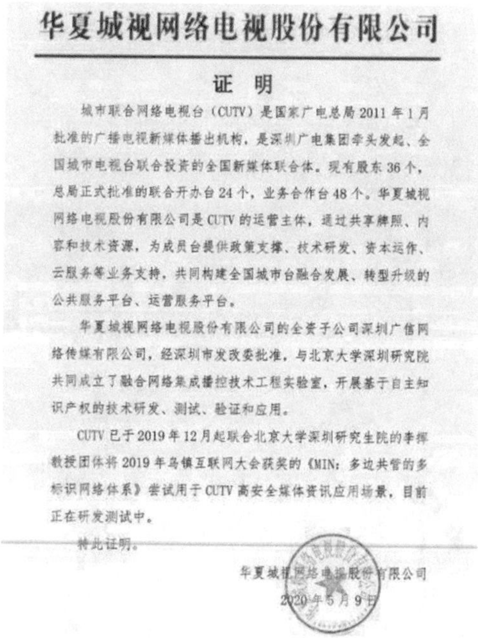

华夏城视网络电视股份有限公司

证　明

城市联合网络电视台（CUTV）是国家广电总局 2011 年 1 月批准的广播电视新媒体播出机构，是深圳广电集团牵头发起、全国城市电视台联合投资的全国新媒体联合体。现有股东 36 个，总局正式批准的联合开办台 24 个，业务合作台 48 个。华夏城视网络电视股份有限公司是 CUTV 的运营主体，通过共享牌照、内容和技术资源，为成员台提供政策支撑、技术研发、资本运作、云服务等业务支持，共同构建全国城市台融合发展、转型升级的公共服务平台、运营服务平台。

华夏城视网络电视股份有限公司的全资子公司深圳广信网络传媒有限公司，经深圳市发改委批准，与北京大学深圳研究院共同成立了融合网络集成播控技术工程实验室，开展基于自主知识产权的技术研发、测试、验证和应用。

CUTV 已于 2019 年 12 月起联合北京大学深圳研究生院的李挥教授团体将 2019 年乌镇互联网大会获奖的《MIN：多边共管的多标识网络体系》尝试用于 CUTV 高安全媒体资讯应用场景，目前正在研发测试中。

特此证明。

华夏城视网络电视股份有限公司
2020 年 5 月 9 日

network MIN-VPN based on MIN was developed. MIN-VPN is used for uploading videos, images and program contents to the backstage of broadcasting control and editors of CUTV, a city united television station under Shenzhen Radio and Television Group (Fig. 5.50).

5.5.2 Routing Strategy and Mobility Management Scheme in ST-MIN

For different characteristics of the satellite network and the ground-based network, we propose a hyperbolic routing algorithm and a delay-based distributed adaptive routing algorithm in the satellite network. The multiple identifiers are addressed based on the MIN and MIS, and the path selection and forward of different identifier packets are achieved through MIR. The routing strategy and mobility management scheme of ST-MIN is shown in Fig. 5.51.

The routing algorithm based on hyperbolic distance adopts a simple greedy strategy with little routing information. The current node only needs to calculate the hyperbolic distance between each neighbor node and destination node, and selects the shortest path for forwarding. Greedy embedding of a complex network in Euclidean space requires high dimensions leading to the relatively complex network embedding and distance calculation. In a hyperbolic embedding network, a

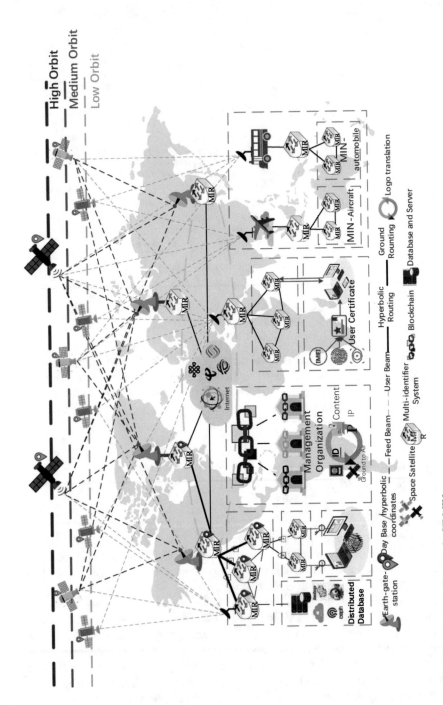

Fig. 5.51 The routing architecture in ST-MIN

hyperbolic plane can embed any network topology of various size and node degree without dimensionality reduction and high-dimensional computation. Based on hyperbolic coordinates, the greedy routing reaches a high routing success rate. Theoretically, good hyperbolic embedding in the network makes the routing success rate reach 100%. For the scale-free network, the greedy routing algorithm based on hyperbolic coordinates approaches the optimal routing path.

The network identifier space is designed with hierarchical structure, which is determined according to the actual demand and topology stability. The bottom of the network identity space consists of individual users, who belong to different network autonomous domains. Hyperbolic coordinates are regarded as hyperbolic identifiers of AS nodes to route between different domains. The hyperbolic coordinate of each domain node remains unchanged for a long time, because the topology of the network between nodes in each hierarchical domain is relatively stable. In the lowest domain, due to frequent topology changes, we adopt the intra-domain routing protocol, such as OSPF, etc., to calculate the overhead of different paths according to link states, then the router selects the path with the lowest overhead as the forwarding path.

The delay based distributed adaptive routing algorithm is suitable for satellite networks with intersatellite links. The algorithm calculates the propagation delay and queuing delay of each candidate next hop to obtain the probability of each next hop being chosen, then forward the packet to the next hop with the highest probability. In addition, when the load of the satellite network is low with a good network condition, the data transmission between satellite network devices should be carried out through the satellite network first. When the load of the satellite network is too high or the link fails, packets will be sent to the station in the ground-based network. Hence, it is an adaptive routing algorithm which reduces the delay of packet transmission and the possibility of network congestion and gives the control method when congestion occurs.

The routing process in the ST-MIN is as follows: (1) The routing process between devices in the satellite network is carried out through the satellite network first. In case of network congestion or link failure, the ground-based network is used as a backup. (2) In order to select the optimal gateway station for data transmission, the routing between satellite network equipment and ground based network equipment should comprehensively consider the geographical location of satellite network equipment, and the hyperbolic distance between the gateway station and the target ground-based equipment. (3) The method of minimizing the hyperbolic distance between neighbor nodes and destination nodes is adopted to routing between ground-based network equipment.

The mobility management scheme in ST-MIN, saves the geographic location information and hyperbolic coordinate information of nodes in rendezvous nodes (RV nodes), which are distributed across various domains. The distributed rendezvous system (DRS), which is formed from these nodes, enables the network to identify and locate terminals by running the data synchronization protocol. By this way, ST-MIN supports users to use terminals during the mobile process.

5.5.3 5G Business

The 5th generation mobile networks (5G) are the latest generation of cellular mobile communication technology, which is extended from 4G (LTE-A, WiMax), 3G (UMTS, LTE) and 2G (GSM) systems [12–14]. 5G aims at provide the service with high data rates, low latency, energy savings, low costs, large system capacity and large-scale device connectivity. The first phase of the 5G standard in Release-15, required the completion of early commercial deployment. The second phase in Release-16 has been completed in April 2020, and submitted to the International Telecommunication Union (ITU) as a candidate for the IMT-2020 technology. The ITU IMT-2020 standard stipulate multiple requires, such as a speed of 20 Gbit/s, wide channel bandwidth and large capacity MIMO.

5G network is a digital cellular network, where the service area covered by the operator is divided into many smaller geographic areas called cells. Analog signals representing sound and images are digitized in the phone, then are converted by an analog-to-digital converter and transmitted as a bitstream. All 5G wireless devices in the cell, communicate with local antenna arrays and low-power automatic transceivers (transmitters and receivers) in the cell via radio waves. The transceiver allocates channels from a common frequency pool. These channels can be reused in geographically separated cells. The local antenna is connected to the telephone network and the Internet through a high-bandwidth fiber optic or wireless backhaul connection. When users move from one cell to another, the mobile devices will automatically switch to the antenna in the new cell.

The sovereignty network is developed based on the identity centric network (ICN), it combines with the in-network caching, and inherently supports multiple paths, so that it can support the 5G communication well. The in-network caching ensures good mobility. When users move to another coverage area of the base station, it is only needed that their device send another interest packet. Because the requested content has cached in a certain node on the path of the last request, the data is returned directly through finding the nearest cached node on the path. The identity centric network inherently supports multiple paths, which means that ICN allows mobile devices to connect to multiple base stations at the same time without affecting the data transmission beyond the current base station coverage. Within the sovereignty network, the base station of 5G acts as a node in the identity central network, which is carried out directly following the data transmission mode in the identity central network. If the base station of 5G is located outside the sovereignty network, named an IP node, it will be an important issue to supervise the data accessing the sovereignty network through the 5G base station, that is, how to manage mobile users leaving the sovereignty network. We design the data transmission process shown in Fig. 5.52 to solve this problem.

(1) A wireless terminal device with an identity identifier, communicates with the base station via Overlay IP.

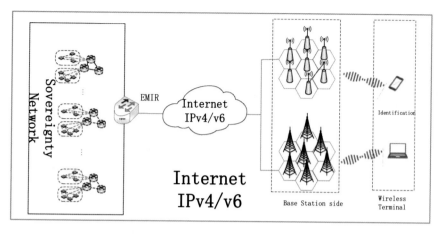

Fig. 5.52 5G support for IP nodes from the sovereignty network

(2) The base station sends the data to an outbound node of the target sovereignty network following the traditional IP transmission mode.

(3) The outbound node audits the user's identity. If approved, it is allowed to access the data, otherwise denied.

(4) Hence, the sovereignty network supports the 5G business and mobility well.

5.5.4   Switching Scheme Between Satellite and Gateway Station Based on 6G

With the development of ground network, whether the 6G technology can be used in the low-orbit satellite network has attracted lots of attention. The switching technology and network architecture are researched, so that ordinary users can seamlessly switch between the 6G satellite base station and the 6G ground base station.

The ST-MIN should guarantee the continuity of service when terminals move in different wireless cells. Assuming that the low-orbit satellite MIN is also equipped with a 6G base station and complies with the 6G standard, a seamless handover scheme between the terminals in satellite cells and ground cells is analyzed and designed.

The satellite beam and the ground station beam have different time delay and frequency offset for the 6G terminal on the ground. During switching, time and frequency needs to be synchronized between the terminal and the new cell. Figures 5.53 and 5.54 show the variation of channel delay and frequency offset when the beam of a satellite on 600 km orbit passes a terminal on the ground.

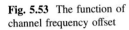

Fig. 5.53 The function of channel frequency offset

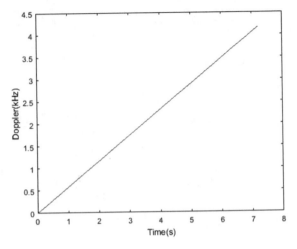

Fig. 5.54 The function of the channel round trip delay

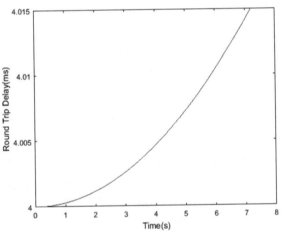

Under such conditions, the randomly access technology used in the ground network cannot complete the time-frequency synchronization process. In order to complete the switch between the ground cell and the satellite cell, the randomly access technology of the 6G standard needs to be enhanced. Besides, it's necessary to design the leader sequences, sub-carrier interval, sequence splicing mode, which enables access to the 6G cell covered by the satellite network. Firstly, the terminal judges whether the target switching cell is a cell covered by the satellite network. Then the enhancement scheme can be adopted in the switching process.

Due to the regularity of satellite movement, the network predicts the switching of terminals and adopt the noncompetitive randomly access process to reduce the switching time between cells. As an example, Fig. 5.55 shows a classic noncompetitive randomly access process. The original cell sends the leader sequence required for switching to the terminal, and the terminal sends the sequence directly

Fig. 5.55 Noncompetitive randomly access process

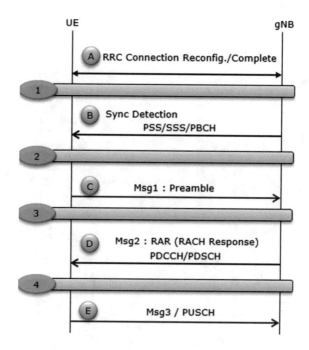

to the target cell. Furthermore, according to the regular of moving of satellite, the time-frequency synchronization of fixed terminal can be predicted, so as to simplify the sequences required for users to access the target cell to shorten the time required for access. We estimate the time-frequency offset prediction ability in simulation and measurement in an actual environment to guarantee the fast switch.

Due to the complex topological structure of ST-MIN, cell switching also involves the switching between different core networks and different Public Land Mobile Networks (PLMNs). In the future work, it is necessary to analyze the signaling process under different circumstances at the same time, and further improve the switching process of 6G protocol standards.

5.5.5 Experiment and Evaluation of ST-MIN

1. The Building of ST-MIN Testbed

Starting in April 2020, an ST-MIN testbed was built in cooperation with China Satellite Communications Corporation (or China Satcom). At present, it has passed the primary test and verified the feasibility of ST-MIN. The prototype network is shown in Fig. 5.56. The test network deployed several representative small multi-identifier subnets, including MIN-IDC (Multi-Identifier Network Internet Data Center) in Kashgar, Chengdu, and Beijing, and MIN-IDC in Peking

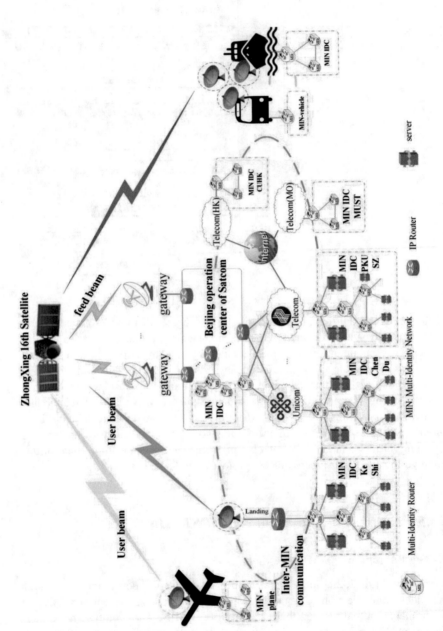

Fig. 5.56 The testbed of ST-MIN

University Shenzhen Graduate School, Chinese University of Hong Kong, Macau University of Science and Technology, and so on. Multiple subnets are connected through the ZhongXing 16th Satellite. IP tunneling is used to communicate between subnets, and the link-layer protocol is used to transfer the multi-identifier network packets directly within the subnets.

2. Two-level Multi-identifier Management System Deployment Test

Based on the ST-MIN testbed, one server from each subnet are selected as a blockchain node and to compose the first level blockchain of our multi-identifier management system. The first level blockchain including eight nodes respectively from Peking University Shenzhen Graduate School, China Satcom, Chinese University of Hong Kong, Macau University of Science and Technology, Hong Kong University of Science and Technology, South China University of Technology, Jinshan Cloud Co. Ltd., and China Unicom.

In the private network of Satcom, the second-level consortium blockchain is deployed based on ZhongXing 16th Satellite communication system. The second-level management system of Satcom contains a total of 5 nodes, which are used to manage the space-based network communication identifiers. The experiment shows that the two-level management system can run normally and the multi-identifier management system has great flexibility in the level expansion.

3. Basic Communication Test of ST-MIN

A simple network file transfer program is implemented to do the basic communication test on the ST-MIN testbed. This program includes a server and a client. The server is installed in the host named wt3 in IDC of China SATCOM in Beijing, and the client is installed in the host named node11 in the IDC of PKUSZ in Shenzhen. The client downloads file from the server with a simple transmission control protocol based on MIN's network protocol. This transmission control protocol can use a fixed number of transmission windows to transfer data reliably and every packet size it sends is 8000 bytes. The test network topology is shown in Fig. 5.57. The total bandwidth of the transmission link is 20 Mbps. Eight kinds of a fixed number of transmission windows are used to do the test, and every test repeats ten times. The transmission results are shown in Fig. 5.58. As the transmission window increase, the transmission rate increases almost linearly. Further transport testing requires the design of a good transport control mechanism based on ST-MIN, which is beyond the scope of this article.

4. Analysis and Comparisons

Compared with IP networks, the key advantages of ST-MIN include the following: (1) Multiple identifiers and transmission modes are allowed to coexist, and a more appropriate identifier is used to meet different scenarios, such as hierarchical identifier in the ground network and geospatial identifier in the space network.

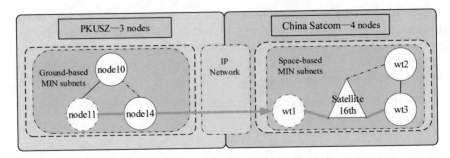

Fig. 5.57 Basic communication test topology

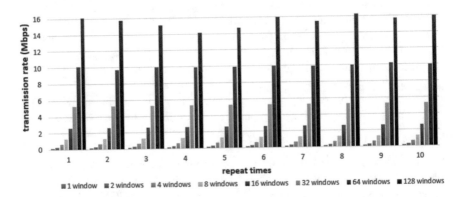

Fig. 5.58 Basic communication test result

(2) ST-MIN has more endogenous safety features, including trust computing, packet multi-signature, and self-authentication identifiers. (3) Identifier co-management and co-governance technology, the voting management of the identifier is realized through the consortium blockchain technology. (4) Identify extensibility, instead of using fixed identifier and communication mode, the ST-MIN reserves interfaces for future identifier and communication mode expansion, which makes the resistance of future network architecture innovation less.

References

1. World Internet Conference (2019) The 6th world internet conference. https://2019. wicwuzhen.cn/. Accessed 29 Dec 2020
2. Gubbi J, Buyya R, Marusic S et al (2013) Internet of Things (IoT): a vision, architectural elements, and future directions. Future Gener Comput Syst 29(7):1645–1660
3. Li H, Qi Z (2019) Thinking on secondary node construction of industrial internet identifier resolution. Inf Commun Technol Policy 296(02):68–72

4. Sadeghi AR, Wachsmann C, Waidner M (2015) Security and privacy challenges in industrial internet of things. In 2015 52nd ACM/EDAC/IEEE Design Automation Conference (DAC), pp 1–6
5. Khan MA, Salah K (2018) IoT security: review, blockchain solutions, and open challenges. Future Gener Comput Syst 82:395–411
6. Li JQ, Yu FR, Deng G et al (2017) Industrial Internet: a survey on the enabling technologies, applications, and challenges. IEEE Commun Surv Tutorials 19(3):1504–1526
7. Baccelli E, Mehlis C, Hahm O et al (2014) Information centric networking in the IoT: experiments with NDN in the wild. In: Proceedings of the 1st ACM conference on information-centric networking, pp 77–86
8. Zhang YW, Chi C (2019) Zhu SY (2019) Information and communications technology and policy. Inf Commun Technol Policy 08:43–46
9. Jia XQ, Luo S (2019) Hu Y (2019) Industrial Internet identification and its application research. Inf Commun Technol Policy 04:1–5
10. Wei GH, Li H, Bai YJ, Li GX, Xing KX (2020) Space-terrestrial integrated multi-identifier network with endogenous security. Space Integr Ground Inf Netw 1(02):66–73
11. Liu G, Huang Y, Li N et al (2020) Vision, requirements and network architecture of 6G mobile network beyond 2030. China Commun 17(9):92–104
12. Boccardi F, Heath RW, Lozano A et al (2014) Five disruptive technology directions for 5G. IEEE Commun Mag 52(2):74–80
13. Zhou YQ, Pan ZG, Zhai GW et al (2015) Standardization and key technologies for future fifth generation of mobile communication system. Data Acquisition Process 30(4):714–724
14. Liu D (2019) Promote the integrated development of 5G and industrial internet. http://www.caict.ac.cn/kxyj/caictgd/201911/t20191128_270414.htm. Accessed 29 Dec 2020
15. Like BW, Like SW, Italiano I et al (2013) The Cyber-Industrial-Complex. Theriskyshift Com
16. Wu JX, Li JH, Ji XS (2018) Security for cyberspace: challenges and opportunities. Front Inf Technol Electron Eng 19(12):1459–1461
17. Li H, Wu JX, Yang X, et al (2020) MIN: Co-Governing Multi-Identifier Network Architecture and Its Prototype on Operator's Network. IEEE Access (8):36569–36581
18. Li H, Wu JX, Xing KX et al (2019) Prototype and testing report of a multi-identifier system for reconfigurable network architecture under co-governing. Scientia Sinica Informationisnis (49):1186–1204
19. Wang YM, Li H, Xing KX et al (2019) Identifiers management of industrial internet based on multi-identifier network architecture. ZTE Communications 18(1):36–43
20. Lin CJ, Liu XW (2019) The construction and application of identifier resolution in automotive industrial internet. ZTE Communications 18(1):55–65

Printed in the United States
by Baker & Taylor Publisher Services